The Royal Beasts
and other works

The Royal Beasts
and Other Works

William Empson

Edited with an introduction by
JOHN HAFFENDEN

University of Iowa Press
IOWA CITY

International Standard Book Numbers 0-87745-195-8 cloth,
0-87745-196-6 paper
Library of Congress Catalog Card Number 87-51312
University of Iowa Press, Iowa City 52242
Copyright © 1986 by the Estate of Sir William Empson
Introduction and Notes copyright © 1986 by John Haffenden
This edition copyright © 1988 by the University of Iowa
All rights reserved
Printed in the United States of America

Contents

Introduction

This volume of creative writings by William Empson contains texts that are for the most part previously unpublished. Apart from a piece of occasional light verse written when he was thirteen, they cover the period from 1926 to 1942 – years which saw him through Cambridge University and a hectic life as a professor of literature in the Far East, and finally into a senior wartime role as BBC Chinese Editor. The collection therefore complements the poems Empson himself first collected in *Poems* (1935) and *The Gathering Storm* (1940).

Arranged in chronological order, the works begin with a play he wrote at about the time of his twentieth birthday in 1926. A one-act melodrama, *Three Stories* featured in a double bill performed by the Amateur Dramatic Club in Cambridge early in 1927 (with Empson himself taking a part). That production predated the publication of any of his poems, and it therefore has a special status as the first public showing of Empson's imagination. Long lost sight of – even Empson honestly believed it had been destroyed – the text somehow survived sixty years of his nomadic life. Two groups of poems (five poems which Empson published as an undergraduate but omitted from *Poems*, and a larger section of previously unpublished poems) valuably extend our knowledge and appreciation of his output in the early years. They include both trial efforts and notable successes in a variety of forms – light verse, centos, passages of a libretto, and an epithalamion-cum-autobiography – as well as two significant poems from the later 1930s. Next, 'The Royal Beasts' (1937), Empson's only known work of prose fiction, which comprises sections from a regrettably unfinished fable. Empson once defined what he called 'the specific novel-reading pleasure' as 'that of getting inside a life different from one's own and establishing kinship with it';[1] and he achieved just that generous imaginative aim in 'The Royal Beasts'. Writing from an enforced exile on a Chinese mountain, and taking on the combined roles of theomachist and comic teratologist, he fashioned his story so as to dart penetrating questions into the theological and cultural complacency of the Western world. Lastly, in his full plan for a ballet 'The Elephant and the Birds' (1942), Empson ventured into an entirely different medium for the purpose of re-establishing common ground between the cultures of East and West, and of proselytising for the dramatic power of Far Eastern dance. As early as 1927 he had insisted on the fundamental importance of 'our strong and critical curiosity about alien modes of feeling, our need for the flying buttress of sympathy with systems other than our own';[2] both 'The Royal Beasts' and 'The Elephant and the Birds' (and indeed his career as a whole) exemplify his passionate belief in the principle he had laid down as an undergraduate.

Although Empson first became known to the literary world as the precocious author of *Seven Types of Ambiguity* (1930), he started off as a playwright and poet some time before he ever wrote a serious word of criticism. Indeed, as a young writer in 1929 his chief ambition had been to publish a volume of poetry. As luck and his publisher arranged things, however, his first collection of poems appeared only in 1935, in an edition of 1000 copies (*Poems* now has some rarity value, since 400 of the copies were destroyed in 1940). But he had been publishing poems in Cambridge periodicals since 1927, and had gained wider recognition with a selection published in *Cambridge Poetry 1929* which was much debated in university circles and singled out for praise in a review by F. R. Leavis:

He is an original poet who has studied the right poets (the right ones for him) in the right way. His poems have a tough intellectual content (his interest in the ideas and the sciences, and his way of using his erudition, remind us of Donne – safely), and they evince an intense preoccupation with technique. These characteristics result sometimes in what seems to me an unprofitable obscurity, in faults like those common in the Metaphysicals . . . But Mr Empson commands respect.[3]

As for the respect he enjoyed among his peers, his American friend and contemporary Richard Eberhart recalled with some sentimentality in 1944:

In Cambridge everybody talked about Empson's poetry. His poems challenged the mind, seemed to defy the understanding; they amused and they
enchanted; and even then they afforded a kind of parlor game, whiling away
lively hours of puzzlement at many a dinner party. The shock and impact of
this new kind of poetry were so considerable that people at that time had no
way to measure its contemporary or timeless value. They were amazed by it.
Eliot was already enthroned. The 'Oxford Group' had not yet got fully under
way. And Cambridge was buzzing with activity.[4]

Empson had gone up to Magdalene College with a scholarship to
study mathematics; and he proved to be conspicuously successful,
becoming Senior Optime in the first part of the mathematics Tripos in
1928. Just a year later, he won a starred First in the English Tripos.
Among his other activities at Cambridge he had written a good many
book, film and theatre reviews for *Granta* and the *Cambridge
Review*, as well as helping to found a new magazine (*Experiment*);
and he had acquired a prominent reputation as a waggish and
eccentrically learned mathematician and littérateur. 'He was brisk,
quick-moving, florid,' Richard Eberhart recalled. In his last month as
an undergraduate his college magazine affectionately satirised him in
this spoof 'Headmaster's Report': 'I hear from his form master that
Bill has been caught writing poetry again this term, but I think that
more games will soon knock that nonsense out of him . . . he seems
very destructive with his logarithm tables and often scribbles
wantonly in his books.'[5] The anonymous writer could feel confident
that his contemporaries would readily pick up the private joke about
their local genius.

But he made his very first mark as a playwright. A few references in
his journal-notebooks suggest that he became involved in the theatre
virtually from the beginning of his undergraduate career. Against a
date given simply as 'Sunday 8th', for example, there occurs the
tantalisingly terse entry: 'Wrote sadist play.'[6] (It is well known that he
could produce work at an exceptionally fast speed, but that sounds
preternatural even by his standards.) On an unknown date shortly
afterwards ('Sunday'), he expresses misgivings about becoming
caught up with fuddled theatrical fanciers: 'Apparently the Plectron
club, which I appear to have joined, is rather exclusive and concerned
with dramatic criticism. What do *I* know about it? And how on earth
did I get there? . . . I am there like a fish, talkative, in champagne.'

Then at last, on 4 March 1926, he writes, 'I have had in mind, for a week or so . . . the idea of a play'; but even that entry goes on disappointingly – 'I shall take the easier step of describing it here' – though it does include a full outline of the play he would never write.[7]

There is no information at all as to when he wrote *Three Stories*, but a fair guess would put it in the first term of his second year. Some time after the production, however, the text of the play seems to have disappeared from sight;[8] in 1963, for instance, Martin Dodsworth reported in a good account of Empson at Cambridge:

His one-act play *Three Stories* was given a single performance by the ADC in a triple bill at the beginning of February, 1927, in his fifth term at Cambridge. The critics of both *Granta* and the *Cambridge Review* were greatly impressed by it, and it put its companion pieces quite in the shade. We can gather a little of what it was like from the *Granta* review:

'. . . He had achieved an almost complete mastery of his Oedipus complex, and used it for very intelligent purposes. A theme of the rebellion of an idealist young man led from an excellent Shavian comedy to plain, honest melodrama, and was framed within romantic scenes in heroic couplets and contrasted with a scientific disquisition fathered on Dracula. It sounds very complicated, but, if we interpreted it rightly, it amounted to something like this: that the ethical problems of life differ from the scientific problems only if one conceives them romantically, and even then, the apparent romanticism achieved, they become scientific again. The last line of the play, in which the hero, having slain his businesslike ogre, is compelled to proclaim himself a 'managing young man' we thought a triumph.'

It is a pity that the manuscript of the play is now lost, since it was obviously an original and characteristic piece of Empson, already putting into practice some of the ideas developed in *Some Versions of Pastoral*. Mr Empson (in conversation) has explained that the basic structural idea of the play was to take a story and interpose a scene of apparently total irrelevance in the middle. This was obviously too much for the *Cambridge Review*'s theatre critic, who remarked groggily that 'if Mr Empson will content himself with a conventional three-act comedy as a medium, and refrain from wild experiment, at any rate until he has had more experience, he should have some considerable success.' ('Empson at Cambridge', *The Review*, Nos. 6 & 7, June 1963, pp. 4–5)

Fortunately Empson's otherwise untidy habits did not include any *deliberate* jettisoning of papers, so we can now judge his three-ply experiment for ourselves – as text if not performance.[9]

Given his conspicuous undergraduate success as a writer and above all as a scholar, he was soon tipped for an academic career, and his starred achievement in Tripos won him a Bye Fellowship for postgraduate study. But careless fate stepped in and dashed his immediate prospects. As he was being moved bag and baggage from an annex into Magdalene College proper, a college servant discovered that he had some contraceptives in his possession; the news also emerged that he had been in the habit of entertaining a woman in his rooms until a very late hour of the evening. Empson's inadvertence might not have been particularly damaging in itself except for the fact that the servant gossiped about it to other servants, who in turn noised the news about town. Since a public scandal appeared to be imminent, the Master felt obliged to convene an extraordinary meeting of the Governing Body in order to scotch it. Although Empson explained himself with great honesty and made no attempt to plead silly excuses, the Governing Body decided by a majority decision to exact the maximum penalty – both to deprive him of his Bye Fellowship and to remove his name from the books of the college (as the University Statutes empowered it to do, since sexual misconduct was deemed to be a University offence).[10] Empson's brilliant future seemed to be shattered, and he returned home to Yorkshire. His mock-heroic response to being expelled from Cambridge is the sharply witty poem in this volume, 'Warning to undergraduates', which puts to good use the octosyllabic couplets of Samuel Butler's burlesque *Hudibras*. Written probably within a few weeks of the fell event itself, it is testimony to his generosity of spirit that he could so quickly translate a painfully humiliating setback into a form of 'smilingness' (to borrow Byron's word). Certainly he felt very distressed by what had happened, but he refused to repine for long. For the immediate future he hoped to take up some form of journalism; and in any event he had other literary hopes.

Quite coincidentally, in the very month when he gained his degree and lost his place as a postgraduate (June 1929), Empson offered a collection of 'about twenty poems' for consideration by his friend and contemporary Ian Parsons, who had recently joined the firm of Chatto & Windus. As far as Empson was concerned, his poetry had top priority – for almost as an afterthought in the same letter he asked with characteristic modesty, 'I was thinking of offering a gram-

matico-critical essay to the Hogarth called the Seven Types of
Ambiguity: you don't do small essays (15,000 words) do you?'[11] It
was the first outside news of a study that would presently become a
watershed in literary criticism. (At an uncertain later date he
discovered – to his apparent surprise but to no one's regret –
'Ambiguity is growing on my hands . . .') Parsons felt hesitant about
the poems – 'it is rather difficult to make a decision on so little work' –
but asked to see them in any case; he received them on 14 June, along
with this unconfident but beguiling letter:

> Most of them you have seen already. There are twenty-three of them. I doubt
> if I have turned out enough even now (dear me; I mean turned out of the
> collection, of course, not 'output' in a professional sense) (though that would
> be true too); I should be glad of your advice.
>
> When I am not actually faced with explaining them I feel notes aren't
> wanted: but I think people would be more easily tempted to read verse if
> there was plenty of critical writing thrown in, demanding less concentration
> of attention, and with more literary-magazine or novel-reading interest – I
> know *I* should. And there is a rather portentous air about compact verses
> without notes, like a seduction without conversation. Arguably I ought to
> wait till I have more of them.

Parsons felt eager to take the critical book, but not the poems; so that
towards the end of July he wrote again: 'I am so glad to hear that
Ambiguity is progressing so swiftly and satisfactorily, and I am
already very anxious to discover your seven varieties . . . Meanwhile I
am sending you back with this the MS of the poems you sent us
originally.'

Seven Types of Ambiguity was accepted for publication on 13 April
1930, and Parsons duly took an informal lien on the poems; if the
criticism did well, it might help to float the poetry. But subscription
sales of *Seven Types* amounted to only 146 copies by late in 1930,
which did not augur well. The reviews were nevertheless extensive
and resplendent; a new critical star had undoubtedly arrived, and
F. R. Leavis again hailed him in the *Cambridge Review*: 'His book is
the work of a mind that is fully alive in this age, and such a book has
a very unusual importance.' Furthermore, remembering how much
the poems had fascinated him eighteen months before, Leavis closed
his review with this helpful prompt: 'And, immediately, there is that
book of poems which he has given us a right to demand.'[12] *Seven*

Types of Ambiguity brought Empson international fame at the age of twenty-four, but it did not immediately sell well. In fact it was not until February 1933 that Ian Parsons asked again about the poems; but being a loyal friend and publisher he pressed for them once more in May 1934, and finally accepted Empson's submission in December that year.

In an essay reviewing Empson's full poetic career after the publication of *Collected Poems* in 1955, A. Alvarez praised the 'enquiring originality' of the early poems and pinpointed Empson's importance as 'a stylist of poetry and ideas'; he observed too that

the poetry is an outcome of a peculiarly strong and sensitive feeling for the intellectual tone of the time. Empson seems to create less out of personal situations than out of an emotional response to something he has already known with his wits, intellectually.[13]

Such a Romantic critical assumption was by no means new. Curiously enough, even Empson's mentor I. A. Richards had suggested it in an early review (1929), which equivocally admired the young poet's topical intellectualism while trusting to the future for him to discover some basis of enduring emotional drive:

such intellectual excitement as he provides is one of the few literary commodities that *prove themselves*. We may value this adroitness in emotional logic variously, but we cannot deny it. And enough sensibility may be suspected beneath the startling compression of his verses to carry him some distance if he should later find a direction in which to travel. He may be merely bottling a contemporary atmosphere – but he may have an explosive mixture of his own.[14]

Although Empson was certainly a product of the rational humanism favoured by Cambridge in the 1920s, Richards surely misled his readers with the suggestion that Empson's intellect had most of the say and stood in danger of bypassing his feelings. In fact, Empson's apprehension of the place of the physical sciences, biology and anthropology in the modern world had charged his poetry (according to his friend and contemporary, Kathleen Raine) with distressing questions about the way in which man tries 'to impose order on fields of knowledge and experience so contradictory as to threaten the mind that contains them with disorder – the compulsion, as Empson writes, to "learn a style from a despair".'[15]

Wordsworth in his 'Preface' to *Lyrical Ballads* foresaw the day when

The remotest discoveries of the chemist, the botanist or mineralogist will be as proper objects of the poet's art as any upon which it can be employed, if the time should ever come when these things shall be familiar to us, and the relations under which they are contemplated by the followers of these respective sciences shall be manifestly and palpably material to us as enjoying and suffering beings.[16]

It may reasonably be claimed that Empson in his poetry largely fulfilled the prophecy, and not as an impersonal discipline for the mind alone; he carried 'sensation into the midst of the objects of the science itself', as Wordsworth had predicted. The poetic imagination he brought to the late 1920s 'had to adjust itself to a new scientific world-view at once alarming and inspiring,' Kathleen Raine recalled. Feeling that any enormous shifts in scientific knowledge of the physical world must radically challenge received ethics, Empson treated the conflict in a spirit of painful perplexity. He wrote in an early article:

The scientific view of truth . . . is that the mind, otherwise passive, collects propositions about the external world; the application of scientific ideas to poetry is interesting because it reduces that idea of truth . . . to a self contradiction.
    And yet one must not accept such a contradiction as final . . .[17]

The kinds of issue that concerned him as a poet figure in a review dating from January 1930:

In the nineteenth century one was only a pile of billiard balls, jerking about according to mathematical rules; scientific determinism spelled horror and despair. It is a real and terrible ghost . . .
    All things are alike determined, all things are alike free.
    Science is . . . a product of the mind; a product, too, of the universe which allows it to yield results; and cannot make final statements about either. There should, then, be some mode of thinking other than the scientific one, but to mix the two will only confuse both.[18]

While the areas of learned reference in his poetry may be outside the normal order for perhaps a majority of poets, there can be little doubt that Empson felt it upon his pulse when he wrote that 'the notion of an atom's probability is a mystery, and very *like* what one feels about people . . .'[19] Nor was his concern confined to a brief undergraduate spell ending in 1929. In a notebook dating from 1934, for instance, he was still chewing over the freedom–determinism paradox at a time when he was otherwise taken up with studying Buddhist iconography. 'The point about determinism is not that we want our actions to be causeless – random – but that we want them to have a different sort of causation from the physico-chemical one. This isn't got by dropping cause like JS Haldane (on his own account, which seems wrong) or by any discovery of random action in physics or chemistry.'

Like E. M. Forster when he worried that 'the post-war world of the '20s would not add up into sense,'[20] Empson took to his troubled heart the contradictions of the age. Accordingly, at the beginning of his most productive period as a poet (1927–29), he wrote in a review of The Prospects of Literature, by Logan Pearsall Smith, what amounts to his own statement for the times:

That in the disorder of this age there is no formula one can lose oneself in expounding . . . that the writer must therefore build for himself, with slow labour and due regard for fame, a private cosmos, is hardly deniable, and here stated very prettily. But just now, when there are lots of novelties . . . what is of most importance is to find out which is valuable. This period has, in fact, a formula, that the writer's business is to digest fads, and how can he do it without hunting them? And how can the result avoid a certain tentative and dishevelled air, less like the eating of pastry than of the first oyster?[21]

Feeling far less comfortable with this state of affairs than that review would admit, he constantly disparaged the simple-mindedness of anyone who presumed to make up a synthesis out of radically opposed accounts of the world. His impatience with facile thinking is evident, for instance, in a review of C. E. Payne's The Pre-War Mind in Britain (1928): 'She has the "scientific" mind; she is fond, for instance, of repeating two opposite things earnestly, in the hope of implying a synthesis which combines them . . .'[22] He made just the same protest in another early review (1927): 'It is a fallacy that men of great abilities can produce what Mr Eliot calls a "synthesis" simply by explaining their mental habits; they must do it by producing a work of art.'[23] That distinction between 'mental habits' and imaginative creativity he knew to be vital for his own poetry; it is small wonder that he later felt exasperated by certain critics who judged his own metaphysical poetry to be over-intellectualised.

'How much twentieth-century poetry, examined in cold blood, really resembles Donne or Marvell?' John Wain once asked.

I should say that only John Crowe Ransom, Robert Graves since 1926, and possibly the early dandified Eliot, ever consistently recalled the metaphysical way of setting about poetry . . . So that, historically speaking, the renascence of (in any precise sense of the word) 'metaphysical' poetry boils down to a few poems by a few poets.

Empson, however, is one of these poets.[24]

In a retrospective BBC programme (1952), Empson stressed the fact that he had indeed modelled the argumentative conceits of his early poetry on the example set by John Donne (as Leavis had recognised in 1929). But he stipulated too that there were good reasons for its specific density: 'The object of the style, in my mind and I believe in Donne's mind, is to convey a mental state of great tension, in which conflicting impulses have no longer any barriers between them and therefore the strangeness of the world is felt very acutely.' The explanation he later gave in an interview with Christopher Ricks consistently enlarged upon the idea that his poetry worked 'on the basis of expressing an unresolved conflict', while crediting Robert Graves as an exemplar of the principle:

he thought the poem ought to be about a conflict which is raging in the mind of the writer but hasn't been solved. He should write about the things that really worry him, in fact worry him to the point of madness. The poem is a kind of clinical object, done to prevent him from going mad. It is therefore not addressed to any public, but it is useless to him unless it is in fact clear and readable, because he has to – as it were – address it to the audience within himself. It isn't expressed unless it's a thing which somebody else can read, so if it's obscure it actually fails in this therapeutic function, it isn't saving his sanity.[25]

If Empson's best poems are the fruit of mental puzzling, therefore, they express above all else an intelligence that is passionate about its preoccupations. 'The first or only reason for writing verse,' he wrote in 1937, 'is to clear your own mind or fix your own feelings.'[26] Edwin Muir justly observed in 1956, 'The passion in Mr Empson's poetry is uncomfortably real, almost raw, and the control is difficult. He moves us by the spectacle of a shocking struggle for control.'[27] The constantly operative terms of his creative drive were 'tension', 'conflict', 'contradiction', and 'argument'. And not only as an undergraduate in the late 1920s. He held to the first lessons of his imagination when in 1933 he wrote about Virginia Woolf's *Mrs Dalloway* that 'like most post-war good writing, [it] makes a blank statement of conflict.'[28] Yet later, at a time when he had virtually given up writing poetry (1939), he still praised Eliot's *The Waste Land* in terms which have a direct relevance to his own verse: 'a frightful tension requires a frightful concentration of style.'[29]

While some of the apparently esoteric allusiveness of the poetry can be overcome by studying the sciences with which Empson was familiar, John Fuller acutely identified its real difficulty when he wrote that 'the straits Empson sometimes gets into result from the attempt to maintain a polymetaphorical structure, a storeyed edifice of meaning'. But 'meaning is the key,' Fuller properly added.[30] Although even the best poems of *Collected Poems* make enormous demands on the reader with their intricate intertextuality and condensation of structure, Empson deplored the notion that one could ever feel content to admire a poem without understanding it; he considered it a 'lethal formula'[31] to place pride of sensibility above critical intelligence. Even worse, such a critical formula implies that the poet can somehow articulate feeling at a remove from reason (like the Imagist pretenders),[32] thus purveying a contradiction which Empson thought a slander on the creative imagination.

Empson's best poems measure up to the exacting standards of his critical statements. Nevertheless, Michael Wood has reasonably pointed out what might appear to be a divergence between Empson's poetry and his criticism:

the most striking thing about the poems for me is their radical difference in tone and feeling from the criticism. They are cramped, clogged, and diffident whereas the criticism is reckless and easy. The reason for this may be simple enough: it's exciting to discover fruitful complications in a great writer, but it's no fun to face and articulate oppressive contradictions in your own life.[33]

Wood wondered too whether the 'real source' of this apparently 'remarkable' contrast was 'the contradictions being faced in the poetry or a certain hampered, mechanical approach to the actual writing of poetry'. But what Wood posed as alternatives cannot in fact be split apart from one another: the contradictions that incited Empson required of him a condensed mode of poetic composition.

Empson never made high claims for his poetry – indeed, he often called it 'too specialised'[34] – but his best poems (he justifiably remarked in another interview) are 'complicated in the way that life really is'.[35] As Geoffrey Hill perceptively wrote in 1964, Empson's poetry and criticism are actually linked by virtue of the fact that both are 'essentially pragmatic'; and he pinpointed this fundamental connection: 'Empson's interest in both poetry and criticism is fixated on the perennial problems of conduct and belief.'[36] John Fuller has likewise written, 'Empson *is* in fact a poet of vision, where the only true vision is a question of discovering what man's position in the world really is.'[37]

Empson is reported to have said in December 1939 that he 'considered his early poems in the nature of experiments, trial balloons or something of the sort.'[38] By that reckoning, the poems in the present volume must be taken as even more experimental than the excellent poems he collected in *Poems*. However, if they are 'tentative and dishevelled' (to use his own words quoted above), they are not negligible – simply because they demonstrate just how diverse an apprenticeship he served as a poet. The five uncollected poems in part 3 of the text Empson himself rejected as decidedly inferior to the poems of *Poems* (1935); they are reprinted here for convenience, in order to preserve in an accessible form those poems that he chose to publish at least once upon a time. In part 2, apart from the nonce-verses he wrote at the age of thirteen (which delightfully anticipate his mature quarrel with the Christian religion), several of the previously unpublished poems date from his undergraduate years. The prose poem 'Address to a tennis-player', for instance, is an association-exercise on the theme of the calling and sacrifice of St Peter. The centos too show the nineteen-year-old Empson trying to match his erudition with the skill of versifying. Likewise, in a wire-drawn exercise in free verse dating from the same year (1926), the speaker of 'Song of the amateur psychologist' draws us down the endlessly spiralling staircase of a wine cellar: the poem is a metaphor for Empson's early interest in psychoanalysis, and it suggests that the labyrinth of the mind is in fact bottomless. Empson recalled in 1965, 'One of my earliest memories is of clutching a candle in my shaking hand and climbing over heaps of coal as I wound up the thread left by my sister across the vasty and labyrinthine cellars of Yokefleet Hall

[the family home in Yorkshire].'³⁹ The same image may lie at the back
of the tautly-written portrayal of a resourceful 'Young Theseus' in the
more mature 'Myth', which dates from his twenty-third year.

Yet a further undergraduate experiment is 'Two songs from a
libretto' (1927). Although too little of the libretto survives to give any
clear idea of its intended plot, one can infer that Empson meant
somehow to combine literary satire with a tale about a young girl being
pressed into a loveless marriage by her ignorant and wickedly venal
aunts. Both begun and apparently abandoned just as Empson turned
twenty-one, it follows up the romantic melodrama of *Three Stories* and
seems to anticipate something of the character of T. S. Eliot's *Sweeney
Agonistes* and even of Auden's early plays. But it may be going too far
to guess at anything of the sort from such fragmentary material; all the
same, one passage has real merit: the girl's first song is a genuine
achievement, finely affecting in its poignant measure.

Along with 'Warning to undergraduates' (discussed above), the
wry epithalamion 'Letter vi: A marriage' (1935) is one of Empson's
few excursions into directly autobiographical verse. Nothing in the
poem is fanciful, and perhaps all one really needs to know about it is
there on the page; treating 'the traditional theme' of lost love, it is
piquant and wittily self-deprecating.

Whatever the relative merits of these various early experiments and
fragments, no high claims need to be made to justify their inclusion in
this volume. It is appropriate, however, to extend to them an
observation that Empson himself made in a review of the uncollected
verse of a fellow poet he much admired: 'Even in the minor works of
Dylan Thomas, a glittering or searching detail is always liable to crop
up; besides, his major poems are hard to plumb, but the ideas get
repeated, so that a weaker but simpler use of one of them may turn
out a great help.'⁴⁰ For the same reason, Empson evidently felt averse
to keeping any literary remains 'under wraps' (as he put it in the same
review); and he claimed in another but not unrelated context, 'I
stubbornly won't hide anything.'⁴¹

The verses beginning 'Not but they die, the terrors and the dreams'
are especially interesting because of their relationship to another
poem, 'The Teasers' (*Collected Poems*, p. 67), which begins 'Not but
they die, the teasers and the dreams'. In his BBC reading on 15
December 1952, Empson said about 'The Teasers':

I think it was nearly very good, above my level altogether, but I feel its final form is rather a cheat, with a solemn last verse giving a moral which the poem hasn't earned. I wrote a lot of other verses and cut them out, rightly I am sure, but I ought to have got better ones. It is a case where the poetry of conflict becomes rather too flat, just as Shelley's kind of poetry did when he thought it was sufficiently evocative to say 'O world, O life, O Time'. I can't say what this poem means, partly because I don't remember, partly because I don't want to, and partly because it doesn't matter since the poem failed to say it. It is very tempting, in this kind of poetry, to put in a moral at the end in suitably ambiguous terms and hope it will sum up the conflict. Sometimes I think it would be better to cut out the last verse of this poem and sometimes I feel that would only make the poem sillier. But it is a wonderful form; I do not feel humble about that part, only about not filling it enough.

The lines published in this volume may be either a new poem altogether – though prompted by Empson's fondness for the opening locution 'Not but they die', followed by a less ambiguous variant of the phrase 'the teasers and the dreams' – or a reconstitution of the verses he cut out of 'The Teasers'. Certainly 'The Teasers' itself is in a form that Empson himself invented (though he could not sustain it through the whole poem) – 'a new kind of quatrain, made out of three iambic pentameter lines, by breaking the second line into two short lines at the caesura,' as George Fraser described it in a notable essay[42] – whereas the poem here is in terza rima. Empson also said elsewhere that although he wrote additional verses for 'The Teasers' he felt his 'grumbles were so trivial that only the general verses would do . . .'[43] Nevertheless, his comment that the poem failed to achieve any definite meaning has not stopped good critics from trying to work one out. George Fraser's essay 'On the Interpretation of a Difficult Poem' (1955), for example, is in part a response to an analysis by John Wain (1950). Wain found the poem guilty of formal carelessness, but identified the nature of the teasers and the dreams as 'our inward afflictions and aspirations – in Bacon's noble phrase, the "desires of the mind".'[44] In turn, Fraser classified the poem as 'a short dramatic and philosophical monologue', and judged that its central concern is 'erotic energy as the lawless source of a much wider human energy'[45] – as Christopher Ricks agreed in his resourceful essay 'Empson's Poetry' (1974).[46] While Empson himself regarded all such interpretations as little better than guesses, it so happened that he reviewed the volume in which Fraser's essay appeared (*Speculations*, ed. John

Wain), and seemed partially to confirm the drift of Fraser's argument when he observed: 'The idea of my poem was to go on saying things which applied at once to the high and the low passions, the lusts and the ideals'; but, he reiterated, 'other impulses were at work which produced verses I later disliked, and the cut version is inadequate.'[47] It is therefore quite possible that 'Not but they die, the terrors and the dreams' does in fact comprise those verses including 'other impulses' which he came to dislike; in any event, they have less to do with eroticism than with philosophical morality. In so far as they enter ambiguous caveats against self-preservation, for instance, they can be seen to reflect the second line of 'Reflection from Anita Loos': 'It is not human to feel safely placed' (*Collected Poems*, p. 66). To opt out of taking risks and into the sanity of playing safe may well be equivalent to dying; the healthy mind does not happily settle for ducking out of the action, since a sense of failure and remorse may result from electing the 'short view' which restricts emotional responsiveness. The verses are querulous and sardonic, so making an interesting comparison to the more firm-minded argument against 'madhouse' in the later poem 'Let it go'; and it is possible that Empson rejected them simply because they might have appeared to endorse the idea of shrinking from life, whereas they actually incorporate grave misgivings about that very policy. Although the rhythm of the lines breaks down by the end of the four stanzas, the image of the magnifying glass as being 'able for the flame' is a masterfully ambiguous conclusion: it suggests both that the man who has opted for short-sightedness (or non-involvement in life) can still start a fire with the burning point of his magnifying glass and that he reserves to himself the illusory ability to take a good look at the flames (or passions) generated in other people – to whom he stands in the relation of a spectator.

Lastly, 'The ages change, and they impose their rules' is a straightforwardly political poem, and unashamedly vatic.[48] In a way that is altogether far-sighted and calm-minded, it announces that the fate of the later twentieth century is necessarily to put up with the international balance of power. The subversive strength of the poem comes from its ably satirical use of one of Empson's favourite forms, the villanelle, for it rings the changes on one rhyme in proclaiming that the new 'rules' are kept up by 'fools'. Like both 'The Teasers' and its new companion 'Not but they die, the terrors and the dreams', it probably dates from Empson's most consciously 'political' period – between 1937 and 1940 (though the chronological order of the last two poems in the hitherto unpublished group may well be interchangeable).

Empson always maintained in fact that the burden of the poems he wrote in the later 1930s was fundamentally political; in response to Michael Wood's article 'Incomparable Empson' (1975), for example, he drafted a lengthy testament headed 'Empson's Defence':

Nursing myself back into literary work after the war was rather a business, closely connected with trying to get a complete cure from a stomach ulcer; I first, for about a year, wrote an essay on Buddhist sculpture before 1000 AD, which got lost afterwards [it is discussed later in this introduction] . . . but there was no such need to start writing poetry again, and the theme which all the modern poets I admired had been working on, which I had been working on too, had been blown out like a candle.

I suppose I look ridiculous when I claim to have been a political poet too, like Auden and Spender and all those geared-up propaganda boys in Oxford (whereas I was in Cambridge); and it is true that I never learned the technique so was never considered a political poet. But my second volume of verse *The Gathering Storm* means by the title just what Winston Churchill did when he stole it, the gradual sinister confusing approach to the Second World War. Of course the title was chosen after writing the poems, during the early years of the war, but nearly all the poems really are considering this prospect, with which I had been fairly closely confronted, in China, Japan, Indochina and Korea. Well then, after the war had been won, I was in the same cleft stick as my brother poets, and I am inclined to congratulate myself upon stopping writing.

Notwithstanding his own explanation, the question most often asked about Empson's career is still: why did he stop writing poetry, or why did he decide not to publish any of the poems he may have written in the years after *The Gathering Storm* (1940)? John Fuller modified the question like this: 'If there is any explaining to be done about Empson's publishing career it is, surely, not why he more or less stopped in 1940, but why he wrote fewer poems after 1930 and how the poems of the thirties are different from poems of the twenties (ten a year on average before 1930, just over two thereafter).'[49]

An answer can be approached by way of glancing at a novel by Martin Amis, *Success*, which includes the following piece of idiomatic dialogue:

'Why? Why not let it go?'
'You don't want that and the whole thing there,' I said.[50]

The context of the exchange is that the first speaker, Ursula, has felt so desperate about her life as to attempt suicide, to let go of life altogether. Amis is in fact alluding to Empson's poem called 'Let it go' (*Collected Poems*, p. 81), where the offhand title means quite the opposite of what Amis knowingly (and with deliberate ambiguity) suggests in his novel. This is the second of the poem's two stanzas:

> The contradictions cover such a range.
> The talk would talk and go so far aslant.
> You don't want madhouse and the whole thing there.

The poem is 'about stopping writing poetry', Empson said.[51] What he meant is that you can avoid 'madhouse' only if you *positively* (not negatively, as for Amis's character) let go of those conflicts that cannot be resolved. The final line of the poem is as much persuasive as declarative: it begs one certain answer to the implied question 'do you?' Surely no one would willingly talk themselves into the certainty of mental disequilibrium that is suggested by the auxiliary 'would' in the penultimate line? The acknowledgement that the creative imagination can never argue away real contradictions is a large part, I think, of the reason why Empson gave up writing poetry at a comparatively early age. I believe he relinquished poetry not in despair but in the recognition that contradictions can mean vitality rather than desperate stalemate.

'Let it go' argues for moral and mental health; but that resolve is reviewed even more positively in 'Sonnet', which proposes:

> A more heartening fact about the cultures of man
>   Is their appalling stubbornness. The sea
> Is always calm ten fathoms down. The gigan-
>
>   -tic anthropological circus riotously
> Holds open all its booths.

The idea that Empson was willing to renounce poetry because he had learned that while one is unable to synthesise or solve contradictions (philosophical, political and religious) the sane approach is a positive and appreciative acceptance, is supported by a review dating from 1940:

What is heartening about people is their appalling stubbornness and the strong roots of their various cultures, rather than the ease with which you can convert them and make them happy and good. Probably a whole political outlook can turn on this.[52]

During his years in the Far East, in fact, he had discovered that there are viable philosophical alternatives to the conflict long apparent in the West between the findings of science and the ethical freedom of the individual. Even as late as 1956, in a review of Joseph Needham's *Science and Civilisation in China*, he rehearsed one of the tensions that had been central to his best early poetry – the conflict between the new scientific world-view (including the paradox of determinism mentioned above) and the old ethics ordained by the Christian dispensation. By implication, he felt, Needham reaffirmed his judgement that he had done well to let go of the issues that provoked the passionate argumentation of his early poetry:

The European mind has kept on getting itself hag-ridden by philosophical dilemmas . . . and the chief dilemma is this: either the universe is merely a fortuitous concourse of atoms, or else the atoms . . . only do what was ordered by a man-like lawgiver, who is God; in either case, our minds cannot be expected to do what we want of them . . . It feels wonderful to Dr Needham (instead of invincibly stupid) to see how the Chinese mind habitually winced away . . . from the belief that there had to be a personal lawgiver before the laws of Nature, at all their levels, could exist, with at their summit the Natural Law of man.[53]

'I feel myself that the line of thought which [this book] suggests is the only one offering a future to mankind,' he concluded. He had begun to think along such lines early in the 1930s, and indeed it was his experiences and reflections in the Far East that gradually engendered both 'The Royal Beasts' in 1937 and 'The Elephant and the Birds' in 1942.

As I said at the beginning, the poems in this volume (apart from the teenage verses twitting supernatural supervision) all date from the period 1926–?1937, but they are certainly not the last word from Empson the poet. In more than one interview he stated that he had written some poems in Peking between 1946 and 1952, but he thought them all bad. Just how much poetry he wrote in the post-war years is not at all clear, and in any event it became a habit for him to declare that he had long since finished. Yet Professor Philip Hobsbaum, who knew Empson at Sheffield University in the 1950s, suggested to me a short while ago, 'you would be doing us all a service if you could dig up any of Empson's later poems. He always said he was writing but that the poems were no good because he wasn't old enough. Writing poetry was like taking baths, he said: necessary only for the young and the old. Middle-aged gents exempt.'[54] At the age of sixty, on the other hand, Empson said in a newspaper interview that he had stopped writing poetry 'because what I was writing seemed too tight, not on principle. I went on until the war, until I was thirty-four.'[55] Whether he was in fact *not* writing poetry in his later years or simply diffident about it, no evidence has yet come to light that any poems survive from (say) the last thirty years of his life. If there are some late poems still remaining to be discovered, however, it is most probable that they would take the form of lucid and lyrical shots at the 'singing line' he always admired. As a newspaper profile reported when he retired from Sheffield University in 1971,

His creative energies became absorbed in criticism. 'I've been very wrapped up in my present work. Escape from these duties may enable me to write verse again.' But any new poems will not be 'an expression of unresolved conflict,' a state of mind, Empson feels, that has been invoked as 'a reasonable ground for ignoring the reader.' . . . Now, he says, the poet, whether working out his unresolved conflicts or not, 'can't keep his sanity unless he's intelligible.'[56]

II

The full story behind both 'The Royal Beasts' (1937) and 'The Elephant and the Birds' (1942) covers more than ten years of Empson's life after his graduation and dismissal from Cambridge. It was a peripatetic decade of professorships and brilliant literary productivity. From 1931 to 1934 he taught as a professor of English in Japan, a country which at that time waxed ugly with military imperialism. Following a three-year break in London which he occupied with writing literary criticism, he took up another post in the Far East – at Peking National University – where he arrived (as ill luck would have it, on a Japanese troop train) in the autumn of 1937. The Japanese had moved upon Peking and forced the three great universities of northern China to combine in exile in the province of Hunan,[57] where their new recruit shortly caught up with them. As the invading forces penetrated ever more deeply into the country, Empson committed himself to the Chinese and worked with them towards the southwest. He stayed with his student charges until the war in Europe grew imminent, and left China only in order to help at home. Throughout the decade, and notwithstanding the turbulent and itinerant circumstances in which he found himself, he still sustained his major work in literature. *Some Versions of Pastoral* (1935) he wrote during his disconcerting time in Tokyo; in war-torn China he drafted many of the essays later collected in *The Structure of Complex Words* (1951); and at the same time he managed to produce the understandably modest output of poetry gathered up in *The Gathering Storm* (1940). Besides all that, he energetically pursued an absorbing and time-consuming hobby – hunting Buddhas – a hobby which led him towards writing 'The Elephant and the Birds'.

But first, 'The Royal Beasts': strictly speaking a fable,[58] the story supplies the imaginative link between Empson's early interest in biological and anthropological science (including Darwinian evolutionism), as well as in versions of pastoral, and the later challenges to Christian dogma he enunciated at length in *Milton's God* (1961). Begun in a provocative 'holiday' humour, it tells how a group of newly-discovered African mutants – rational creatures with the characters of sub-human primates – cannily refuse to be classed as human beings. Empson's sympathetic and clever hero Wuzzoo sets off a serio-comic series of reactions which disjoint the cultural presuppositions of Western man. Firmly locating itself in the tradition of Swift, Aldous Huxley and T. F. Powys, the tale is rich in theological and sociological implication, and generously satirical.

It is not possible to determine exactly how long Empson worked on 'The Royal Beasts', but the starting-date is clear: he began it in China in the late autumn of 1937, during the early part of the Sino-Japanese war, in a Bible College on a sacred mountain – Nan-Yueh, near Changsha in Hunan province, where he had joined the staff of the refugee universities. (One of the manuscript pages of the novel is written on the back of a typescript draft of two stanzas of the poem 'Autumn on Nan-Yueh'.) 'The mere journey south was a dangerous adventure which people did separately,' Empson wrote in a draft memoir. 'Over twelve hundred students got through . . .' The location was picturesque to a degree, but the conditions of life were cramped, primitive and bitterly cold: in order to provide themselves with some warmth the staff and students had to burn charcoal on iron plates, an activity so perilous that at least four students suffered from carbon monoxide poisoning – it 'turns the blood cherry pink,' Empson recorded with scientific calm.

'Imagine camping out with a set of dons,' he buoyantly suggested. 'Keep in mind what dons are':

You must think of Oxford and Cambridge contriving to sink their differences and combine in the Highlands, struggling to arrive . . . with their lecture notes and the clothes they stood up in, getting no new buildings, getting hardly any books . . . and starting the lectures without a break for the next academic year . . . I know the quality of the men I have to sleep with. I suppose there is no other country in the world where that type of man would take the migration and its startling hardships, not merely without false heroics, but as a trip that leaves you both waiting to collect news about your special branch of learning and also interested in the local scenery and food.

'As to rice,' he added on another page, 'I think the stuff tastes better when it's burnt, though certainly it is more comfortable eating if you take out the gravel.'

In view of the almost complete lack of books, the exiled professors had to teach from memory. Although Empson modestly stated, 'I know enough verse by heart, but I can't do prose,' one of his students remembers his prodigious pedagogical feats:

It was almost unimaginable that anyone could compile a textbook of English literature. Empson, without saying anything, typed out Shakespeare's *Othello* from memory . . . On another occasion, persuaded by his students, he recited long passages of Milton's *Paradise Lost*. His typewriter provided us, totally out of 'nothing', with Swift's *A Modest Proposal* . . . But we were more impressed by his attitude towards work, and his way of working. He never boasted about his work, and never intended to let his work be known by others.[59]

As the *only* foreigner with the refugee universities, Empson felt to some extent isolated and was seemingly withdrawn – 'I live very much out of the world here,' he wrote – spending part of his time pacing around the college buildings or hiking over the shoulders of the mountains: 'The heart of magic is the sense of power; and any tolerable walker gets a sense of power here . . .' He also suffered the isolation of being unable to speak the language: 'To be sure my

ignorance of Chinese (which I have studied, so like a deaf old lady I
have embarrassing gaps of intelligence, and am not the fool I choose
to look) is a means of protection. But I hope I am not yet so frightened
as to put down mere laziness (a proud thing) to fear.'

The passages in this volume are all that survive of 'The Royal
Beasts'; they are best introduced by the following undated and
unposted letter that Empson addressed at the time to Solly Zuckerman,[60] who had recently published two authoritative studies of
mammalian physiology and sociology, *The Social Life of Monkeys
and Apes* (1932) and *Functional Affinities of Man, Monkeys, and
Apes* (1933). (In view of the fact that Empson forgets the exact
spelling of the name Zuckerman, it is most unlikely that he was
writing with those books to hand; and in that event it is remarkable
how closely he recalls the complex morphological problems he had to
face in postulating his imagined race of Wurroos.)

Dear Dr Zukermann,

I am starting to write a fantasy novel, about a Central African tribe which
is not of human stock. It would be giving too much trouble to ask your
advice, but I propose to put down the main points of the novel in a letter, and
would be grateful if you feel interested enough to answer. Various Peking
universities have had their arts departments moved onto a sacred mountain
in Hunan, a rather isolated place, and it seems best to have a novel to write,
now I have got there.

The boundary between a separatist Dominion and a British Crown
Colony, in an inaccessible and mountainous part, has been taken over from a
previous treaty with an African chief, and is therefore defined in terms of
tribal areas not of territory. All land up to the last tribes south of the
mountains belongs to the Dominion. Then a gold mine is discovered at the
foot of the mountains in the territory of this new tribe. Britain has reached a
condition where there is an urgent need for gold. The governor of the colony
takes up the claim that these men do not constitute a tribe, and the case goes
to the Lords. Britain I think wins the case, and then in a second case it is
decided that the creatures are persons in the same sense as Joint Stock
Companies, so that British Law applies to them. All the Christian sects
demand to send missionaries, and the Japanese for purposes of cultural
penetration claim that Buddhism is the only religion open to non-human
species. The difficulty is to stop the novel with a good enough bang. I am
rather afraid that they will all have to die of a plague of colds. A great deal of
the stuff needs technical knowledge that I can't scratch together here.

About the creatures themselves. I want them attractive enough to excite
sympathy and clever enough to stick to their case. They are well informed

about the Dominion treatment of negroes and determined to keep out of it; they swear by their gods they are not men. (Rather tempting to make them swear they are parrots on totemistic grounds; business of hushing this up.) They are covered with valuable fur, and to keep this off the market they demand the status of Royal Beasts, like sturgeon. They have a rigid breeding season with some kind of bodily change; a sexual skin is hardly pretty enough and apparently does not go with a breeding season. One could say they are a Lemuroid stock, but they have a broad nose and muzzle; all the lemuroids seem to have a rat expression which I don't want. Having a breeding season means that they have become rational without using Freudian machinery, interesting to try and work out. They rebuke mankind a good deal on this point. But they pick fur all the year round, have a craving for it. The hero is presented with a Persian cat and throws it out of the window, much shocked at being incited to an obscene perversion. They are incapable of interbreeding with man, at least such evidence as is timidly brought into court leads to that view, because it was acquired in a criminal manner, so it cannot be a strong argument. However their blood can't be transfused with any human group, and they have long furry tails. I don't think there would be much difficulty in getting a united front of scientific experts in court to say they weren't men, though some experts would say they were a closely allied species. You might easily get the law refusing to concern itself with the scientific definition, though, and saying that a man in law is a rational creature capable of observing contracts or what not. The Catholic Church would I think undoubtedly claim that they were men, on such grounds as were used in its great sixteenth century decision that the Tierra del Fuegans were; but I need to find out what grounds were given then.

It seems possible to make them a very recent mutation, all descended from one ancestor three or four generations ago. Hence all their customs are in a state of flux, they need a new language and so on. There was a 'language' before but with no object-nouns as it was entirely concerned with distinguishing social situations. In that case the Catholics might claim that they have only had souls since the mutation, a clear example of the divine purpose. But this would only make the story rather more unplausible, I suppose.

Apart from fun with politics and theology the interesting question is whether an intelligent race with a breeding season could develop at all, and whether it would be very unlike ourselves mentally. They get no social training from family life and no source of mental energy from repressed sex; most of the year they are a herd like wolves and sheep. One must suppose a period of very hard conditions in which they survive by learning to make concerted plans under a leader. I was tempted to make them vegetarians with a strong head for alcohol, but it is only in hunting that you get much scope for concerted plans. If they were water animals they might make plans like beavers, but there seem to be no water monkeys. Possible reasons are that the primate body does not swim fast and catches cold easily. A water animal with the use of fire might have entertaining customs, but does not seem plausible. I take it they can't with decent plausibility be made grazing animals, with hay being demanded at the big political dinner, because no monkey digests cellulose. (It is no good making them an entirely new kind of creature because there must be serious doubt whether they are men or not.) They have retreated to a single mountain area which they defend against negro attacks; the negroes are afraid of them, don't talk much about them, and when they do say things that sound like romancing. This makes it reasonable enough that they haven't been discovered. But it is not clear what large animals they can hunt up in the mountains. They must have an elaborate social structure of personal dominance, I think, reflected in the old language; because otherwise their lives seem too blank to develop intelligence. Rice-growing, come to think of it, would be a very neat employment for them; once they had taken to the mountain they would have to do a great deal of centralised waterwork to make the stuff grow, and the planning would require dominant leaders. Or some plant like rice; rice could hardly be got to them. The dominating situation arises during the breeding season only, when the herd originally split up into pairs for a short period. It is not clear how this could spread over into the placid herd situations between breeding seasons. The sexes are then hardly distinguished, but you discriminate a good deal about your furpicking partner. The hunting cooperation seems an easier thing to invent, partly because somebody is already dominant over the animal hunted, partly because the object is more in view. An intelligent race without either domination or pervasive sex I find too hard to imagine. To be sure one could run the novel on making them simply a tribe with evidence it wasn't human stock, but this seems hardly interesting enough.

You see the kind of topic. Grateful if you care to send comments.

Lord Zuckerman has no specific recollection of being consulted by Empson, then or later, but he has recently read the transcript and comments in a letter to me (7 April 1986) that he found it 'fascinating. Nothing in [Empson's] text is an affront to biological wisdom, and the Wuzzoo and all the others like him are beautiful, fantastic creatures. I particularly liked the way he brought in the breeding season.' Empson's fabulous beast may come as no shock to a seasoned biologist, but it is certainly designed to startle the European conscience at large.

As soon as he appears, Wuzzoo (the confusingly-named chief representative of the Wurroos) is seen to be covered with thick black fur, and he has a long tail and floppy ears. Accordingly, in spite of observing the evident fact that this creature is rational, articulate and perspicacious, the liberal but puzzled colonial administrator George Bickersteth provisionally decides that he must be put upon the footing of 'the family dog'. Although considerations of primate taxonomy and phylogeny are not seriously in question on the creature's first encounter with a human being, his initial status as a precociously intelligent pet cannot rest for long. Empson's intention in describing the creature so exactly is to invite the human race to puzzle over a cultural and philosophical dilemma: what social and spiritual value would we accord to a newly-discovered lower mammal that is yet capable of reason? This quick issue is signalled when Mrs Bickersteth (a character who surely owes something to Lorelei Lee and her friend Dorothy in Anita Loos's *Gentlemen Prefer Blondes*) discovers that the Wurroos have a demarcated breeding season. Although Empson did not particularly favour the looks of the genus *lemur*, he had (as he told Zuckerman) considered the idea that the Wurroo might be of 'lemuroid stock' – principally because of this peculiarity of breeding habit, which virtually requires it to be taken as a sub-order of primate. Monkeys and apes are 'like man' in experiencing 'a smooth and uninterrupted sexual and reproductive life' (as Zuckerman points out in a happily suggestive phrase).[61] The Wurroos' yearly season of anoestrus is 'unknown even among the great apes': so argues the advocate before the House of Lords on behalf of the Wurroos' claim that they are non-primate mammals. His presentation of the evidence thus follows the facts set out in Zuckerman's published studies, in particular that an intermittent breeding habit has the phyletic significance of putting such creatures at a remove even from the sub-human primates:

For the purpose of sociological analysis, mammals can be divided into three main groups, the first of which comprises the monkeys and apes (Order *Primates*). The members of the second group are those of the non-primate or lower mammals that have an anoestrus and a demarcated breeding season.[62]

The lawyer for the Wurroos brings forward the further crucial evidence that they are unable even to cross-breed with man: interspecific barriers of that kind obey the implication of the Linnaean concept that 'a species should be unable to cross successfully with a neighbouring but different one.'[63] Accordingly, if the Wurroos have no apparent physiological affinity with mankind, they must have a different morphological status. In sum, if there is no possibility of a Wurroo–human hybrid, and whatever their level of intelligence, the law sets these creatures outside the race of man – which is ironically

just what they desire: they have somehow heard the bad news about
racial oppression, and would prefer to be treated not as a 'tribe . . . a
lot of black men' but as a protected species.

Another point at which Empson hints is that, like apes and
monkeys, the Wurroos are normally polygynous: in one of the
fragments of the text Wuzzoo mentions that he has had three
children. 'I suppose you could call it favouritism rather . . . they were
all by the same female. People thought it rather pretty, you know,
evidently we liked each other a lot and so on.' It is 'rather eccentric'
behaviour, he tellingly observes. 'The idea of permanent sexual
relationships,' Zuckerman states,

conflicts with the annual transition of a sexual animal with functional
reproductive organs, into an asexual animal with non-functioning sexual
organs. This seasonal alteration from sexual to completely asexual behaviour is outside the range of human experience. It is as if an animal were
periodically castrated and then, after an interval, subjected to the operation
of implanting a functional gonad . . . sexual selection, as defined by Darwin,
has no important place in the social mechanisms of those sub-human
primates whose behaviour is known. Affective sentiments . . . are not
necessarily linked with sexual relationships.[64]

It is therefore a bit odd for Wuzzoo to have confined his sexual
relations to one female for three years running, even though the pair
felt affection for one another (which is peculiar in itself). The
Wurroos are in addition fur-picking mammals, which according to
Zuckerman is a fundamental factor in the social behaviour of sub-
human primates.[65]

However, if science and the law must needs determine that the
Wurroo is a sub-human species, does the creature's obvious intelligence nonetheless suggest a spiritual capability? 'Anybody can see
that we are like animals,' Empson wrote in a book review the year
before beginning his fable, 'but the theological issue comes with the
question whether the dividing line is sharp or blurred.'[66] This is the
crux of the story for Empson, and it explains why he took such care to
fashion his exotic creature as an authentic biological possibility: it is
his mode of bringing a creature from outer space literally down to
earth, with the fabulous Wurroo being made analogous to a fantastic
Martian. From his early years Empson thought it impudent and
parochial for Christians to believe that they bore witness to the one

true God and had been offered the salvation of souls through the redemption of Christ's sacrifice on the cross. His direct onslaught against the Christian God became most widely known only with the publication of *Milton's God* in 1961, but for many years he had felt distressed by the nature of the Christian atonement, and he always suggested as much in his published articles. As early as 1928, at the age of twenty-one, he observed in a review of the movie *The King of Kings* that 'there seems little religion in a drawn-out sanctimonious gloating over tortures, whose theological interest is not once adumbrated . . .'[67] Although he wrote about the subject guardedly as an undergraduate, then as later he felt it a repugnant conception of transcendent divinity that God the Father should have found it 'satisfying' to witness the appalling crucifixion of his Son (Empson's sense of the gospel required him to credit Arianism, since he thought it impossible to believe the doctrine of the Trinity – that Christ could be both true God and true man). However, even though he deplored the Christian God – whom he later dubbed the 'Torture Monster' – he did not glibly dismiss the possibilities of religious faith. As a metaphysician from his earliest years he agonised over the meaning and purpose of human life. Even in 1927 he had taken sober heed of Wyndham Lewis's rehearsal in *Time and Western Man* of the fact that recent cultural developments had permanently damaged some of the 'main props of our faith in Western common-sense' – chief among them being (in Empson's words) 'private integrity of thought, by the removal of a fixed God, which has fostered the idea of an unknowable, ever-changing organic flux, and referred all belief to contemporary shifting needs'.[68] Likewise, taking open-minded advantage of living and working in the Far East for a large part of the 1930s, he absorbed himself in codes of conduct and belief which seemed to contradict what he thought the smugness of European Christianity – just as much as Copernicus and Galileo had challenged the view of the world that John Donne inherited. He therefore felt profoundly bothered by the contradictions represented by the alternative systems of belief on our planet. The argument from those contradictions is the felt substance of many of the poems in *Collected Poems*; it is equally the substance of his plan for a ballet, 'The Elephant and the Birds', and – from a humorous but still philosophically searching angle – of 'The Royal Beasts'.

In his article 'Donne the Space Man' (1957), which has a direct bearing on the central issue of 'The Royal Beasts' dating from twenty years earlier, Empson argued that astronomical discoveries have profound theological and ethical consequences at any time of Christian culture, if you follow the logic of the discovery of a plurality of possible worlds beyond our own:

In our time no less than in Donne's, to believe that there are rational creatures on other planets is very hard to reconcile with the belief that salvation is only through Christ; they and their descendants appear to have been excluded from salvation; by the very scheme of God, indefinitely and perhaps for ever. One might suppose, to preserve God's justice, that Christ repeats his sacrifice on all worlds . . . but this already denies uniqueness to Jesus, and must in some way qualify the identity of the man with the divine person. It becomes natural to envisage frequent partial or occasional Incarnations on this earth . . . The young Donne, to judge from his poems, believed that every planet could have its incarnation, and believed this with delight, because it automatically liberated an independent conscience from any earthly religious authority. (*Kenyon Review*, XIX, 3, Summer 1957, pp. 339, 341)

'The Royal Beasts' features not a spaceman but a version of an apeman: the issues Empson raises about his particular creature apply either way. Donne's repeated metaphor of the separate planet, Empson argued in another essay, stood both for freedom and for 'the awful isolation of the human creature'.[69] This further observation from 'Donne the Space Man' has an equally obvious applicability to the puzzle of the Wurroos: 'The present state of scientific enquiry . . . almost forces us to believe in life on other planets . . . it makes the mind revolt at any doctrine which positively requires our earth to have the only rational inhabitants . . . the European maritime expansion made it hit the attention of Christians much more; the number and variety of people found to be living out of reach of the Gospel, many of them not noticeably worse than Christians, came as a shock . . .' (pp. 339–40)

These crucial issues are raised at the end of section III of the text, when the character Mr Thompson adroitly questions the theological consequence of excluding the creatures from the race of man – 'Are these Wurroos for ever, by one act of this court, to be shut out from heaven?' – and they are developed in sections IV and V. Here as in his article 'Donne the Space Man', Empson logically pursues the metaphysical deductions to be made from advances in scientific knowledge of the universe, which would seem to put in question the authenticity and justice of God's one local manifestation on this planet. As Sir Herbert Grierson wrote in 1929,

Like Tennyson, Donne is much concerned with the progress of science, the revolution which was going on in men's knowledge of the universe, and its disintegrating effect on accepted beliefs. To him the new astronomy is as bewildering in its displacement of the earth and disturbance of a concentric universe as the new geology was to be to Tennyson. (*The Poems of John Donne*, Oxford: OUP, vol. II, 1929, p. xxviii)

Empson affirmed Grierson's view: it is 'natural', he stated, 'to suppose that [Donne] believed what he says in the poems – that the unified world-picture of Catholicism had broken up . . . into isolated individuals . . .' ('Donne the Space Man', p. 350). He also took account of the fact that Donne 'read Kepler's book about a *nova* in 1606 and Galileo's about his discoveries through a telescope in 1610' ('Donne the Space Man', p. 344). In one of his early notebooks he worried the unavoidable questions with jottings such as these:

Importance of matter goes with social disorder: not one place like Rome from which to form a hierarchy, so things must somehow carry their merit in themselves.

Matter of earth like matter of heavenly bodies: so matter of earth is not fundamentally inferior.

Kepler claimed that 'Trismegistus called [the sun] the visible God': hence that it could be the centre of the system. The old centre had been the lowest thing, dead matter: the new one was also matter, but divine matter.

. . .

All the world partakes of God in that it partakes of number. Hence a revival of astrology in Kepler's time: matter may tell us anything. But later, surely, matter becomes dead billiard balls, with no very divine qualities.

'Of course, I ought to have said before,' remarks an unnamed speaker in Empson's fable, 'it was an essential claim for Christianity as a powerful centralised religion that you couldn't possibly get to heaven without it':

The justice of God was under a great strain anyway, because the vast majority of men hadn't been given a chance. There were all the great classical pagans before Christ appeared at all, and even then the Chinese didn't hear of him for a thousand years. I daresay it seems easier now that the missionaries have got about a good deal, but Dante felt it all right; how God can be just at all had to be made a supreme mystery with a whole crowd of interlocking allegories.

This line of thought became crucial for Empson not only for its speculative and sceptical value but because the historical Church had made it a life-and-death issue: at the turn of the seventeenth century the Inquisition had indicted Giordano Bruno for his belief in a possible plurality of worlds, and it is justifiably believed that the heresy he thus professed was brought up as one of the charges which led to his execution. 'They wanted the earth to be the only habitable planet so that Christ could be unique,' Empson's spokesman comments in section V of 'The Royal Beasts'. Furthermore, as Empson pointed out in an essay entitled 'Literary Criticism and the Christian Revival' (1966),

Melancthon, as soon as Copernicus published, had denounced him for implying an argument against Christianity: 'Does Jesus Christ get crucified on each of the planets in turn? Or is the Father totally unjust to the Martians?' . . . Professor Marjorie Nicolson was still saying in 1935 (*Studies in Philology*), 'The idea of a plurality of worlds, which Donne had suggested in his earlier poetry, was indeed for churchmen a dangerous tenet, even, as it came to be called, the "new heresy".'[70]

Once possessed by what he regarded as the necessity of defying the Christian God, a passion which can be dated back at least as far as his reading of J. B. S. Haldane's *Possible Worlds* in 1929, Empson took every opportunity to reiterate it. He even enlisted to his camp another literary giant some thirty years after writing 'The Royal Beasts', when he protested (or provocatively conjectured against the Christian orthodoxy of Professor Northrop Frye) that Milton's 'theological position made him want to have man-like creatures on other planets because that would be a decisive blow against the claim of any Church to be the only source of salvation.'[71] Empson's voice of reason in 'The Royal Beasts' argues that 'once there were any number of possible worlds that Christ hadn't died on and where people couldn't possibly hear the gospel the injustice of the thing would become intolerable.' His humane solution follows: 'The only way out is to say that Christ does it on all the different worlds . . . and that gives you quite a different idea of the historical Jesus; for one thing, Christ may just as well have other incarnations as a man.' As Empson explained in a later article (on Dylan Thomas), 'The idea that any man can become Christ, who is a universal, was a major sixteenth-century heresy and has been kept up among the poets.'[72] It would be no less a heresy today, of course, but Empson was at once begging the question and trailing his coat. The religion and morality he adumbrates in 'The Royal Beasts' – which postulates a position (as the text has it) 'ambiguous between pantheism and Arianism, in which the historical importance of the events related in the gospels is reduced to a reassuring unimportance' – owe much to his study and understanding of Mahayana Buddhism. At some point during the 1930s, for instance, he had made these precise and interested notes on the concept of 'Suchness' (which also anticipate his ballet 'The Elephant and the Birds'):

> The Bodhisattva becomes not merely a Buddha, but Buddha, the ultimate undifferentiated reality, suchness . . .
> Between Asoka and AD 1 [there were] important changes in the idea of the nature of a Buddha . . . Everyone might now aim at becoming a Buddha. The term bodhissatva [sic] occurs in the sutras, where it means the state of a Buddha before his enlightenment.

Likewise, his defiance of the doctrine of the uniqueness of Christ anticipates his later applause for Aldous Huxley's formulation in *The Perennial Philosophy* (1946) of the concept that everyone participates in a 'Divine Ground'.[73] The need to bypass Christian doctrine became a moral passion for Empson. A religious position which might somehow conjoin pantheism and the Buddhist doctrine of Karma seemed to him at once more generous and just than the options of heaven or hell: 'the universalising of the idea of Christ,' he suggested in 'Donne the Space Man' (and earlier, in sections IV and V of 'The Royal Beasts'), makes 'individuality less important.'[74]

The entirety of 'The Royal Beasts' is first-draft work; but even without any finish of style or structure it raises all the crucial issues of Empson's ethical concerns and researches during the 1930s, and it gestures forward to the indictment of Christianity that is central to *Milton's God*. Equally it stands on the brink of the imaginative act of cultural and moral equity that he would try to compose between East and West in 'The Elephant and the Birds' five years later. Since Empson in China was kept so busy with his teaching in extremely difficult conditions, which included the constant threat of Japanese bombing raids, it is surprising not that he failed to finish 'The Royal Beasts' but that he wrote quite so much of it. Early in 1938 the combined universities hiked the further distance of 800 miles to the state of Yunnan, where Empson taught until late in 1939. From 1940 until his return to Peking in 1946 he worked for the BBC, where George Orwell was one of his colleagues and closer friends. (Although 'The Royal Beasts' in some respects anticipates *Animal Farm* by about eight years, it is unlikely that the unpresuming Empson ever mentioned his work to Orwell.) As he explained to Christopher Ricks in 1975, 'I dropped all my literary interests, even reviewing, because I got absorbed in the war; I thought the defeat of Hitler so important that I could do nothing else (it was a time of great happiness, looking back, and anyway of considerable pleasure, but I have just a steady trickle of mental productiveness, and it was then all directed into propaganda).'[75] We cannot therefore assume that Empson tired of his novel or thought it an unsuccessful venture, only that he was overtaken by circumstances and other professional commitments. Suffice it to say that he had the manuscript of the novel with him – and possibly worked on it – during the Communist liberation of Peking at the end of the 1940s, and that he certainly felt grateful when a Burmese friend later rescued his well-worn papers: 'When I left Communist Peking he smuggled out for me a small suitcase containing unfinished plays, an unfinished novel about Africa, none of it to do with China; I have never looked at them since but revere Myat Tun for saving them with such firm instructions and energetic adroitness.'[76]

One factor to bear in mind while reading 'The Royal Beasts' is the serious stress Empson placed on his observation (in *Milton's God*) that 'the central function of imaginative literature is to make you realise that other people act on moral convictions different from your own . . . What is more, it has been thought from Aeschylus to Ibsen that a literary work may present a current moral problem, and to some extent alter the judgement of those who appreciate it by making them see the case as a whole.'[77] All the same, and even in its unfinished state, Empson would surely have felt about his fable what he wrote about the contemporary poem 'Autumn on Nan-Yueh': 'I hope the gaiety of the thing comes through.'[78]

III

'I haven't any cultural side to speak of, being now definitely an all-time propaganda hack,' Empson wrote to I. A. Richards on 12 January 1943; 'if I'm not fussing about broadcasts *to* the Far East I ought to be fussing about home BBC programmes *on* the Far East, the second is my artwork which I may do when I get home from the office . . . My office is next door to George Orwell's and I find him excellent company; it is wonderful how he still manages to do some writing.' But Orwell was by no means alone in his ability to keep up with his writing under any circumstances, for Empson goes on in the same letter to declare quite unassumingly: 'I have written a ballet . . . [but] I am afraid nothing more will come of it . . .' (Empson Papers).

'The Elephant and the Birds' (1942) is in many ways complementary to 'The Royal Beasts', for it shows Empson's imagination conciliating rather more than quizzing. Its imaginative burden is to establish a rapprochement between East and West, to exemplify just how much they are alike in their religious myths and cultural heritage in general.

Just as Empson found it unavoidable for his poetry to have what he called 'puzzle interest', the text of his ballet also begins by facing us with a riddle. 'The dance tells the story of two legends,' it opens, 'the Greek story of Philomel and Procne, and the Indian story of what the Buddha did in his incarnation as an elephant.' So the question is, what have the following in common: a lustful Thracian king who ravishes and mutilates his sister-in-law and in return suffers the horror of being induced to dine on his own son; two vengeful women, wife and sister-in-law of the king, who feed him that grisly meal and escape his wrath by being transmogrified into birds; and the Buddha, who dies as an elephant only to be reborn as a man, and who fulfils his mortal destiny by founding a religion whose essence is ultimate extinction? At first sight, there would appear to be little common ground between them. Come now (as Empson would say), they simply will not go together. But it is those very legends that Empson set himself to conflate in the seven scenes of his ballet.

The story of Philomel, Procne and Tereus survives in Greek and Latin versions (and, as Empson reminds us, it plays a part in Shakespeare's terrible *Titus Andronicus*), but it is best known in the version retailed by Ovid in *Metamorphoses*, book VI, the text from which Empson took this strand of his scenario, and which T. S. Eliot also drew upon in *The Waste Land*. In his own introduction to the ballet Empson sketches the original tale so briefly that it may be helpful if I tell it again in a slightly fuller form. After her marriage to King Tereus of Thrace, Procne (daughter of the king of Athens) coaxes her husband into fetching her beloved sister Philomel to live at their court. While fulfilling her wish, Tereus is inflamed by a wicked passion for his sister-in-law and presently rapes her; he then cuts out her tongue when she threatens to denounce him. For fear that she might yet find a way to reveal his evil deed, Tereus secretly imprisons his victim; but she weaves a tapestry depicting the crime and has it conveyed to her sister. Procne rescues Philomel by subterfuge, and together they take revenge by killing Itys (Procne's son by Tereus) and preparing his body as a dish fit only for this king. Gleefully they tell the king what they have done, but only when they have borne filthy witness to his hearty eating. Thrown into a murderous rage, he lunges after them; and upon that cue they are unaccountably transformed into birds – a swallow and a nightingale. (Tereus too becomes a bird; but, as Empson jests in the text, 'we need not worry about his subsequent status as a Hoopoe.')

The other legend Empson brings into play – the story of the Buddha in his incarnation as an elephant – is probably unknown to the majority of readers in the Western world: it figures in the *Jataka*, the enormous Pali canon of stories of the Buddha's former births. The prologue to the *Chaddanta-Jataka*, which is Empson's specific source,[79] tells how a female novice suddenly intuits that in a former life she had once committed a sin against the Buddha, whereupon the Master himself rehearses the full story. When the Bodhisattva came to life as a gloriously pure white elephant, he remembers, he became the chief of a great herd and had two consorts; by chance he appeared to favour the first of his wives, with the result that the second wrongly felt slighted and conceived a grudge against him. She prayed that in her next life she might become the queen of Benares, simply in order that she could arrange for a hunter to slay the six-tusked (or possibly six-coloured) elephant who had offended her; and forthwith she pined and starved herself to death. And so it came to pass: in her next life she did indeed become the queen; and remembering the injury supposedly done to her she despatched a hunter ('a stout knave') to fulfil her vow of vengeance, commanding him not to return without the wondrous tusks she coveted. Although the hunter managed to wound the mountainous elephant with a poisoned arrow, he found himself too weak to cut off his colossal tusks. The elephant bore his mortal agony with perfect patience; and realising that the hunter acted not for his own advantage but had been suborned by his malign mistress he generously sawed off his own tusks, and so died. However, when the hunter finally delivered the trophies to the jealous queen,

> His tusks no sooner did she see
> – Her own dear lord of old was he –
> Than straight her heart through grief did break
> And she, poor fool, died for his sake.

The upshot is that because she grieves for her former sin the 'yellow-robed ascetic maid' subsequently attains to Sainthood. Yet the real moral of the story, which concerns goodness and generosity, redounds principally to the credit of the Buddha himself. As the Bodhisattva surrenders his life he remarks: 'May this meritorious act be to me the cause of attaining Omniscience.' His selflessness accordingly seems to include a portion of self-glorification; an element of what Empson's scenario justifiably terms 'wilful moral splendour'.

Empson clearly hoped that in performance the riddle of the ballet – the marrying of the two legends – would solve itself. Short of having it produced on stage, however, I must unravel it by filling in something of its rich intellectual and artistic background – the background that Empson himself gathered on his travels. His introduction to the ballet suggests that he has only a dim memory of the Chaddanta-Jataka, and indeed is whimsically little concerned with its detail: 'The Buddha in his incarnation as an elephant offered his body to a hunter, I am not sure whether to save the other elephants or to comfort a hunter who clearly needed an elephant, but anyhow it was through this act of wilful self-sacrifice that he contrived to be reborn as a man.' But in fact he had long studied both Buddhism and Buddha effigies, and they are central to his conception of the ballet. The full story of the story behind the ballet thus begins at the latest by

1933, during Empson's period of teaching at the Tokyo University of Literature and Science (Bunrika Daigaku).

Some years after writing the ballet he claimed that his nose had been 'rubbed very firmly in the Buddha'[80] throughout his time in Japan and China. The truth is that he had sought out Buddhist icons with an erudite-amateur interest amounting to a passion. 'The Buddhas are the only accessible art I find myself able to care about,' he wrote in March 1933,[81] underplaying what had in fact become a thoroughgoing involvement with the techniques and meaning of the innumerable images of the Buddha he studied in the Far East. In 1933, for example, he spent his spring break from the university in travelling from Japan to China – with the specific purpose of visiting Yungang (to the northwest of Peking), where in the fifth century AD twenty vast caves had been cut out of the rock, many with enormous Buddhas. During another vacation he went to Korea; and within Japan itself he inspected the early ('very good') statues at Nara, as well as those in Kyoto – where he judged that the later examples of the artistic expression first imported from Korea had been so comfortably assimilated by the Japanese as to become 'a sort of whimsical family joke'.[82] Subsequently, after quitting his post in Tokyo in 1934, he stopped off during the long passage home in Burma, Ceylon and India – again with the specific aim of pursuing Buddha images.

Never put off by the hot hardships and inconveniences of travelling in the Far East, which he took in the spirit of junketing, he nonetheless found himself wondering in a witty letter of 7 March 1933 to his friend John Hayward: 'Always rather embarrassing to wonder what one gets out of travel to make up for its privations; except that it requires so much imagination to stay at home.'[83] He later remembered the fact that Dr Johnson had taken with him to the Western Isles of Scotland Crocker's *Arithmetic*, 'because (he said) you get tired of any work of literature, but a book of science is inexhaustible.'[84] Empson fully agreed with Johnson's point of view, and reported during his visit to India: 'I have bought a textbook of algebra to try and keep the soul alive on the boat.'[85] (During his period of refugeeing with the Chinese in 1937–1939 he prized 'a little book of school Problem Papers' for times of relaxation; but, he added, 'it was worth carrying the poems of Dylan Thomas as well because they were equally inexhaustible.'[86])

The fact that he admired Buddhism so much more than other religions – including Hinduism, for example – comes strongly to the fore in the notes he took in India, where he wrote:

A revival of Buddhism no doubt can't be expected, but it would be fine; it was a vast relief to my feelings, at any rate, ill-informed as they may be, to see a few people in the yellow robe again when I got to the bo-tree of [the Buddha's] illumination at Bodh Gaya. They have put up a very nice temple [the Mahabodhi temple] and rest-house there with curiously Anglican frescoes. Filthy and naked except for a loincloth and pendant asserting that he is the British Empire's official guide, the man who falls on you when you approach the ruins repeats incessantly in English that all statues belong to the Asoka period, from which no statues survive.

Bodh Gaya had been the only place he visited in India which was 'hardly worth the trouble', he later reported to his friend George Sansom (a savant of Japan and at that time commercial counsellor to the British Embassy in Tokyo),[87] but he had 'filled it out with a trot across country to the Barabar caves, empty and well polished' – which he correctly guessed 'might be what Forster was thinking of [in his description of the Marabar caves] in A Passage to India, though they don't fit exactly.'[88]

Given his passion for Buddhist icons, he thought it a gravelling though entertaining irony that the Indians should have connived at British arrogance even in matters of artistic value:

The best single joke of the guide-book is about Calcutta, where there is a superb monster collection of all the periods and arts of India; I was concentrating on the Buddhist statues, and only remember how good it is on them. The only art museum in Calcutta, says the guide-book, is the Victoria Memorial Hall (or some such name), which contains paintings of all the viceroys since Warren Hastings, many taken direct from life.

Not being himself a disciple of Buddhism, however, he felt no need to be too sober about the effigies he inspected so keenly; again in Calcutta, for instance, he observed with amusement that the 'huge lying Buddha under its cast iron . . . summer house' looked 'like the R101 in dock'.

All in all, he took rather a low view of the Indians[89] as well as their predominant religion, and as a direct consequence he found Anuradhapura in Ceylon (his next port of call after Calcutta) 'rather a disappointment':

the Indians here aren't merely ousting the natives as in Burma, and Malaya (with Chinese), but absorbing them: I thought it would be a great relief to get here but it is only the change from the sewer-rat to the water-rat; my guide is a Singhalese Hindu who says soothingly that Hinduism and Buddhism have fused their virtues together in Ceylon, but he brought his nephew today in the car to improve his mind – the nephew he complains might become an archaeologist but is too pious – and the nephew looked at me with the feeble furious pop-eyes of the Indian and wiggled his fingers and said loudly that he was a Hindu. Specially addicted to Siva, his uncle confessed.[90]

Although he took copious if often cryptic notes on his travels, it is much to be regretted that he never undertook the full travel book he often thought of writing, for his occasional jottings display a high level of learning and aesthetic appreciation. Among the few passages he did write up, this piece – which he headed simply 'Two Buddhist Sights' – amply illustrates his ability to evoke a monument and its deep significance:

The Shwedagan, the big pagoda at Rangoon, being garish, praised for size, and last altered in 1871 (the date of the main present form seems not to be known), might be expected not to have great merit but in fact carries out the principle of the bell-shaped pagoda to a rare perfection; the Shmehmawdaw at Pegu was the only other one I saw (seeing only those two towns) which played the same trick, and that not so well. Architecture can seldom deal directly with metaphysics but these objects having no practical purpose and for that matter no inside are free to concentrate on a single root notion, the relation of the Many and the One; every line is concerned to bring bodily before the eyes an abstract and fundamental mode of thought (independent of any one religion, and though made less urgent by individualising Christianity at least as relevant to Taoism and Mohammedanism as to the doctrine of the Blessed One). The mere dome of an Indian stupa remains striking chiefly for its pointlessness; the Burmese type with a curved spire and cluster of attendant bulbs seems to have given the traditional cult-object its proper symbolism.

Outside the two lines of fussy small bulbs, twenty feet high or so, at the bottom of the octagon, which transfer it to the square, is a wide low promenade flanked outside by temples and the gates heading the four stairways; clustered with alabaster Buddhas, pilgrims, people selling things, and dogs dying of starvation. The corners of this outer square, from which one might see three sides of the octagon symmetrically, are largely blocked, and it is best not seen symmetrically. Taking it with two of the sides mainly in view the complicated juts and corbels which step up the octagon, different on alternate sides and thus made to twist round in one direction, seem to climb up out of all this clutter into the single smooth form that you see at a distance, and the lines of the third face in perspective, which would climb the other way, go through 'virtual foci', not meeting but nearing with the effect of an elbow-movement lifting the eye round. All the weight of detail of the lower world is thus forced sideways up into the pure circle of the bell, the bubble, and the beggingbowl, in the dome; straightness is then dissolved into the lush forms of the lotus and the carrotlike bulb of the plaintain, and the curve soars up the handle of the bell to the little diamonded umbralle [? umbrella] of the empyrean. It is a type of architecture in which every detail follows from a single premiss, which is never anything but the sustained translation of one thought.

The ethics of Buddhism struck Empson as altogether more humane than those of Christianity, and certainly more generous in allowing the disciple to improve in moral worth through successive incarnations. In addition, two particularly important factors fascinated Empson about the earliest authentic representations of the Buddha: (i) the expressive enigma posed by the faces of the oldest statues, which managed at once to broadcast the essential meaning of the faith and to transcend national and racial boundaries; (ii) the process by which that image and its message had been dispersed all the way from India to the Pacific. To the casual Western tourist it can often seem that the inscrutable and even bland face of the Buddha is endlessly replicated throughout the Eastern world; Empson's more assiduous eye enabled him to discriminate not only that the image varies from country to country, and indeed from one historical phase to another within each country, but also that the paradigm of the Buddha's expression manages to incorporate two apparently incompatible significations. He had early schooled himself in the ambiguities of literary expression for the book that brought him worldwide fame, *Seven Types of Ambiguity*; subsequently, in the early 1930s, he discerned that the secret of the Buddha's given expression likewise embodied a fundamental ambiguity. From the start of his travels he accumulated a large quantity of notes on his personal observations of Buddha effigies and from his reading in Buddhism, since he planned in due course to write a book about the Buddha expression; then, on 5 February 1936, he published in the *Listener* a short preliminary article ('The Faces of Buddha') describing some of his observations, though he held in reserve the theoretical basis of his argument; and finally, at the very end of World War II, he sat down in London and completed the long-planned monograph, *Asymmetry in Buddha*

Faces, which he decked out with the numerous essential photographic illustrations he had gathered on his travels.[91] Unhappily, through no fault of his own and to his lasting disappointment, that finished work together with the photographs was lost in London soon after he returned to China in 1946. Among the draft papers he left heaped in his den, however, some few passages do survive – most fortunately this opening page which gives the key to his complete theory:

The experts have tended to avoid talking about the expressions of the great Buddha heads, partly because the whole subject of faces is so little understood by science that one can only assert a personal impression. Mr Langdon Warner[92] of the Boston Museum gaily said 'that way madness lies' when I asked him about them. But the faces are magnificent; it is a strange confession of helplessness if we have to keep mum for fear of talking nonsense. I think there is a clear point to be made here which has been neglected by Western critics, a point that lets you understand and enjoy the statues better. It will be agreed that a good deal of the startling and compelling quality of these faces comes from their combining things that seem incompatible, especially a complete repose with an active power to help the worshipper. Now of course the two things must somehow be diffused through the whole face, or it would have no unity; the whole business is very subtle. But the normal way of getting the effect in the great periods is a reliable and simple one; the two incompatible things are largely separated onto the two sides of the face.

I had a chance when I was in Japan to suggest this theory to Mr Anesaki, which I did very timidly, expecting him to treat it as a fad. He treated it as something obvious and wellknown, and told me to compare the masks of the Noh stage. These give something like historical evidence because the tradition of the craftsmen has not been lost (they are very much later than the Suiko statues); it is definitely known that their faces were constructed to wear two expressions.

In an early review (1928) of a book entitled *Opposite Things*, by M. Carta Sturge, Empson had defined a paradox that he felt characterised the whole of human existence: 'Extremely often, in dealing with the world, one arrives at two ideas or ways of dealing with things which both work and are needed, but which entirely contradict one another ... Miss Sturge is expounding this very important process with reference to Hegel; but she is not much concerned with him; she could get it out of the practice of scientists, recent mathematical logic, primitive languages, the doctrine of the Trinity, the corresponding Eastern ideas, and, in fact, out of anything of any importance.'[93] It is no accident, therefore, that he thought the crux of the poem by himself which he most liked, 'Bacchus', was the 'notion . . . that life involves maintaining oneself between contradictions that can't be solved by analysis';[94] nor was it by chance that he became absorbed by the same vital doubleness as soon as he saw it incorporated in the form of the face of the Buddha.

What had also been growing in Empson's mind was the recognition that the Buddha face represented something not necessarily, or even distinctively, national or racial (given its iconic origin in India), but that it perhaps linked cultural elements ranging geographically and historically from a point of contact with the Mediterranean world to the farthest reaches of the Eastern world. Having witnessed in Japan in the early 1930s the effects of a fiercely misplaced nationalism, he became concerned to minimise the importance of national differences and to emphasise what different countries held in common through their religious myths and art, and through their mixtures of race. His article 'The Faces of Buddha' argues that it is a mistake to explain the Buddha expression as 'merely racial':

Graeco–Roman artists in the North-West, about the first century AD, seem to have broken the Indian convention that the Buddha must not be portrayed, and the calm of their Apollo made a conflict with the human and muscular earth-god tradition of Mathura . . . The merely racial difficulty in understanding the faces is indeed smaller than you would expect, and the artists at Angkor no less than Ajanta seem to have amused themselves by putting the same face on to all the races of mankind. (*Listener*, 5 February 1936, pp. 238–40)

Even some three years earlier, while lamenting that he knew 'no decent book about faces later than Darwin's' (*The Expression of the Emotions in Man and the Animals*, 1873), he had stipulated: 'I am sure that the general rules about telling character from faces are the same for the whole human race – allowing for the type the individual varies from – but how much does the type mean? etc. etc.'[95] He felt certain at the least that just as the Buddha image spans nations so it is a damaging fallacy for any nation to assert itself as a fixed race. With reference to the imperialism of Japan, for example, he said in his capacity as BBC Chinese Editor during World War II:

Japanese anthropologists cheerfully admit a Chinese and a Mongol and a South Sea island wave of immigration. Then there's the Hairy Ainu in the north, who certainly intermarried with the Japanese, and the Hairy Ainu is supposed to be Caucasian like ourselves. The beautiful girl of the Utamaro woodcut has a long narrow face with a curled nose, a fine Jewish type, and she only really occurs among the Japanese aristocracy; and that element might come from Arab traders in the South Seas. In fact it's a very complete mixture of race.[96]

As to the artistic origin of the particular face that preoccupied him, Empson had to some extent to rely in the 1930s on the scholarship of a book called *The Beginnings of Buddhist Art* (1917), by A. Foucher, who argued vigorously that all the representations of the Buddha – whether in India, Ceylon, Cambodia, Korea, China or Japan – stemmed from a common prototype established in northwest India. In brief, the burden of Foucher's study is that the image of the Buddha had a Greek origin. Alexander the Great had conquered and colonised Bactria (northern Afghanistan) in 326 BC, after which the western confines of India had been so subjected to a Hellenising influence (especially under Menander, 150–100 BC) as to make it inevitable that the first Buddha images should be created in a style to which scholars apply the heteroclite term 'Greco–Buddhist'. Discoveries at Gandhara (in Pakistan), Foucher asserts, oblige us to decide in favour of the Eurasian prototype of the Buddha image. He seeks to demonstrate as much by describing two statues which appear to share a model: one is a figure of Christ taken from a sarcophagus in Asia Minor, the other a Buddha from a ruined temple in Gandhara. Both statues, he claims, are directly descended from the statue in the Lateran Museum known as the Orator: 'plastically speaking they are cousins-german. The one is a Greco–Christian Christ; the other is a Greco–Buddhist Buddha. Both are, by the same right, a legacy left *in extremis* to the old world by the expiring Greek art.' The initiatory type of the Buddha, he argues further, 'issues from the fusion of a double ideal, that of the Greek Olympian and that of the *Mahapurusha*, or Indian "Great Man", with no borrowing from living reality, if we except the detail of the distended lobes of the ears.' He climaxes his evidence with these words:

Thus, then, we are on the whole well informed as to the where and the when, from the rencontre of the two inverse expansions, that of Hellenism towards the East consequent upon the political conquests of Alexander, and that of Buddhism towards the west by favour of the religious missions of Açoka, was born once and for all the Indo–Greek type of Buddha.[97]

Such seemed to be the state of the art for the historians and aestheticians of Buddhism in the 1930s. But Empson did not take Foucher's writings as his final authority; he continually looked at things for himself, as in this fine perception from a contemporary letter:

I was interested in Japan by the trick of making the upper eyelid overhang so that the eye opens when you come up and pray under it. It seems that you get this in Gandhara stuff but there it doesn't mean anything, and don't get it anywhere else before the Gupta period, when most of them do it, obviously intentionally, even though the eye is half open. The example of 'transition' in the Sarnath museum hasn't learned the trick yet. This seems interesting if true, since it would be a case of 'learning' from the Greco–Roman type things it had never meant seriously. One of the three seated Buddhas at Anuradhapura . . . (the thing is puggy and childishly determined from the front, Mussolini from the side, and the body is ready to jump up and kick about like a monkey . . .) does this eye-trick, and of course may be very early: the guide beat my attempt at denying the date was 300 BC by saying the Singhalese might presumably make Buddhas even if the Indians hadn't started.[98]

The question of the priority of the Buddha prototype – whether it should be acknowledged as Greco–Roman or indigenous Indian (in the style of Mathura) – has come under renewed scholarly scrutiny in post-war years. Wladimir Zwalf carefully sums up the recent scholarly compromise on the issue, which is that the Buddha images of the Mathura school must take first place over the western-influenced Gandhara Buddhas of the northwest frontier: 'the first Buddha images were in the Indian Mathura style, while the Gandharan Buddha grew out of that prototype by incorporating the local Greco–Roman stylistic features.'[99] At best, then, as Christmas Humphreys confirms in *Buddhism*, the artistic history of the Gandhara school 'runs parallel to and independent from the main current of Indian art'. Humphreys also cites the informed view of Ananda Coomaraswamy that – while there is a clear influence of Western forms on all later Indian and Chinese Buddhist art – 'the actual art of Gandhara gives the impression of profound insincerity.' He therefore concludes: 'In brief, the flower of Buddhist art in India, which developed in the Gupta period (AD 300–600) is purely Indian.'[100]

Empson, it needs to be said, never swallowed the tendentious opinion that the Buddha effigy had been created '*de chic*' (to use Foucher's twee phrase)[101] by European artist-strangers. In fact, he anticipated much of this whole debate, but with the sceptical feeling that Indian scholars of the 1930s at least might not always be capable of disinterest in their findings; his contemporary notes include these remarks, which indicate that he had discriminating doubts about the priority of the Gandhara Buddha in advance of some of the scholars:

The old view about the early statues of Buddha, powerfully maintained by Foucher, was that none were made until a Greco–Roman influence provided both the initiative and the stock type. This is now sometimes heartily denied. The ignorant seeker after truth will think the denial likely right, but he will find it chiefly made by Indian experts in whom he can detect a nationalist bias . . . it does no good to the experts; an expert on an obscure subject ought to be quarrelling all the time, because there is nothing else to keep his spirits up. At any rate I couldn't get clear about the state of informed opinion, and must talk boldly about what I saw . . . On the face of it, the Greco–Roman work from Gandhara that we see about in such quantities is too bad to inspire anybody. You might suspect that people only pretended it was interesting in order to insist that India had no original sculpture.

In any event, Wladimir Zwalf's recent scrupulous summarisation that 'the Buddha image evolved in both centres independently and more or less simultaneously'[102] would still seem to justify Empson's conviction that East had indeed met West – through the gradual historical and geographical dispersion of religious art and cultural myth. 'The Elephant and the Birds' postulates that there is no significant contrast between the Greek and the Indian legends it depicts, and that (in the words of the text) 'The general assumption of the story is that a colonial Greek princess has married a north-eastern Indian king some time after the conquests of Alexander the Great, when the two countries are in regular contact.' Still, in the 1930s at least, Empson was seeking not the imaginative collocation of Greek and Indian myths that he later designed in 'The Elephant and the Birds', nor even a syncretism to be defined in terms of Greco–Buddhist art, but merely to trace some provisional sense of the real cultural connections between Europe and the Far East. His deep interest lay in the demonstrable fact that (as he later put it) 'India developed in parallel to the Mediterranean basin.'[103]

Empson situates his ballet in an indeterminate Indian site not unlike Angkor, the legendary city of the kingdom of the Khmers located to the north of the great lake Tonle Sap, at the highest reaches of the Mekong river in Cambodia. The reasons are not far to seek: they again relate to the forced march that the Greek Alexander the Great made into India, and the consequent influence of Greco–Roman forms of art and myth on the art and myth of the East. 'The kings of Angkor,' writes Bernard Groslier, 'claimed descent from an exiled Indian prince and the daughter of the king of the local *naga* [a many-headed serpent, the water-god of the Khmers].'[104] In Empson's ballet, Philomel and Procne are depicted as types of the European temperament, psychologically self-tormenting and fixated on wretched memories; for a while they cannot be reconciled to the Buddha, but by the end of the dance it comes about that they can be. In a similar fashion, Tereus, the deified Greco–Roman king, is shown for a time to be quite unlike and then *not at all unlike* the Buddha as Empson portrays him in all his majesty. In an analogous fashion, the great kings of Angkor found a way to accommodate the Buddhist religion which came to their land from the West, and presently to assimilate within their temples both their old cult of the king-god and their celebration of the newfound lord, the Buddha.

'Let it be said immediately,' wrote Osbert Sitwell (who visited the city ruins at about the same time as Empson), 'that Angkor, as it stands, ranks as chief wonder of the world today, one of the summits to which human genius has inspired in stone, infinitely more impressive, lovely and, as well, romantic, than anything that can be seen in China; than, even, the Great Wall or the Ming Tombs.'[105] Founded in the sixth century AD, the dynasty of the Khmers reached its zenith between the ninth and twelfth centuries. In the early twelfth century the then king, a devout disciple of Vishnu, built what is now the best-known monument of the kingdom, Angkor Wat, a vast funerary temple resembling a pyramid; its several towers and tiers of galleries and portals are approached by a long causeway over canals and water-works. It is the supreme construction of a Cambodian Brahman. Later, at the turn of the thirteenth century, King Jayavarman VII constructed the Bayon, the supreme Cambodian temple of the lately arrived Buddhism, which should by rights have been at odds with the prevailing religion of Hinduism but in fact topped it – or rather perhaps subsumed it – with apparent ease. According to Bernard Groslier, 'Angkor Wat marked the zenith both of Hinduism and the monarchy. The Bayon was the sweetest flower of Buddhism springing from an exceptional king.' Groslier adds this likely and important information: 'it is not impossible that Jayavarman VII, at least to some extent, facilitated by his apocalypse in stone the change-over from Hinduism, which no longer led anywhere, to a Buddhist peace . . .'[106] The Bayon, which is an extraordinary feat of monumental sculpture – 'the *omphalos* of this stone cosmos' – Groslier describes as 'a veritable forest of fifty-two towers rising to 45 metres from ground-level in a vertiginous chaos of stone . . . In the central sanctuary stood the image of the Buddha, incarnation of the king and Lord of the World.'[107] It was to the Buddhist Bayon, therefore, that Empson understandably devoted most of his attention when he visited Angkor during his second sojourn in the Far East.

In their flight from the Japanese invaders the staff and students of the combined Peking universities migrated in the spring of 1938 to southwest China, where they found their final wartime home in the pleasant city of Kunming, capital of the province of Yunnan. The upheaval and the arduous journey onward from Changsha, where Empson first drafted 'The Royal Beasts', had obliged him to stop work on the novel until better days might bring peace enough for him to resume it. But mess and unrest never troubled Empson; he would simply create his own pocket of intense thought within any circumstantial chaos. While most of his colleagues felt only too content to recuperate in Kunming after the heavy trek across the mountains, nothing could stop Empson's quest for Buddhist monuments. Just as soon as he could free himself from teaching, in the spring of 1938, he broke away from his billet in order to slog across to Angkor.

'I find my prejudices are stronger than ever about Hinduism,' he wrote to a friend about the extraordinary lost city, 'the good stuff here was all done while they were more or less Buddhist.'[108] His contemporary notes exercise the same bias in favour of the Bayon:

As the Bayon brings the human head into architecture the Neak Pean was a temple made of a lotus, standing in the middle of a bathing pool. The tearing Indian imagination works on the cool taste and feeling for pattern of the Khmers, and for a brief century they can wield architecture like sculpture. Angkor Vat is not in the same street as this: merely a Hindu temple in good taste – but what is the good of good taste in a Hindu temple?[109]

Perhaps the chief feature of the Bayon is that the builders had carved four huge faces on each of its multiple towers, showing a quality of workmanship which Empson had no hesitation in praising on behalf of what he considered the unequivocally excellent influence that Buddhism brought to Asia. 'The eight-foot faces are extraordinarily sensitive and noble; the Chinese were never able to make the big heads work, and thank God the Indians didn't try. It is awfully bad luck that the Khmers only came in for the end of Indian Buddhism.'

A friend named Norman France had lent Empson a book about Angkor, and very soon – with a spritely irritation generated by his better personal understanding – he reported on it in a letter:

> Your book keeps chattering about how primitive and romantic the Bayon is, and the idea of using big faces in general. I can't see what 'Romantic' has to do with it: the effect is that you are immensely protected and secure (once you are on the terrace with the heads all round you in their places), 'safe in thine eternal arms'. It is almost the opposite to Romance . . . The clumsiness of the Khmer type of arch seems to be necessary to the effect: if you have a tidy rectangular building a big face obviously doesn't belong to it, but the loose stepping-in shape can have vague connections with the human body.[110]

He adds wittily in a postscript: 'I found I wanted to put in the year [1938] because I started imagining Dr Johnson and then Beckford picking up this letter and wondering what it meant. It seems awfully hard luck on Poe that somebody couldn't have picked him up and dropped him in the Bayon – of course in that sort of way the Bayon *is* romantic; but that only goes to show that Romantic is merely a historical term.'

The other remarkable feature of the lost city of Angkor, which certainly added to its mystique after the French naturalist Henri Mouhot rediscovered it in 1860, is that in the years since the demise of the Khmer kingdom its stone masses had been overtaken by the jungle: it had become literally a jungle-city. Consequently, the setting Empson gives his ballet is both forest and court, tree-trunks mixed with pillars. 'The effect to be aimed at, I think,' he writes in the text,

> is a rather contradictory one; the coiling tree-trunks seem to have grown all round the pillars, and yet it is just the same forest scene . . . The forest ought not to be made very hot and thick. I have actually pushed through dense tropical jungle around Angkor till I was bumped by the huge Buddha statue I was looking for, and even then what you see overhead is quite like ordinary

temperate woodland. The designer . . . is asked to have some fun over huge coiling white tree-trunks near the ground; these serpent-like objects have in fact torn apart the stones of Angkor, and the ground jungle there, up to about six feet high, can become impenetrable again within about fifteen years of being cleared. I am all for having the scenery dramatic so long as it doesn't put in the wrong drama.

'The remarks about Angkor of course apply to India too,' he stresses. This is because the point of the ballet is imaginatively to shift Angkor into India, in order to facilitate the idea of convoking and reconciling the Greco–Roman myth of reincarnation and the ideologically complementary reincarnation which is the Buddha's birth-story.

Empson's contemporary notes record the awe he felt in April 1938 on first seeing the buildings of Angkor devoured by the jungle:

The trees at Ta Prohm are as extraordinary as you are told – this *is* romantic if you like. They have white trunks that spread in huge flanges like webbed feet or snow on ridges, and the banyan roots will grow back into the branches if they meet them, or go on wandering like tentacles over the surface for any distance starting as thick as an elephant's foot: one had gone forty or fifty feet down the central path of the courtyard, turned to the left at the end, and wriggled off another thirty or forty feet to disappear at the tower – getting fairly thin by then. They will duck under a roof edge and come out again when it is too hard to lift, and wander over the top. When they get over a gate or tower they spread all round it, stretching and going again, hideously like something inside the body – a cancer but more sinewy. The one that destroyed Neak Pean did a normal trick apparently . . .

Ta Som had the big Kwannon heads over the gateway all swathed and stifled by great tree roots: the eyes buried on this side, the mouth on that. A terrible and grand piece of symbolism . . .

They are now apparently trying to rebuild Neak Pean, and have taken out the great tree that tore it to pieces. Seems doubtful whether my guidebook reconstruction is correct. The great curved animal legs imitating the lotus must have been gloriously lovely if they were as shown, but I could only find small bits of legs lying about, not certainly with that sweeping curve. Some paws and some hoofs.

The Buddhist buildings in his judgement exemplified 'any amount of good sense and public spirit and this immense graciousness of the religion.'

Empson had been given an introduction by Stephen Balfour (the district officer in Hong Kong) to M. Maurice Glaize, the French expert who had been appointed in 1933 to take joint charge of the restoration of Angkor. There is no record that he ever actually met 'the mysterious M. Glaize' (as he called him) – presumably because he had no idea where to locate him in the dense temple-jungle – but he busied himself with drafting letters to him which are full of highly informed and adroit questions: 'How do the Khmers come to be sitting on chairs in the sixth century? Surely the Indians never did, and the Chinese say that their first use of chairs was in late Tang. How far were the Khmers up-to-date in their borrowing from China? Was there a regular trade route? . . . It struck me that the fiveheaded Naga has a shape very like the hand of Buddha when expressing "absence of fear", and I thought this a beautiful idea, but on reflection I found my ignorance very complete. Does the mudra for "absence of fear" come from India, and when does it begin?'

With respect to 'The Elephant and the Birds' his most pertinent questions come up in this passage: 'Is it yet known whom the great heads of the Bayon represent, granting that they are some Bod-dhisattva [sic]? . . . And are we to regard this outburst of building as produced by missionary enthusiasm for Buddhism, or were the religions much confused? Apparently the Chinese ambassador [Chou Ta-kuan, in 1296] arrived at the height of the reaction to Hinduism and thought he was among Buddhists.'[111] Bernard Groslier interprets the dual status of the sculptured heads of the Bayon in these terms:

The Buddhism of Jayavarman VII was that of the Great Vehicle, which allots a special importance to the bodhisattvas, the future Buddhas whose radiant benevolence watches over the salvation of mankind. For it is now man that is the centre of interest, not the cosmos as in Hinduism.

At the same time the role of the king-god was too vital for Cambodia's very existence to be neglected. Jayavarman VII, by a syncretism very characteristic of the Khmers, understood how to combine his faith with his duties as a king. He also built his temple-mountain for the celebration of the universal cults which would ensure the prosperity of the country. Only he took care to harmonise them with Buddhist ideas.[112]

The Khmers were as much consummate syncretists in their religious art as the Indians were eager and adventurous proselytisers for Buddhism: the two countries found a match in one another. According to Groslier, 'In Khmer art, Buddhism retained its icono-graphy and most of its plastic formulas, themselves mainly derived from Hellenistic–Roman sources.'[113] Even if (in view of the more recent scholarship discussed above) Groslier here overstates the case, it nonetheless seems perfectly valid to claim – while making all necessary allowances for evolutionary development across space and time – that some trace of Greco–Roman culture really had reached as far as Cambodia.

Part of the conception of 'The Elephant and the Birds' is to posit a gradual identification between the Greco–Roman Tereus (king-protagonist of the Mediterranean world) and the Buddha (lord of the East), on the basis that the respective myths have common properties, including reincarnation. Empson's 'Eurasian' ballet contends that there is no essential contrast between the two historical traditions. 'The suggestion of confusing the Buddha with the tyrant may . . . seem pretty remote,' the text pleads, 'especially if it is supported . . . by the theory that the Buddha or Bodhisattva heads at Angkor (for instance) were idealised portraits of the reigning kings. But then again, the idea of the divine right of kings is a familiar and recurring one in the West.' Empson need not have felt too apologetic in making this imaginative connection, since (as Groslier has explained) it does appear to have been the case that when Jayavarman VII of Khmer created the great faces of the Bayon he did indeed conflate the image of the Buddha with the image of the deified king. What the Khmers brought together in their sculpture, Empson attempts to bring together again in his ballet.

In a shorter, draft version of his scheme for the ballet Empson wrote that the Buddha 'forms a contrast to the tormented and revengeful women who are reborn as birds.' Accordingly, we need some further understanding of the extent to which Empson himself actually endorsed or advocated the ideal of the Buddha, since – very like 'The Royal Beasts' – the ballet is to a degree a smack at Christianity. The birds of the dance are characterised in terms of European psychology: the nightingale (in the words of the draft) 'not merely incessantly remembers the wrongs it did and suffered but "leans its breast against a thorn", "a thorn its songbook making", and is wilfully determined to torture itself for fear it ever forget,' while the swallow suffers from 'a neurotic refusal to remember and is apparently happy.' Thus both of the women who are metamorphosed into birds have recourse to the complementary tricks of their own temperaments; as the finished text has it, Philomel is 'introvert',

Procne 'extrovert'. They behave like 'independent forces', and as 'impressive rivals to the Buddha'. In contrast, the Buddha conducts himself with the 'majestic humility' of 'wilful self-sacrifice'. So it might appear that Empson is actually distinguishing between the cultural demeanours of Europe and the Indianised East. But 'The Elephant and the Birds' equally stipulates that there is no significant contrast between the Greek and the Indian legends, or between the historical traditions from which they arise. What the ballet in fact attempts is to dissolve certain putative differences between East and West, in terms both of the geographical and historical links Empson traced as a result of his first interest in Buddha faces and of the pre-Christian kinship of cultural manifestations.

His sense of the fundamental importance of the trade routes which facilitated cultural intercourse between Europe and the East is something he catches up again in *Milton's God* (1961), where he extols what he considers 'the most impressive case on record' of 'rapid simultaneous development':

We do not easily realise how impressive it is to have the Second Isaiah and Pythagoras and the Buddha and Confucius all alive at the same time . . . None of these thinkers invented his whole position for himself; he was a centre of crystallisation for a frame of mind which had been growing up for a generation or two. This must have depended upon some idea which was portable . . .

Thus around 600–500 BC China, India and the Mediterranean basin behave like three great trees in a park in the springtime, doing the same things in parallel without apparent contact; and a mood of doubting the practical claims of murderous and expensive priests is about the only thing we can imagine them to catch from one another. The effect of giving up human sacrifice was that thinkers felt free to consider what was just and good for all men. The effect of this again, in various cases, was to make them conceive a God of all mankind, transcendent and metaphysically one with Goodness; though both India and China tended to conceive an Absolute rather than a Person.[114]

The thrust of this part of the argument of *Milton's God* is that, at a date some five centuries before the advent of Christ, most of 'the various universal religions' had rejected the practice of offering human sacrifice as a means of appeasing the Divinity. 'Christianity is the only one which ratted on the progress, the only one which dragged back the Neolithic craving for human sacrifice into its basic structure.' In Empson's judgement, the worship of torture is 'a sexual perversion'; and yet Christianity confronts us with a grotesque irony: 'the symbol of the Religion of Love [the Crucifixion] is a torture.'[115]

As I indicated above, Empson's passion for slating Christianity in favour of the older and more enlightened religions of the world (especially Buddhism) began early. His introduction to a Japanese edition of T. S. Eliot's *Selected Essays* (published in 1933), for example, is concerned above all else to show just how far Buddhism had anticipated the moral teachings of Christianity. Among other observations, Empson points out that Eliot's 'stress on society and tradition rather than the individual is [for the peoples of the Far East] not an argument for Christianity but for Buddhism.' Eliot's 'essential claim,' he argues further, 'is that man can somehow escape the valuelessness of mechanism, though Mr Eliot chooses to put it in Christian language . . . but the claim is inherent, of course, in the very evasive Buddhist concept of Karma.' The burden of Empson's presentation is at once to make Eliot's thoughts on the Christian tradition accessible to the Japanese and to show that such thoughts are already in place in Buddhism. His conclusion is this: 'Either Mr Eliot's support of Christianity from tradition is a claim that the truth is national or racial or otherwise incidental, or the True Orthodoxy must not limit itself to the traditions of Christianity.'[116]

It would be false, however, to suggest that Empson ever evangelised for Buddhism. All the same, he was certainly persuaded that in comparison with Christianity Buddhism showed a better historical record and also that, by grace of the doctrine of Karma, it offered its disciples infinite opportunities for amelioration. 'Karma transformed by Buddhism, which made the ethical character of an action depend upon the motive and not the external performance,' he noted in the 1930s; and again: 'For Buddhism final release is brought about by a process of training of the self, in which it is released by stages from the bonds or fetters that hinder complete insight.' In the context of 'The Elephant and the Birds', this explains why Empson writes in the scenario: 'The women whom the torture of the world leads into evil are reborn as birds, and must suffer so far for their Karma, but of course a murder in a past life would never prevent a bird from being reconciled with the Buddha.' Empson observed too that there must be an implied background of unsatisfactoriness (and even evil) to the ideal held in common by Christianity and Buddhism that the world must be made into a better place, especially since the most worthy men unselfishly sacrifice themselves for the sake of improving it. Likewise, in an unpublished essay dating from the early 1930s – on the Ideal of the Good – he undertook to assess the implications of Freudian therapy by comparison with the ideal of Buddhism, and clearly signalled his approbation for the practical morality of the latter:

the actual aim of the healing work on which the Freudian world picture was based is simply release from torment. The Freudian disciple Money-Kyrle [in *The Development of the Sexual Impulses*, 1932] carried this to its logical conclusion when he argued that after a completely satisfactory psychoanalysis a man would be free to kill himself.

This aim is also the lofty ideal of the Buddha, whose theology has a better reason for avoiding immediate suicide . . . The Buddhist believes that if he kills himself directly he will be reborn in a lower existence, so he must woo his real death by the more circuitous technique of good works. This makes the religion a practicable system for men who take their theories seriously enough to act on them.

However 'evasive' or 'circuitous' (Empson's words) the doctrine of Karma might appear, it still seemed to him to have higher ethical claims than the Christian eschatological doctrine of a God who simply punished or rewarded; for that same reason Empson disparaged any conception of immortality, as in a later review (of *The Judgment of the Dead*, by S. G. F. Brandon) which is perfectly consistent with the stand he had assumed nearly thirty-five years before:

The difference between right and wrong does not depend upon an arbitrary decision by a divine tyrant, and Professor Brandon could have learned this from the other half of Christian theology, let alone the other half of the Old World – India and China and their satellites. Why is it taken for granted that the belief in life after death (always a very strained thing) actually produced better behaviour? ('Heaven and Hell', *Listener*, 30 November 1967)

As an obviously direct consequence of his philosophical approval of the Buddhist doctrine of Karma, Empson became continually eager in the post-war years to salute works of imagination by other writers which suggested a belief in reincarnation. Most notably he rebuked those critics of W. B. Yeats who 'prattle about his Religious Values and his Religious Symbolism without ever once letting on what he actually believed,' which – according to Empson's interpretation of poems such as 'Byzantium' – was no less than reincarnation. 'When the doctrine cannot be ignored [in Yeats],' he wrote, 'critics present it as pokey and lower-middle-class. But it is less unjust than Christian immortality, and more ancient, and still believed by the majority of the inhabitants of the Eurasian land mass.'[117]

Some critical misunderstanding about Empson's position arose when in 1955 he published *Collected Poems*, which is prefaced by his own version of the so-called 'Fire Sermon' that the Buddha preached at Mount Gaya. Empson scrupulously explained that he had naturally first looked up the sermon because it featured in Eliot's *The Waste Land*; he felt so fascinated by it that he simply wanted to produce a 'workable' English translation. He never espoused Buddhism, he insisted in a letter published in *Essays in Criticism*; nor could he ever endorse the fierce message of the Fire Sermon in particular, because it is '*unlike most of Buddhism*, and leaves Christianity far behind, in maintaining that all existence as such, even in the highest heaven, is inherently evil' (my italics).[118] In an undated draft of that letter, however, he had included the remark that 'though it is only an accident that I have the Fire Sermon to start my Collected Poems . . . still I seriously want it there, and would have made a row if for some technical reason I couldn't have it' – for one crucial reason, as he explained further: 'The Europeans have got to realise that Asia really exists.' In another undated draft letter (to his friend John Wain), he expressed similar sentiments: 'I feel I failed to get enough attention for [the Fire Sermon]. However, I suppose I was guilty of religiosity a little, hinting perhaps "We all feel that life is inadequate for us".' But this is not to accuse Empson of bad faith; he would have insisted that the Fire Sermon appear in his *Collected Poems* not as an article of personal belief but as an arrest to any reader's parochial preconceptions. He felt that the Buddha's words should be given prominence, that is to say, principally because Christians must never be allowed to believe that they have a prerogative in the truth. As he added in the draft letter to John Wain quoted above, 'a belief in the world-spirit is not belief in the Father who could be bought off torturing all mankind by the Satisfaction of having his Son tortured to death.' The conclusion he drew from looking at both versions of divinity, the Christian person and the Eastern impersonality, was simply this: 'one should stop believing in this all-executive Father, but accept an impersonal "Divine Ground" . . .'[119]

Allowing for his splendidly jocose tone in addressing a student audience, the same serious sentiment is the burden of his response to another review of his *Collected Poems* that had appeared in a periodical at Sheffield University:

To be sure, the coolness of Buddhism towards Heaven, and towards the supernatural in general, is one of its most attractive features. On one occasion when the Buddha was preaching, the magic of his words became too much for him and he rose forty feet into the air, but he shouted down to the audience begging them to pay no attention; it would be over in a moment, and wasn't of the smallest interest compared to what he was saying. Any lecturer can sympathise with this point of view . . . The basic position, of course, is that Buddhists believe in abandoning selfhood, sometimes interpreted as merging oneself into the Absolute or the impersonal Godhead. If you are good but rather a busybody you are liable to be reborn as a god yourself, which may hold up getting to Nirvana indefinitely; just as over here a too virtuous scholar is liable to be made to do administration. ('Everything, beggars, is on fire', *Arrows* (Sheffield University), 1957, p. 5)

Although Empson never actually subscribed to any religious faith, his sympathies inclined towards a philosophical conception of an Absolute or impersonal Godhead that runs close in spirit to the sutras of Mahayana Buddhism. 'I am afraid,' he wrote in another place, 'that nothing can purge Christianity of the Father who was satisfied by the Crucifixion; an impersonal Divine Ground, as in Aldous Huxley's *Perennial Philosophy*, is the only Supreme Being that can be worshipped without moral shame.'[120] Huxley's formulation of the Perennial Philosophy, published in 1946, gathers together numerous texts from the wisdom of the ages, but without enacting a legalistic creed. It is fundamentally concerned with composing a way of life, a system of ethics, by which man might actualise a unitive knowledge of God (or the Buddha-womb): 'the Atman, or immanent eternal Self,' Huxley wrote, 'is one with Brahman, the Absolute Principle of all existence.'[121] God is to be experienced as at once immanent and transcendent, supra-personal as well as personal. Just as radically, Huxley also endorsed Empson's judgement on one directly conse-quential matter:

if we approach God with the preconceived idea that He is exclusively the personal, transcendental, all-powerful ruler of the world, we run the risk of becoming entangled in a religion of rites, propitiatory sacrifices (sometimes of the most horrible nature) and legalistic observances. Inevitably so; for if God is an unapproachable potentate out there, giving mysterious orders, this kind of religion is entirely appropriate to the cosmic situation. The best that can be said for ritualistic legalism is that it improves conduct. It does little, however, to alter character and nothing of itself to modify consciousness.[122]

Empson's partiality for the Perennial Philosophy explains why he implicitly endorsed Dylan Thomas's kindred leaning in a review dating from the very next year: 'Dylan Thomas's religion is pantheistic and absorbs the Godhead into the world.'[123] Equally it explains why he always spoke of his empathy with Thomas, and why he later characterised the qualities of Thomas's poetry in terms which rehearsed his own earlier definition of the Buddhist paradox: 'his chief power as a stylist is to convey a sickened loathing which somehow at once (within the phrase) enforces a welcome for the eternal necessities of the world.'[124] Empson himself believed likewise, that the Perennial Philosophy enabled one to feel 'morally free to recognise that the world contains wonderful things as well as horrible things.' ('Resurrection', *Critical Quarterly*, 1964, p. 178)

Given Empson's hostility to the Christian God of sacrifice, and his sympathy for an uncanonical commixture of pantheism and reincarnation, a question still remains with regard to the way he presents the Buddha in 'The Elephant and the Birds': why does the ballet focus on the Buddha in his self-sacrificial aspect as a Bodhisattva? The answer returns us to Empson's first investigations into the meaning of the Buddha face. In the mid-1930s his discovery of the ambiguity of the Buddha expression, together with his understanding of the way cultural ideas passed between Europe and the Far East, had led him to speculate about possible mythico-religious links in a way that significantly anticipated 'The Elephant and the Birds'. In terms of the international and inter-racial representation of the Buddha face, for example, he had observed during his visit to India in 1934 that the Buddhist art of Ajanta 'throws in all the races of the world and some perfectly good Christs (when the Buddha is in a self-sacrificial incarnation).'[125] More especially, the development of the ideal of the Bodhisattva as a sacrificial incarnation indicated to him that there is surely less of a divide between Buddhism and Christianity than has commonly been supposed:

An idea that you must be somehow satisfied as well as mortified before entering repose goes deep into the system, and perhaps into human life . . . a Bodhisattva . . . has escaped these doctrinal puzzles and become clearly sacrificial. They are saints who have given up their Nirvana, their heaven, till they have helped their last fellow-creature into heaven before them, and the face is meant to show it. In a sense they have given up their deaths, not their lives, but the conception appeared in the first centuries after Christ and along the caravan routes to Europe; the two religions may very well be connected. ('The Faces of Buddha', *Listener*, 5 February 1936, p. 238)

Likewise, as early as 1933, in another of his untitled and unpublished essays – an essay centrally concerned with the Buddhist ideal of death – Empson can be seen checking the European conviction as to the singular significance of the Atonement by relating the sacrifice of Christ to the longer historical perspective, which supplies much to the credit of Buddhism:

Merely to die for other people like Christ is of course a quite harmless exercise, often performed by the Buddha in previous lives. [But] . . . there is about [the Bodhisattvas] nothing of the Christian tragedy: they have sacrificed their deaths for the sake of man, not their lives.

These logical puzzles need I think to be stressed in praising Buddhism; the worship of death here goes both with a plan for a better life and a fundamental doubt about the nature of death when attained.

As the text of the ballet again explains, 'self-sacrifice is not a new idea to Europe, and the Greek legend is already a Buddhist anecdote.' Empson also learned (from the great scholar-translator Arthur Waley[126]) that in China the concept of the 'suffering hero' pre-dated even Buddhism. The king or emperor had always been regarded as someone who takes upon himself the sins of the people; T'ang, the founder of the Yui dynasty, for example, offered himself up as a sacrificial victim.

Even though 'The Elephant and the Birds' figures the Buddha in the self-sacrificial mode that Empson otherwise deplored, it stresses two features above all in the way it treats his sacrifice: (i) unlike Christ (according to Empson's interpretation of the Atonement) the Buddha does not die to appease a jealous God the Father; and (ii) we must in any case have equal reservations about the Buddha's conduct in that respect. 'This ballet is not a Buddhist tract,' Empson properly insists in the text; and again: 'the pacifist moral story about the Buddha elephant offering his body is grotesque because it overplays its moral . . .' That judgement was not new for Empson. Six years before, on 3 September 1936, he had written for the BBC a short talk which criticises the pragmatic unreason of the pacifist ideal. 'The Traps of Idealism' includes these pertinent remarks:

There is at least one case, I think, of a genuine ideal, which many people are the better for, and yet which you positively ought not to live up to; I mean the ideal of death. That is, the whole set of feelings that in the end death is the best. This is not what is ordinarily called idealism, and it is different in different cases. I shall try to make clear what I mean. As a rule people called idealists want to improve the conditions of life in the world, but the ideal of death is apt to be mystical and individualist. But it needs to come into this talk; it is the trump suit in most of literature and most of religion, and it raises the whole question I am talking about particularly sharply. The essential thing in understanding a tragedy, for instance, or in feeling rightly about it, is to realise just what levels of thought are in play. For instance, the ideal may be directly religious, a desire to leave the struggle of the world and enter the peace of heaven. It may seem wrong to call this an ideal of death, because Christianity has always tried to make heaven seem like real life; but the Christian ideal is very close to that of Buddhism, the other great religion of mankind, and Buddhism has always gone in for putting the final heaven further off from the ordinary worshipper (who will have rebirths on the world before he gets to it) and then insisting that this heaven is a kind of death. But in literature the use of this ideal is commonly not direct; the idea of death is continually used, instead, as a frame or test for any conception of happiness. In effect the man says, 'I want to think about death here, because to do that makes me feel sure that I want what I am trying to get. It is worth trying for.' This is clearly very different, and there are a lot of things in between. Mr T. S. Eliot remarked the other day, answering someone who had said that the great thing was to have faith in life, that the only real thing was to have faith in death. I am not at all clear what he had most in mind there, but it is clearly a resounding saying in its way. And yet anyone who has had to deal with somebody threatening suicide must have felt the nuisance of all this background of splendour; you do not know how to stop the ideal from coming in too quick.

In other words, the ballet does not seek to adjudicate between the Christ and the Buddha; it is not a partisan piece. A further indication of Empson's ambivalence towards Buddhism, for example, can be seen in some small modifications that he made to the text between the draft and the finished version. In describing the Bodhisattva's death as an elephant, the draft version comments with something close to admiration: 'It was through this *feat* of wilful self-sacrifice that the Buddha *succeeded* in being reborn as a man . . .'; the final text has it that 'through this wilful *act* of self-sacrifice' the Buddha '*contrived* to be reborn as a man' (my italics). The adjustment of phrasing suggests that Empson desired to qualify the impression that he might otherwise be offering a wholehearted endorsement of the Buddha; so does the eventual omission from the text of a phrase in the last sentence of the draft which states that the Buddha 'acts as a point of rest' between the tormented and anamnesic birds.

Although the ballet draws short of arbitrating between one faith and another, however, it does attempt to show that the European world and the Eastern world have in some fundamental respects mirrored each other's cultural traditions and manifestations. 'Both stories take for granted the idea of reincarnation between human being and animal,' Empson writes in the text; the only difference is that 'the reincarnations go opposite ways around.' Furthermore, picking up both his liking for the humane opportunities of reincarnation and his knowledge of the ancient cultural interflow between Europe, India and the Far East (in particular as he had traced it through his study of the Buddha effigy), he adds tentatively but advisedly: 'Pythagoras believed in reincarnation, and the Greeks had probably been in touch with Indian beliefs.' In that sense, therefore, the ballet is an exercise in reuniting the two halves of the world; an attempt to pinpoint and illustrate certain age-old congenerous features of their cultures.

Yet a final question might well be: why a ballet anyway? At first blush, indeed, a dance starring an elephant does not sound promising. Even Empson's text admits that it could be difficult to convince the dancer that the style conceived for the elephant 'appears regal and does not appear a form of galumphing'.[127] But again, his decision to write for the medium of dance stemmed from his personal observation and appreciation, together with a theory to back it. In Japan in the early 1930s he had attended performances of the Noh plays: after a fashion of loud and deathly slow ceremoniousness that came to delight him, the ethos they expressed made a match *in specie* with his thinking about Buddhism. His contemporary notes on Japanese dance include these remarks: 'The movements are able to seem at once quick and evasive and monumental: the sad and unillumined transitions of thought of a firm, almost complacent, mind; "there is no other way to keep the necessary contradictions from leading to chaos", and the music goes steadily into the sky with a wail like gnats.' Both the music and the movements of the Japanese style of theatre made him reflect on the differences in cultural disposition between East and West. In effect too, they chimed with the philosophical 'notion' informing many of his own poems, that 'life involves maintaining oneself between contradictions' – for the elephants (says the text) 'are always balancing'.

Even outside the theatre, on his travels through the Far East, Empson constantly attended to the characteristic qualities of singing voices; his notes include these remarks, for example, written at an unidentified port of call:

I was woken by singing at the jetty instead of the donkey engine. It seemed a deep Buddhist chanting in spite of the swinging rise and fall of this simple jerky tune, and the trebles kept coming in with a tearing spiritual triumph, like a spinning and mounting ball, like the last movement of the sixth Brandenburg. I tried to pick out the men doing this, but apparently all voices had all ranges. The singing is used quite blankly as a means of lifting weights . . .

And again:

I remember wandering out in the middle of the night in Tokyo because the air was full of singing full of appealing and passionate exaltation, very far from what the Japanese usually like as music, much more what Europe wants of music in the sense of individual freedom and generosity . . .

The coolie singing both here and in Japan has kept a sense of free and bodily exaltation which belongs much more to the music of Europe than the East, and the reasons would go a long way into the difference of the two styles.

When he came to write 'The Elephant and the Birds', however, one memory again held a primary significance in Empson's imagination. During his visit to Angkor in April 1938, he happened to stay at a cheap hotel where on the first evening he sat down to a vermouth and watched some native girls performing 'ancient Cambodian dances to illustrate the apsaras . . .' *Apsaras*[128] are the attractive celestial nymphs whose dancing forms, intertwined in twos and threes, figure extensively on the bas-reliefs of Angkor Wat; according to Osbert Sitwell, they are 'given to dancing, flying and throwing flowers'.[129] Noticing that our man in Angkor took a lively and intelligent interest in the dances and the dancers, the waiter offered to procure one of the girls for him (although the hostelry was not in fact a brothel). Did Empson accept the offer? Probably not (or at least he left no word to suggest otherwise), which may be surprising in view of Bernard Groslier's lyrical evocation of the *apsaras*: 'Nude to the waist, they wear skirts of gorgeous material with flying panels spread flat on either side according to the conventional perspective . . . nothing can detract from the exquisite grace of their pose, the rhythm of their gestures, the fantastic charm of their plaited tresses and jewelled diadems. They are dream creatures, for whose sake one might almost dare death to enter the paradise in which they disport themselves.'[130] But then, apparently, the live local girls of Angkor were not particularly good performers. All the same, it was their dancing as *apsaras*, and then in an elephant dance, which set the seed in Empson's imagination that matured four years later in the form of 'The Elephant and the Birds'. 'I have only seen it done by the dancing girls at Angkor,' he writes about the elephant dance in the text, and 'nobody could imagine that these exquisite little pauses were galumphing.' Thus the very key to Empson's sense of the emotional and philosophical meaning of the dance – which also connects back to the informing idea of his poetry that 'life involves maintaining oneself between contradictions' – appears in the letter he wrote to Norman France on 11 April 1938: 'Interesting about the dancing, though, that it was very slow and required very good balancing (which the girls couldn't do); one thinks of apsaras as skipping about, and they seem better sculpture if you realise they are moving slowly over a difficult point of balance.'

Empson had substantially developed this idea of balancing in the essay 'Ballet of the Far East' (1936), and I must conclude by quoting it at some length – not only for its evangelising, but because it deftly knits together all the thoughts on East and West that pattern out 'The Elephant and the Birds' as a complete work of art (as well as the character of the Wurroo music in 'The Royal Beasts'):

In the West, the supreme God is a person, in the East He is not; their ideas about man follow from that . . . It is much the most fundamental line of division between the civilisations of the world, and we need to understand the people on the other side . . . Of course Europe has always known about pantheism (since Pythagoras), but the important thing is that people can get an idea into their bones, and when they agree, intellectually, to the other side they cannot see how it works out in practice. Almost the only kind of man who can tell you how it works out in practice is the artist who has worked with it in his bones. So it is a good thing, if possible, to tie the points about the ballet on to the difference of theology . . . Also it keeps us from calling the difference a mysterious matter of race (slit eyes or what not). The man who made the supreme expression of the Far Eastern view of God and man was the Buddha, and he was an Aryan, the same race as ourselves . . . And in fact there is no peculiar racial difficulty about understanding Far Eastern art once you see the ideas behind it . . .

The Noh theatre is fantastically slow . . . the music has a direct effect on the nerves. It is based on eight slow beats, taken separately by different percussive instruments. Now the scientists seem to agree that we feel differently about rhythm according as it is slower or faster than a heart-beat, and nearly all European music goes faster than a heart-beat . . . All our instruments are meant to go bouncing along very frankly, like a nice well-intentioned dog; in their music you sit still and strengthen yourself like a cat . . . I think it is true to say that European music is a much larger creature than Eastern music; it is the fresh air. But the fundamental difference in all these things goes back to the view taken of God and of the individual man. A rhythm quicker than the heart-beat is one that you seem to control, or that seems controlled by some person; the apparently vast field of our music is always the frankness of the West, always the individual speaking up. Music based on rhythms slower than the heart-beat can carry a great weight of emotion and even of introspection, and of course incidental runs will go quick, but it remains somehow impersonal. I only want to say here that you must take the music seriously as something that fits in with the whole story, and the story may well be the other half of the truth about the world . . .

If you have got used to the Far Eastern stage it is very hard to take the Russian ballet as seriously as all its audiences do. Beside dancing like this, the Russian ballet is a glorified form of romping. In dancing of serious power, the dancer can stand still for several minutes and make you watch the imperceptible movements of his breathing like a cat watching a mouse. Now Western music cannot stand still; it is not built to give a dancer these opportunities. If we ever get what there is so little hope of at present, that is, a reasonable attempt to take the world as one place and use the best things in it, then it will be obvious that Far Eastern music is the normal kind of music for serious dancing. Sensible people who love the European ballet will tell you that the permanent thing about it is its eternal youth. This is quite true, but it is a limited kind of pleasure. In all the other arts the Far East has one thing and we have another, and it is stupid to say that either is better. But in dramatic dancing the Far East makes us ridiculous. ('Ballet of the Far East', *Listener*, 7 July 1937, pp. 16–18)

It is a pleasure to acknowledge the help I have received during the preparation of this volume. First and foremost I must thank Lady (Hetta) Empson, who has most generously encouraged the work and positively invited my many intrusions into her home. Lord Zuckerman kindly gave me the benefit of his reading of 'The Royal Beasts'; and Wladimir Zwalf (Assistant Keeper in the Department of Oriental Antiquities, British Museum; editor of the splendid *Buddhism: Art and Faith*) expertly pinpointed Empson's white elephant and bore with my ignorance on other questions. For their valuable help in various capacities I am grateful also to the following: Mr B. F. Cook (Keeper of Greek and Roman Antiquities, British Museum); Mrs C. Cruickshank (Archivist, Faber & Faber); Mrs E. E. Duncan-Jones; Professor Richard Eberhart; Dr Michael Halls (King's College, Cambridge); Professor Philip Hobsbaum; Allegra Huston; Professor Yukio Irie; Dr Michael Leslie; Dr Richard Luckett (Magdalene College, Cambridge); Dr Christopher Norris; Professor Christopher Ricks; Mr J. A. Simson; Dr Alice Stewart; Miss Sun Yu-mei; Mr Julian Trevelyan; and Professor Wang Zuo-liang. The letter by John Hayward (Appendix to 'The Elephant and the Birds') is published by kind permission of Mrs R. H. Oakeley. Lastly I am grateful to my agent Andrew Best and my editor Andrew Motion, for providing aid and agitation in just the right proportions.

Notes

1. 'Life in the Far East', *New Statesman & Nation*, 29 June 1946.
2. 'Where The Body is . . .', *Granta*, 2 December 1927, p. 193.
3. F. R. Leavis, 'Cambridge Poetry', *Cambridge Review*, 1 March 1929, p. 318.
4. Richard Eberhart, 'Empson's Poetry', *Accent*, 4:4, Summer 1944; rpt. in *On Poetry and Poets*, Urbana: University of Illinois Press, 1979, pp. 117–18. Further evidence figures in a letter of 3 December 1929 from Randall Pope to E. E. Phare: 'The Empson cultus is ubiquitous. Public readings of his poems are given, as you

probably know. Leavis mentions him in every lecture. Some poem of his is to be found in nearly everyone's rooms; even in the possession of people who would not dream of reading the work of an ordinary poet.' (E. E. Duncan-Jones)

5. 'Some old college mss.', *Magdalene College Magazine*, no. 61, June 1929, p. 81.

6. All quotations for which no specific source is given derive from the collection of Empson's private papers (including miscellaneous notebooks, loose-leaf notes, drafts of published and unpublished writings, and correspondence) hereinafter designated 'Empson Papers'.

7. The full diary entry is interesting because it tells us about the kind of situation that Empson considered possible for theatrical treatment:

'Soame Jenyns mentioned to me the enjoyably over-civilised trick of society people during the last war – I think Lady Diana Manners would be the word to conjure with – of having an admittedly bogus telegram brought in at the height of a dinner-party, the husband, or son of the house, is killed. And because nobody could view those envelopes with a real detachment, because they were actually playing with fire, it would be a mild thrill as well as an aesthetic pleasure to see how accurately, with what courage, tact, delicacy, strength of will, she would return the envelope to the tray, perhaps swallow once, and look fixedly at the opposite wall for a moment, and then continue with no real break in the conversation, and a hardly more conscious charm, elegant, witty, cultivated, enduring to the end. Well, that must have been great fun at the time, but my idea (first arrived at, I think, in conversation with Herklots) was the obvious Pirandello trick of having two telegrams, one of them real. Everybody accepts the first one as artificial, except the lady herself, who sees that the wording is slightly different from what she had arranged, and that the butler has something, evidently, on his mind. She is tortured by uncertainty but of course the game has to be played out, and the guests think she is doing it rather badly. After a little while the second telegram, the invention, is delivered to her. It becomes obvious to the dinner-party that something is wrong; they are caught by a quite unexpected anxiety. A bluff old creature, rather out of place, will find courage to say "Not bad news, I hope?" But she, knowing now that it is true, and shielding her conscious mind with the first course of action that comes to her, is struck by the fact that this is the wording she had expected, this is the situation she had planned for, and to the stammering horror of the rest of the party she repeats word for word, gesture for gesture, all the conventional behaviour that she had decided upon as most suitable to the evening, repeating every epigram as if new, telling the same funny story with the same gesture, and this difference only, that she does it far more perfectly than before. You can see now what she was trying to do when her anxiety prevented her, and that gossamer of easy elegant conversation becomes detached and isolated by a real despair, it seems to shimmer more brightly "over the black mouth of a gun."

'Yes but war plays are dreadfully tiresome by this time, and you can't do a dinner party on the stage. I shall not write it.'

8. 'That I'm sure was destroyed. It wasn't very good anyway. But I tried quite a lot to write plays. The failed plays were lying around in quite a quantity for some time. I don't know whether they're still in a drawer, so to speak' ('William Empson in conversation with Christopher Ricks', *The Review*, nos. 6 & 7, June 1963, p. 26).

9. Anyone interested in coming up with a deep reading of *Three Stories* may like to have at their disposal a further point of information of possible interpretative significance. Given that the play juxtaposes a socio-psychological story about an angry young man of the twenties and a 'scientific disquisition fathered on Dracula' (in *Granta*'s good phrase), it is interesting that the same association popped into Empson's mind more than seven years later (May 1934), but in an apparently very different context: 'Puzzled to know why reading a version of Aquinas on God was so eerie and horrible – thrilling as a fugue might be, that one would expect, but this was like reading Dracula or a Freudian case. The reason (which I don't remember seeing elsewhere) is that God there is point by point, in some points with much subtlety of observation, an extreme case of dementia praecox: only he is not mad but right: filling the heavens – a personal God could not be sane' (Empson Papers).

10. Empson in conversation; a letter of 10 November 1929 from F. R. Salter (Fellow of Magdalene) to I. A. Richards (Magdalene College, Cambridge); an undated letter from Empson to Julian Trevelyan (Julian Trevelyan); and Ronald Bottrall's memoir-verses 'William Empson' in Roma Gill (ed.), *William Empson: The Man and His Work* (1974), rpt. in *Poems 1955–1973*, London: Anvil Press, 1974, pp. 104–7. I. A. Richards was absent abroad at the time of the crisis, and had no opportunity to intervene on behalf of his outstanding pupil.

11. The source of my account of the correspondence between Empson and Ian Parsons is the archives of Chatto & Windus.

12. F. R. Leavis, 'Intelligence and Sensibility', *Cambridge Review*, 16 January 1931, p. 187.

13. A. Alvarez, 'A Style from a Despair: William Empson', *The Twentieth Century*, no. 161, April 1957, pp. 346, 353.

14. I. A. Richards, 'Cambridge Poetry', *Granta*, 8 March 1929, p. 359.

15. Kathleen Raine, 'And Learn a Style from a Despair', *New Statesman & Nation*, 5 November 1955.

16. *Lyrical Ballads* (ed. Derek Roper), Estover, Plymouth: Macdonald & Evans, second edn. 1976, p. 36.

17. *Criterion*, 9:37, July 1930, p. 770.

18. 'The Sceptical Biologist' (rev. of *The Sceptical Biologist* by Joseph Needham), *Nation & Athenæum*, 18 January 1930, p. 544.

19. Ibid.

20. E. M. Forster, *The Hill of Devi and other writings* (ed. Elizabeth Heine), London: Edward Arnold, 1983, p. 71.

21. 'Loganberry Jam', *Granta*, 25 November 1927, p. 154. Cf. another notable review, 'Poetry' (on *Triforium*, by Sherard Vines): 'Mr Vines is the most sensible poet of the moment; he has swallowed more of the latest intellectual fads than anyone else who has remained comfortable . . . but his peace of mind is based, not on renouncing anything, but on that solid and learned variety of gratification which one associates with a High Table. The fully digested despair, the habit of writing poetry about a profound nervous dissatisfaction, the Byronism of the scholar which Mr Eliot has cultivated, is not Mr Vines's game at all' (*Granta*, 23 November 1928, p. 161).

22. 'Playne but Worthy', *Granta*, 27 April 1928, p. 376.

23. 'More Barren Leaves' (rev. of *Proper Studies* by Aldous Huxley), *Granta*,

18 November 1927, p. 123.

24. John Wain, 'Ambiguous Gifts', *Penguin New Writing*, no. 40, 1950, p. 125. See also Joseph E. Duncan, *The Revival of Metaphysical Poetry*, Minneapolis: University of Minnesota Press, 1959.

25. 'William Empson in conversation with Christopher Ricks', *The Review*, nos. 6 & 7, June 1963, p. 34.

26. 'A London Letter', *Poetry*, vol. 49, 1937, p. 222.

27. Edwin Muir, 'Neat, Muted and Despondent', *Observer*, 14 October 1956.

28. 'Mrs Dalloway as a political satire', *Essays in English Language and Literature* (Tokyo), vol. 1, April 1933, p. 4.

29. 'A Masterly Synthesis' (rev. of *Modern Poetry and the Tradition* by Cleanth Brooks), *Poetry*, vol. 55, 1939, p. 155.

30. John Fuller, 'An Edifice of Meaning', *Encounter*, 43:5, November 1974, p. 78.

31. Untitled rev. of Dylan Thomas, *Collected Poems*, *New Statesman & Nation*, 15 May 1954, p. 635.

32. See, for example, 'William Empson in conversation with Christopher Ricks', p. 35: 'Most poetry today is in the Imagist tradition, and it simply isn't the fashion to understand things; people understand these things in prose perfectly well.'

33. Michael Wood, 'Incomparable Empson', *New York Review of Books*, 23 January 1975, p. 32.

34. 'William Empson in conversation with Christopher Ricks', p. 33.

35. Empson in interview with Christopher Norris and David Wilson (TS copy supplied by Chris Norris).

36. Geoffrey Hill, 'A Dream of Reason', *Essays in Criticism*, 14:1, 1964, pp. 92, 100.

37. Fuller, 'An Edifice of Meaning', p. 76. (For a fuller discussion of the canonical poems, see Haffenden, 'The Importance of Empson: The Poems', *Essays in Criticism*, 35:1, January 1985, pp. 1–24.)

38. Eberhart, 'Empson's Poetry', p. 117.

39. 'The Variants for the Byzantium Poems', in *Using Biography*, London: Chatto & Windus, 1984, p. 182.

40. 'Some more Dylan Thomas', *Listener*, 28 October 1971, p. 588.

41. Unpublished draft version (Empson Papers) of 'Mr. Empson and the Fire Sermon' (*Essays in Criticism*, 6:4, October 1956, pp. 481–2). If Empson had not actually espoused Buddhism, why did he insist on prefacing his *Collected Poems* with his own version of the Buddha's Fire Sermon? His stubbornness exposed him to some critical and personal misunderstanding – such as A. Alvarez's comment (in 'A Style from a Despair: William Empson', p. 353) that 'the later poems seem to be less personal discoveries than expansions of the passage from the Fire Sermon which Empson has put at the front of the *Collected Poems*' – which is discussed later in this Introduction.

42. G. S. Fraser, 'On the interpretation of a difficult poem', in John Wain (ed.), *Interpretations*, 1955; second edn., London: Routledge & Kegan Paul, 1972, p. 226.

43. Sleeve-notes, 'William Empson reading Selected Poems', Hessle, Yorkshire: Marvell Press, *Listen*, LPV 3, 1959.

44. John Wain, 'Ambiguous Gifts', p. 124.

45. G. S. Fraser, op. cit., p. 229.

46. Christopher Ricks, 'Empson's Poetry', in Roma Gill (ed.), *William Empson: The Man and His Work*, London: Routledge & Kegan Paul, 1974, p. 204.

47. 'The Calling Trumpets', *New Statesman & Nation*, 10 December 1955, p. 800.

48. In connection with his favourite poem 'Bacchus', Empson wittily protested: 'Critics have often said that my earlier poetry was tolerably close to the rhythms of the spoken language, whereas I ended in the dead rhetoric of the end-stopped ten-syllable line. But if you are trying to be vatic it is natural to be end-stopped and uncolloquial, and to say that a poem mustn't be vatic is doctrinaire; even though I have against me the strong and improbable combination of Dr Leavis and Professor Robert Graves' (in Paul Engle and Joseph Langland (eds.), *Poet's Choice*, 1962, p. 86).

49. Fuller, 'An Edifice of Meaning', p. 78.

50. Martin Amis, *Success*, Frogmore, St Albans: Triad/Panther, 1979, p. 142. 'I'm saying what lots of people would have said in prose,' Empson said about the poem 'Let it go' in his conversation with Christopher Ricks (p. 32).

51. Sleeve-notes, 'William Empson reading Selected Poems'.

52. Untitled review of W. H. Auden, *Another Time, Life and Letters Today*, 1 August 1940, p. 180.

53. 'The Wisdom of the East', *Observer*, 19 August 1956.

54. Philip Hobsbaum, letter to Haffenden, 27 June 1985. In a letter of 15 September 1957 to D. S. Carne-Ross, Empson declared with his characteristic brusqueness on the subject: 'No, I'm afraid I haven't been writing any more poems. About ten years' time if I am spared would be the plausible date I should think. What odd things people talk about.'

55. Quoted in Byron Rogers, 'Man of words', *The Star* (Sheffield), 31 March 1967, p. 4.

56. Ian Sainsbury, 'An "old fogey" retires', *Morning Telegraph* (Sheffield), 20 July 1971.

57. Beida (to which Empson had been appointed), Qinghua and Nankai were amalgamated as the Southwest Associated University (commonly called 'Lianda') for the duration of the Sino–Japanese war.

58. It fulfils the criteria comprehensively set out by H. J. Blackham in *The Fable as Literature*, London: Athlone Press, 1985.

59. A memoir by Professor Wang Zuo-liang published in *Waiguo Wenxue*, no. 1, 1980, p. 2 (translation by Miss Sun Yu-mei).

60. Solly Zuckerman (b. 1904) was Sands Cox Professor of Anatomy in the University of Birmingham, 1943–68; since 1974 he has been President of the British Industrial Biological Research Association; he was created a life peer in 1971.

61. S. Zuckerman, *The Social Life of Monkeys and Apes*, London: Kegan Paul, 1932, p. 51.

62. Ibid., p. 54.

63. Zuckerman, *Functional Affinities of Man, Monkeys and Apes*, London: Kegan Paul, 1933, p. 93.

64. Zuckerman, *The Social Life of Monkeys and Apes*, pp. 63, 311.

65. Ibid., p. 304.

66. 'Animals', *Spectator*, 30 October 1936, p. 768.

67. *Cambridge Review*, 19 October 1928, p. 34.

68. 'Ask a Policeman', *Granta*, 21 October 1927, p. 47.

69. 'Donne and the Rhetorical Tradition', *Kenyon Review*, vol. 2, 1949, p. 581.

70. *Rationalist Annual*: rpt. in Karl Miller (ed.), *Writing in England Today: the Last Fifteen Years*, 1968, p. 170. See also Frances A. Yates's crucial chapter on Giordano Bruno in *Renaissance and Reform: The Italian Contribution*, London: Routledge & Kegan Paul, 1983. Empson's conjecture that Christ might die on (and for the inhabitants of) other worlds helps to explain an otherwise obscure line – 'No star he [i.e. Christ] aimed at is entirely waste' – in the poem 'Reflection from Anita Loos' (*Collected Poems*, p. 66).

71. 'Senator Milton' (rev. of *Five Essays on Milton's Epics*), *Listener*, 28 July 1966. (For Milton's real interest in Galileo's researches, see *Paradise Lost* (ed. Alastair Fowler), Harlow: Longman, 1971, notes to I, ll. 286–91; III, ll. 589–90; V, ll. 261–3; also Marjorie H. Nicolson, 'A World in the Moon', *Smith College Studies in Modern Languages*, XVII, 1936.)

72. 'Dylan Thomas', *Essays in Criticism*, 13:2, April 1963, p. 206.

73. 'Resurrection', *Critical Quarterly*, 6:2, 1964, p. 178; and see further below.

74. 'Donne the Space Man', *Kenyon Review*, 19:3, Summer 1957, p. 353.

75. Empson, letter to Christopher Ricks, 19 January 1975.

76. Letter to Martin Buxton, 30 March 1963 (Empson Papers).

77. *Milton's God*, paperback edn., Cambridge: CUP, 1981, p. 261.

78. *Collected Poems*, London: Chatto & Windus, 1955, p. 119.

79. See E. B. Cowell (ed.), *The Jataka, or stories of the Buddha's former births*, Cambridge, 1895–1913; rpt. London: The Pali Text Society/Routledge & Kegan Paul, 1981. The *Chaddanta-Jataka* is no. 514.

80. Undated version of letter published as 'Mr Empson and the Fire Sermon', *Essays in Criticism*, 6:4, October 1956, pp. 481–2 (Empson Papers).

81. Letter to John Hayward, 7 March 1933 (King's College, Cambridge).

82. Notes (? or part-letter), written in Kyoto (Empson Papers).

83. As note 81. Empson had another attack of conspicuously misplaced self-deprecation when he wrote in one of his contemporary notebooks: 'The point of travelling to a country is that that makes it seem sensible to think about the place. Nothing is learnt (by me anyway in my weakness) that you couldn't look up' (Empson Papers).

84. Untitled review of Dylan Thomas, *Collected Poems*, *New Statesman & Nation*, 15 May 1954, p. 635.

85. Undated letter to George Sansom, written literally at sea (Empson Papers).

86. As note 84.

87. Sir George Sansom (1883–1965) held a variety of consular posts in the Far East between 1904 and 1940; Sir Charles Eliot (British Ambassador to Tokyo, 1919–26) wrote of him in 1921: 'For sheer intellectual power he is in all probability easily first in the Government Service in Japan.' He was knighted in 1935, and after the war became first Director of the Far Eastern Institute at Columbia University. His publications include *Historical Grammar of the Japanese Language* (1928), *A Short Cultural History of Japan* (1931), and *History of Japan* (3 vols, 1958–64). See also Katharine Sansom, *Sir George*

Sansom and Japan: a memoir, Tallahassee, Florida: Diplomatic Press, 1972.

88. Letter to George Sansom, 2 September 1934, from Anuradhapura, Ceylon. Empson's contemporary notebook records tersely: 'Bodhgaya [*sic*]. Not worth it. One very good Gupta? figure on a four-side-sculpted stupa? in front of new main Buddha' (Empson Papers).

89. On the question of Indian politics in the 1930s, for example, he recorded in his contemporary notes: 'I remember meeting an Indian at some party in London, a specialist on pots or something, and after we had sat passively on a sofa for a while I asked him what were his views on Indian politics. Placidly, finally, only just audible in the uproar, he said "The soil needs blood." Not a silly remark, not silly at all, but you don't want to have it said at a party' (Empson Papers).

90. As note 88. In another, undated letter to Sansom he conceded: 'I began to like Hindu stuff a bit in Colombo, safely at the end . . . How do you suppose a Burmese sculptor aged 50 came to put up in 1909 . . . a colossal lying Buddha in a full-blown style of cubism? The result is no more than amusing, but there it is, cubism' (Empson Papers).

91. 'I have been musing a theory that the impressive faces of the Buddha are always asymmetrical, with the calm of withdrawal from the world on the left side,' he wrote in an undated letter (1938) to Maurice Glaize (Empson Papers). In the mid-1930s he approached a number of editors with a view to periodical publication of the work in progress. On 11 October 1935, for instance, he wrote to George Sansom from London: '[Herbert] Read will take something on split faces for the Burlington at some indefinite future date' (Empson Papers); in late July 1937 he wrote in a temporarily discouraged mood to T. S. Eliot: 'I daresay it's rather a good thing if I don't churn out an ignorant book on Buddhas. The article I should like to have in the Criterion, as it can't be published anywhere with the photographs; but to go without photographs it wants re-writing a bit' (Faber & Faber). He also discussed the artistic representation of facial expressions with Roger Hinks (1903–63), who was at that time an Assistant Keeper in the Department of Greek and Roman Antiquities in the British Museum and author of a monograph, *Greek and Roman Portrait-Sculpture* (1933). In a letter to George Sansom posted from Athens (2 October 1934), Empson remarked: 'I had a very clear idea of the Greek Archaic Smile in my mind, as a fundamental form with a Theory attached to it, and it is a shock to find that hardly any archaic statues have it. Quite a lot of simpering goes on, of a pert coy type which may be observed on modern Greeks, and even that belongs to the 6th century rather than the 7th, but the pulled mouth of nervous strain and intellectual success I thought had something to do with what Otto Ranke says, that Greek thought depended on a unique repression of Mother-Impulses, seems very unusual: they were doing a great variety of faces right from the beginning' (Empson Papers).

92. Langdon Warner (1881–1955). Assistant Curator of Oriental Art, Museum of Fine Arts, Boston from 1906 to 1913, he was field fellow of the Fogg Museum, Harvard University, at the time when Empson talked to him in Boston (c. October 1939). Katharine Sansom described him as 'a jolly sort of buccaneer . . . the gentlest of men and a passionate aesthete', and recalled further that he had undertaken 'amazing journeys in China, where he discovered lost caves filled with superb sculpture and paintings' (*Sir George Sansom*

and Japan, p. 20).

93. 'The Negation of Negation', *Granta*, 9 March 1928.

94. *Collected Poems*, pp. 104–5.

95. Letter to John Hayward, as note 81.

96. 'These Japanese', *Listener*, 5 March 1942, p. 293.

97. A Foucher, *The Beginnings of Buddhist Art*, London: Humphrey Milford, 1917, pp. 130, 135, 136. It is possible that Empson first came across the story of the Bodhisattva-as-elephant in Foucher, who devotes a chapter of his book ('The Six-Tusked Elephant', pp. 185–204) to comparing Pali, Sanskrit and Chinese versions of the story.

98. Letter to George Sansom, as note 88.

99. W. Zwalf (ed.), *Buddhism: Art and Faith*, London: British Museum, 1985, p. 91.

100. Christmas Humphreys, *Buddhism*, Harmondsworth, Middlesex: Penguin, 1951; 3rd ed., 1962, p. 210.

101. Foucher, *The Beginnings of Buddhist Art*, p. 134.

102. Zwalf, *Buddhism: Art and Faith*, p. 91.

103. *Milton's God* (1981), p. 239.

104. Bernard Groslier, *Angkor: Art and Civilisation*, London: Thames & Hudson, 1957; revised ed., 1966, p. 218.

105. Osbert Sitwell, *Escape with Me!: an oriental sketch-book*, London: Macmillan, 1939, p. 90.

106. Groslier, *Angkor*, p. 161.

107. Groslier, *Angkor*, p. 158.

108. Letter to Norman France, 11 April 1938 (Empson Papers).

109. See also Empson's remarks in a notebook: 'All very well [D. H.] Lawrence praising Ajanta, a sex-fearing and [sex]-hating religious product, but why didn't he admire Hinduism – the only big religion which gives sex the place Lawrence wanted, and with results obviously nauseating in life and art . . .

'Ajanta is much queerer than the Vatican frescoes, though the comparison makes it less weird. Without any of the febrile frustrated sexuality of later Indian stuff they are much more sensual than the big Italians, and they were made for monks not ruling priests, and they seem not to feel the conflict in any way' (Empson Papers).

110. Letter to Norman France, as note 108.

111. Letter to Maurice Glaize, 18 April 1938 (Empson Papers). His autograph notes from three days before make a decisive judgement – 'The arrangement of the big heads is the important thing, and that is original Buddhist work all right' – and comment on one of the faces: 'Curious effect of making it Chinese looking: it is the technique of the great Vishnu at Elephanta' (Empson Papers).

112. Groslier, *Angkor*, p. 155.

113. Ibid., p. 218.

114. *Milton's God* (1981) pp. 237, 241. Cf. Empson's remarks in an article 'The Gifts of China': 'The catalogue [of the Chinese Exhibition at the Royal Academy] seems eagerly certain that China developed in total independence from the two other civilisations of the Old-World land mass, India and the Mediterranean, except at two or three permitted points of entry . . . But, considering the vast gulfs of Old Stone Age time, it can't be chance that the

three great trees in the park started flowering almost together; and civilised China emerged notably later than the other two' (*Sunday Times*, 30 September 1973, p. 27).

115. *Milton's God* (1981), pp. 241, 251.

116. 'Introduction' to T. S. Eliot, *Selected Essays*, Tokyo: Kinseido, 1933 (n.p.).

117. 'A Time of Troubles', *New Statesman* (23 July 1965), pp. 123–4. See also 'Yeats and the Spirits', *New York Review of Books* (13 December 1973), p. 44.

118. 'Mr Empson and the Fire Sermon', *Essays in Criticism*, 6:4, October 1956, p. 481.

119. 'Resurrection', *Critical Quarterly*, 6:2, 1964, p. 178.

120. 'Preface' to John R. Harrison, *The Reactionaries*, London: Gollancz, 1966, p. 12.

121. Aldous Huxley, *The Perennial Philosophy*, London: Triad Grafton, 1985, p. 17.

122. Ibid., p. 42.

123. 'How To Read a Modern Poem' (1947), rpt. in John Hollander (ed.), *Modern Poetry: Essays in Criticism*, 1968, p. 246.

124. Untitled review of *Collected Poems*, by Dylan Thomas, *New Statesman & Nation*, 15 May 1954.

125. Letter to George Sansom, 2 September 1934 (Empson Papers). He elaborated on the observation in a further (undated) letter to Sansom written the same year: 'Very odd to find a regular Christ in Ajanta for the Buddha in a sacrificial incarnation – a heavy drooping eyelid with the eye swooping up from under it, entirely unlike the Buddha's, and the droop of the figure, and even the little Italian beard and the droop of the moustache' (Empson Papers).

126. Letter to Empson from Arthur Waley, n.d. (18 January) (Empson Papers). Empson had also commented in his notes of the 1930s: 'Chinese no sense of sin; Indians tormented by purity-anxiety. Neither any tragedy; both doubtful about sacrificial deities. This seems a neat demonstration of the independence of the two groups of ideas' (Empson Papers).

127. Although vague plans for a production were laid in 1942 (with sets to be designed by Leslie Hurry), they presently came to nothing (see Appendix). At an uncertain date some while later, Empson addressed this letter to Rabindranath Tagore (obviously the news had not reached him that Tagore had died in 1941):
Dear Tagore,
I thought I would like to show you this plan for a ballet, which I thought of around 1942 and have been expanding lately. The British won't do it but the Americans might. You might have some useful comments, but don't be bothered with it if you aren't interested.
    W. Empson   (Empson Papers).

128. It now seems to be agreed that the plural spelling is *apsarases*; I have kept to Empson's form to avoid confusion.

129. Osbert Sitwell, *Escape with Me!*, p. 98.

130. Groslier, *Angkor*, p. 100.

A Note on the Text

My brief in editing this volume has been to provide an accessible and readable presentation of the works. To that end I have normalised some points of punctuation and corrected infrequent misspellings, but I hope that my 'sleazy editing' in general has not violated any significant areas of Empson's intended meaning.

The text of *Three Stories* is taken from the author's own typescript, for which no earlier state survives. It is likely that Empson wrote the play directly onto the typewriter, in order to provide copies for the three actors, and he therefore had understandably little concern for precise punctuation; he sometimes used a run of commas, for instance, where normal grammar would invite at least one semicolon, and he regularly omitted question marks: I have silently supplied such points for the sake of syntactic clarity.

Most of the previously unpublished poems survive in only one version. I have adhered to Empson's own typescript copy in the one or two cases where a holograph version also survives (variations between holograph and typescript versions are in any event minor), and I have retained forms such as 'seizin' and 'liefless' for their possible interpretative significance.

Except for two small authorial revisions to the poem 'Essay', the uncollected poems are copied from their first periodical appearances; there seemed to be no urgent call for editorial intervention, so that I have retained what is now the outdated form 'ski-ing', for instance, as well as the spellings 'appalls' and 'artifact'.

There is only one draft copy for 'The Royal Beasts', written partly in typescript and partly in autograph: my primary task has therefore been not to collate different versions but to transcribe each section just as Empson wrote it. Apart from correcting the odd misspelling, editorial decisions have on the whole been minor: Empson began by giving Mrs Bickersteth the first name 'Ellen', for instance, and in later passages chose to call her 'Mary'; I have used 'Mary' throughout the text to avoid confusion. Similarly, the names 'Wurroo' and 'Wuzzoo' occasionally confused even the author himself; I have corrected obvious mistakes such as 'these Wuzzoos', while retaining mistakes attributable to a character rather than to the author – as when the colonial governor Sir Reginald refers to 'this Tuggoo plan'. Other silent emendations have been of a usual copy-editing order: Empson italicised words such as 'impasse' and 'posse', for instance, and it would seem to be unnecessarily distracting to follow his usage in such cases. The entirety of the text is clearly a first draft, and Empson abandoned it well before he needed to make any final structural decisions of the kind outlined on the separate sheet at the end of the text and in the letter to Lord Zuckerman that I have quoted in my introduction; the order of the sections therefore represents an editorial decision, and it is based simply on what seemed to be a natural sequence of events for the story in its unfinished state. For the rest, my only significant editorial problem has been to transcribe as faithfully as I could manage those passages that Empson wrote in autograph; I have tried not to falsify anything, but I am sure it is not beyond me now and then to have misread a word penned or pencilled on a mountain-top (though I should immediately say that Empson's ability to write under any circumstances does not excuse errors that I may have introduced in transcription). Square brackets around a blank space normally mark a single word in Empson's hand that has completely defeated me.

Finally, the text of 'The Elephant and the Birds' is taken directly from Empson's own typescript, and editorial interventions have been confined to some small questions of spelling and punctuation.

Three Stories
A one-act melodrama
[ADC Productions, February 1927]

Dramatis Personae:
GERALD
MARGERY
JAMES

Apronstage. Red footlights. The backcloth is a noble wild prospect. To the right, very high hanging and far, a Gibbs Dentifrice castle; foreground a gloomy battlement and clouds. Enter Gerald from the right declaiming.

GERALD: It burns my heart, it sets on fire my veins,
Princess Princess to see you bound in chains.
Youngest unworthy the third son lowborn,
Granted, I scaled the turret for your scorn.
Call not my cause unworthy, my limbs weak,
Show me the monster only that I seek.

MARGERY: Rash youth, take heed, waste not yourself in vain,
He is too strong I am too sure of pain.
It is with sorrow only, child, with fear,
I should receive you as defender here.
I ask your comfort only for my boon
And thus give welcome, do not die too soon.

GERALD: Now, by my father's cabin in the hills,
By my young heart your lone high beauty fills,
By my two brothers searching in the plain,
He shall be dead ere I approach again.

Which way has walked this conjuror I kill?
Princess Princess, tell me, I will, I will.

There is a pause with Gerald on one knee, facing the audience, his sword drawn, and in the middle of the stage. Then the backcloth runs up and James's study lights go on. James is on a revolving chair in the middle of the back stage, with James's desk behind. He is very bothered and puzzled. As he is speaking the chains without tumult fall from Margery; they hang to the stage side and she walks briskly to the further bookcase.

JAMES: South Borneo? But my dear Gerald, what d'you mean? Who – who – whoever put that into your head? (*The telephone bell rings.*)

GERALD: Just a minute. (*He lays the sword carefully and symmetrically in the middle of the front stage, and goes to the telephone. Margery, sitting on the folding steps, blows dust off before opening a book from the top shelf.*)

JAMES: Hell take that telephone; as soon as you're doing anything important it's dead certain to interrupt you, I've never known it do anything else.

GERALD: Hello. (*Margery with a little gasp of surprise and pleasure looks at the cover again, finds the index, and takes out the next two volumes.*)

JAMES: Margery, go and stop Gerald from making a fool of himself; he'll do what you make him.

GERALD: (*rhythmically*) Hello.

JAMES: Oh do say something, Margery; you can't approve of this ridiculous business, do you? Do go and –

GERALD: Hello. Oh what? Sorry, I was saying Hello.

MARGERY: (*entering the three volumes in her catalogue*) I should think it would be just the thing for him, James, he badly wants something to do.

JAMES: But – but –

GERALD: Say what you like, James, I'm going to go somewhere and do something; I'm not going on hanging about here, philandering with your wife and pilfering your – What? Yes, this is that. No, thank God, I'm his secretary; what d'you want?

JAMES: But – Half an hour ago, Gerald, not that, you were grumbling about overwork and saying you wanted a holiday. Soon as I get *Careful Susan* under way we'll all be buried in work. What's come over you, Gerald, you're so stupid and tiresome? More money, you'd ask for it.

GERALD: Yes, I'm here all right, Charlie – I see – synopsis of famous authors. Not what they believe again, surely, they've done it already? What?

MARGERY: You want him to potter about and look after papers for you, he won't.

JAMES: Rubbish. Secretary. Very good position. Man of *his* age.

MARGERY: It's a woman's job. (*pausing*) Gerald's a very male boy really, you mightn't think it to look at him.

GERALD: *I* see. What does he think of the tendency of modern morals in 400 words. That'll be a nice change, won't it? All right, go ahead, what'll you give?

MARGERY: Gerald's really a very ambitious fellow, only he's ashamed to say so. He wants to be kept seriously busy and excited and in command of things and first frightened and then proud of himself and bothered all the time.

GERALD: Lots and lots more, you aren't trying, Charlie. Why, the old man always does it, don't you see, it's an accepted thing? You can't leave him out, it'd spoil the set.

MARGERY: (*up the ladder*) Personally I'm very properly a female, I love pottering; I've never been happier in my life than I am now.

JAMES: Won't you stop talking, one of you, I'm sure there must be some ridiculous mistake. Of course I never said that.

GERALD: Well, you can't have it at a penny under 25 guineas, Charlie, that's only about 240 – 400 – only about a shilling a word, after all, and where would a synopsis be without grandpa? Why, all the other authors would demand their money back. Good gracious no, I said *twenty-five*.

MARGERY: (*beginning to flap a duster in the emptied top shelf*) In fact, I can't think why I never started doing this library years ago. I'm sure it's been crying out to be done, and of course there's no occupation in the world like fidgeting about a library. I always say –

GERALD: Oh shut up, Margery, how can I listen to the telephone while you're –

JAMES: Don't go rattling on like that about yourself, woman. Here we all are wrestling with this enormously important decision Gerald has just sprung upon us, yes that's the only word I can use, sprung, sprung upon us, and you –

GERALD: Oh do be *quiet*, James; how *can* I handle all your business affairs over the telephone at breakneck speed if you *will* go making a heavy scene about your private feelings?

JAMES: (*flapping*) Gerald, Gerald, you said you were going to –

GERALD: Put it in a novel, man, put it in a novel, don't come bothering me.

MARGERY: (*bellowing behind her duster*) Oh I do like just fidgeting about and being perfectly placid when there's a perfectly appalling noise –

GERALD: What? No I wasn't; what, did I say that? Sorry, wash out, I was just having a chat with James. Do say it all again.

MARGERY: Really, I don't know how any woman could want more than a good library to catalogue, (*shaking out the duster*) and an amiable preoccupied old husband who doesn't take up time. (*She caresses him. He is very preoccupied.*)

GERALD: As a coquette you are so crude as to be painful. If you want to do it, do it better. Good gracious no, I wasn't talking to you, Charlie; you aren't coquetting, you're just plumping out for more than you'll get.

JAMES: What the hell does it matter how much I get a word? You might think I was a pauper. I'm – I'm terribly upset (*his pen flies away*). I can't think of anything. Margery, do go and pick it up again, there's a dear girl. What with this appalling –

MARGERY: Splendid. Throw it again.

GERALD: Oh very well then, I'm busy. Ten guineas, go back and croon over your hoard. You're lunching here on Thursday, remember. Goodbye. Really, James, I'm sorry to keep talking to somebody else all the time, but there's nothing more to say, you know. The dramatic moment is past, the decision made.

JAMES: Did I seriously understand you to tell me a moment ago you were going to leave us at once and become a missionary in South Borneo? Say it again, Gerald, say it as if you meant it.

GERALD: I'm going to be a –

JAMES: You see – he can't keep his face straight. My good boy, what would be the use of it, you aren't a Christian, are you?

GERALD: I am one of the highest and most typical products of Western, that is Christian, civilisation. If I'm not officially a Christian so much the worse for official Christianity. Working for a new inter-racial synthesis, for a more complex fusion of those systems of value, those mental syntheses, those civilisations [which] are now oil and water, I shall be dealing with the most serious and absorbing problems of the human mind. Intellectual snobs like you who laugh at me are wearisome and revolting. As for the Christian fables, it is essential that they should be taught by men who do not pretend they are history, and who [know] precisely from what point of view it is they are important and interesting to the modern world. What is the good of teaching the modern Chinaman, who has been trained from infancy to fear and despise the degenerating influences of superstition?

JAMES: What's the good of teaching the wild man of Borneo, that's what *I* want to know? What on earth made you choose a Godforsaken hole like that for?

GERALD: Oh, I didn't. Is there such a place? I just used the first word that came into my head.

JAMES: Had only just thought of it, child?

GERALD: Yes, well, after all, something had to be done.

JAMES: Gerald, as your old friend, as a very sincere well-wisher, I can only ask what, and why? (*Pause*) And anyway you aren't a parson, child, you'll have to spend years passing exams.

GERALD: Oh well then, I shall go as a sub-missionary or an assistant curate or I shall exercise diaconal functions or something like that. Dash it all, they ought to be jolly glad to have me.

JAMES: Gerald, as an old friend of your mother's, I do want you to confide in me. Why have you taken this extravagant step without once consulting your true friends. What is it, Gerald, what's gone wrong?

GERALD: Good heavens, man, can't you see I'd do anything and go anywhere to get away from *you*? Extraordinarily dull you are this morning, James. Now you've made me put myself in the wrong by saying it straight out.

JAMES: Margery, Margery, what can one say?

MARGERY: (*from the bookstand*) If you ask me, James, I shouldn't say anything; I should go and roll the lawn. It wants rolling, and it'll give both of you time to remember what the other man said and make up your mind what you really want to do about it.

JAMES: Margery, of course you're quite right. I shall come back and answer you, Gerald, when I think of something to say. I refuse to try to be dramatic and think of things on the spur of the moment. It's a vulgar theatrical trick anyway, and you always say what you don't mean to. (*He goes.*)

MARGERY: Splendid. Bravo. Down with plays. There, Gerald, you see the modern mind refusing the dramatic assumptions, knowing itself too subtle for them, too complicated, too – too –

GERALD: Too feeble, that's all (*as he crossly crosses to James's chair*).

MARGERY: (*They meet.*) Now, Gerald, you may kiss me. Calm, peaceful and collected. Tell me why you're kicking up all this fuss and what you've really got on your mind. Don't be in a hurry, it's a big lawn. (*They laugh and do it again.*) Well, what is it?

GERALD: (*He is puzzled and looks round.*) I can't bear, Margery, seeing you paw . . . (*tearfully*) that *Buffer*.

MARGERY: Oh, don't say you're jealous, Gerald. It *is* so tedious and vulgar. (*Quite discouraged she goes back to the bookshelf.*)

GERALD: Rubbish, you don't know what jealousy is. I'm not personally jealous, at all. I see you with a quite cold and detached horror, as one of the thousands of victims of this commercial civilisation, the clever savoury wellsexed young women who moulder complacently, *queens* of virtue, beside bored impotent old grandfathers who oughtn't to be let leer at them from behind railings.

MARGERY: (*roaring with laughter*) Sesame and lilies. Beautiful, Gerald.

GERALD: (*striding about*) It's all wrong, Margery, the system of society is all wrong; you oughtn't to be paid for marrying old men and taxed for marrying young ones.

MARGERY: Gerald!

GERALD: *I* don't want you, you can go to bed with the gardener's boy if you like, but do for God's sake stop titivating that propertied old eunuch and calling it a quiet life.

MARGERY: Is that really what's the matter with you, Gerald? (*Down steps with books and leans back on table.*)

GERALD: (*He sits down.*) I don't know. Why shouldn't it be?

MARGERY: Well, if you're so very impersonal you may as well stay here. I am one of thousands, remember, and the social customs in Western Somaliland are probably even more deplorable. Why should you –

GERALD: Coldhearted pig.

MARGERY: But of course I entirely agree with you, Gerald. In fact, it's rather the pious thing to say just now, isn't it? Ludovici and all that.* In fact at Girton they gave us a positive course of lectures entitled '*Go* to bed with the gardener's boy, or Virtue its own reward'. And I'm sure I'm a nice natural girl and always careful to do what the earnest people tell me.

GERALD: Margery, don't be brutal, what are you snubbing me for?

MARGERY: I think we are a little at odds on the tub-thumping issue, Gerald. I know it sounds very vigorous and intelligent to walk up and down and use a lot of rude words, but it's very distracting and a little tiresome. I mean, it isn't as if I hadn't read the books you keep quoting all the time.

GERALD: But of course I keep quoting, Margery. This civilisation has a very bad conscience, and we *all* know it, but we're *all* actuated by the people who say so. What else can I do but quote them; they all quote each other, don't they?

MARGERY: Well, if you're frankly quoting, you should do it gracefully, allusively and flatly, with a lot of little prepositions and no fuss. You should assume they've read it, and give tabloids.

GERALD: But I'm not *thinking* in tabloids, I don't *feel* like a literary allusion. Why should I go –

MARGERY: Use defensive satire in case anybody wants to laugh at you, always talk as if you won't think the same next week, and say 'of course' to avoid drama.

---

*A. M. Ludovici (1882–1971), author of *Lysistrata* (1924) and *Woman: a vindication* (1923; reissued 1926). Empson's notebook-diary for 4 May 1926 includes the following entry: 'We are in the midst of a grave national crisis [the General Strike] . . . I wanted to speak against Ludovici and the Heterosexual Healthiness; the natural man does not need 96 women, he is male for a honeymoon, and then while the woman plans the autumn baby the man swings back to the homosexual, he wants men-friends, a social evening, "civilisation"; they have both had enough of it. A purely heterosexual man is dangerously uncivilised . . . To make sure the family, Freud has shown, we took sex aside and turned it Oedipose; to make sure civilisation, the focus has shifted again, and we "love our neighbours." Civilisation is not a plurality of harems . . .'

GERALD: But I don't *want* to. Can't you see the two things don't *mean* the same?

MARGERY: Things don't *mean* things, Gerald, you know you aren't allowed to use that word.

GERALD: Sorry. I mean they don't refer to the same reference.

MARGERY: Of course they couldn't have just the same reference, Gerald, or we couldn't tell them apart.

GERALD: Margery, I'm crying to you for help, I open my inmost heart to you, and all you do is to sit with your head in a cupboard and talk like the Mad Teaparty.

MARGERY: But I told you I agree with you, Gerald. I'm just filling in the time while you're thinking what to say next, getting the *quotations* in order and what not.

GERALD: (*screaming*) Fish.

MARGERY: Anyway, you ought to talk like the Mad Teaparty: he was a very intellectual man.

GERALD: What *you* said wasn't. It was perfect nonsense, they might perfectly well have exactly the same reference and quite different – (*without a change in the voice rising higher and higher*) Oh Margery, I love you, *what* are we talking about, Margery, be fair do you care a rap about me or not?

MARGERY: There, Gerald, I'm sorry, I was tiresome. But we can't help it, you know. I mean, for the moment I've teased you enough to relieve my feelings, but I can't bear you being rackety and vulgar.

GERALD: Cruel beast, all because I offended you about the gardener's boy.

MARGERY: Liar.

GERALD: But it's quite true, I know. Margery, I'm suffering and it's not good for me to suffer, it makes me talk too fast. Love me, Margery, love me much, and I shall be oh like a sheep and never say a word. (*He sits down plump in James's chair, and is from now on looking at the sword.*)

MARGERY: Gerald, I do; so don't. And I do think I should be happier with you because it's quite true what you say, there seems to be no doubt the old man's reasonably impotent and I'm a nice natural girl, in fact we might even run to a baby or two. But listen to me, Gerald, we must have lots of money, quite half as much money as James has got, I don't mind how you get it, only we must be quite safe about it and I mustn't be cut off from some sort of intelligent society. If you can do all that, Gerald, though I'm a very contented young woman anyway, I'll come. Mind you, whether I'd say that if I thought you were in the least bit likely to *do* it, is another question. (*Gerald, amused, sits down again and lights a cigarette; she goes out.*)

The hall of Dracula's castle is of grey stone. Impressive arid building with a high roof. In the middle of the stage is a massive door, even when battered, and on either side of it a small window, placed high up, can be looked out of if you climb the three high steps or windowseats built into the wall.

Smith runs in from the wings very fast, looking once over his shoulder; he flings himself at the door and rattles at it, tearing the bolts about. Hits it with his fists for a little, and hangs panting to the doorknob. He steps back and looks about, climbs to the window to try the bars, no good, looks up at the other one, finding an iron bar on the step. He waves it, triumph, and flies back to the door (this is lit by the red footlights and a strawcoloured lantern over it). Dracula comes on left, the other side, stands waiting. Smith, tearing at the lock, turns with his lever, and sees him. He throws up one arm and his head as if he was going to faint or attack him, but in the middle of this begins speaking, carefully.

SMITH: Good afternoon, sir, I thought you must have gone out (*the arm finds wall behind him*); that is, I hadn't expected you to be in. What a splendid old door this is of yours, I was just admiring it. There is something almost frightening, don't you think (*he has turned round*) in the austere security, the unconquerable, passionless quality there is about it? A very convincing piece of work, I should like to do a sketch of it, if I may, some time.

DRACULA: You speak very truly, sir, of security. We are very safe, from interruption, here. You have seen, I fancy, the cliffs on which this castle is built; you know well, sir, that no man can enter, or indeed leave, alive, but by the forcing of this door. And, have no fear, my dear sir, it is impregnable; we shall be alone together; and your stay under my roof, if I may say it without presumption, will be as quiet, as unruffled, as I make no doubt, sir, it will be prolonged.

SMITH: I'm sorry to have to disappoint you, Dracula, but the fact is, now you mention it, I shall have to go away almost at once. I have been recalled to England on urgent family business. I am sure it is most annoying, no one could regret it more than I do myself. Have you such a thing as a timetable in the house?

DRACULA: There has been no letter, no telegram. It would be an event in this part of the country. I trust, sir, you have not been in some way deceived?

SMITH: (*He laughs shrilly.*) Very sharp of you, Dracula, I shall have to expose myself then. The fact is, I have been a great fool, I came away from England leaving a most – that is, a wholly essential family arrangement quite unattended to. It's very absurd, and most disappointing, I know, but really I shall have to go and see to it at once.

DRACULA: While I have not the least wish in the world, sir, to appear to be curious, I must confess myself at once puzzled and concerned. Can it be you have left the gas burning in your bedroom? Depend upon it –

SMITH: You must excuse me, I'm very sorry, er, that is, private –

DRACULA: Can it be, sir, that you have omitted to make your will? They tell me the English always take that precaution before leaving their country; they consider themselves in continuous peril till they return. In that case, while I cannot endorse, I can at any rate sympathise with your in no way flattering anxiety.

SMITH: I, I am afraid I must go. I am afraid. (*backing to the door*) I *must* go.

DRACULA: (*suddenly with decision*) You must forgive me, sir; indeed I apologise a thousand times. I have been guilty of unpardonable impertinence, harassing your departure, and attempting to pry into your affairs. Let me make the most rapid amends in my power. If you pack your bag tonight the carriage will be ready for you tomorrow morning, and will drive you at once to the station.

SMITH: As a matter of fact, after all it's not far to the station, and if I pack my bag at once and catch the night train on foot I shall feel that is my mind will not rest until I –

DRACULA: Sir, I have already opposed your wishes with too much eagerness, it only remains for me to assist you so far as I can. You may, of course, leave the castle as soon as you are prepared to do so.

SMITH: You are – You are most kind. I am sure I am sorry to be so discourteous. I feel, that is, I shall go and pack my bag.

He goes out. Dracula is rather amused. After a pause he takes the lantern from above the door and hangs it before the window, left. He goes out briskly to the left. A wolf, almost at once, howls, far away, and then several, nearer. Soon there is a loud but not continuous howling outside the door, and Smith comes back from the right, with a large handbag. Hearing him they set up a great clamour, he drops the bag, and runs up to the right hand window. He jumps back, and comes slowly down, feeling for the wall behind him.

SMITH: Black. Black. Writhing and turning, waiting, writhing and turning for me, they are hungry they are waiting for me, they cumber they make dark the ground. Black it is darkened for me, it is your gathering of devils, black as the legion of your fiends. They are waiting, they are writhing and turning . . . Ah, the clear white teeth, the clear white teeth, they shall gnaw and tear, gnaw and tear me, and the slobbering of the gums. Teeth, teeth, they shall gnaw and fumble, you watching, the snap and crunch, teeth on my arms, my elbows, my fingers as you throw me forward; I am to be gnawed they shall lay bare my bones. (*Dracula comes in on the left, so that he comes into the straw-coloured area, and is holding a large key.*) Your army is calling, general, what are we to do, why have we been called so quickly? Give us food, they say, where is the meat we are to strip, and the bones we are to draw the marrow [from]? Here at your call, Dracula, the brutes obey you, and I do you homage; Dracula, you are more than mortal, you are beyond the binding of the world. To your calling, you have all power, Dracula, and I tumble, I tumble. You have me, I am less than a man.

DRACULA: You flatter me perhaps unduly, Mr Smith, but it is quite true I have my own little methods of handling, my own outlook upon, even perhaps my own intimacy and communion with, that material world of which, if I may say so, you and your friends have always had so strangely limited, so artificially secure a conception. And now, while it is more than painful, sir, while it is indeed a great sorrow to me that you must leave in such haste, still if you are quite sure, of course, if you are certain your business is so pressing – (*there is a new burst of howling as he begins to rattle the key in the lock*).

SMITH: Now I come to think of it, Dracula, I don't believe any of that; I don't think you're a magician at all. I did just now, I know, but somehow – soon as you say it in long words, as soon as I see what you really mean, you – you remind me, that's all, I remember I don't really believe it at all. (*Dracula shoots back the upper bolt. There is a roar of welcome and a bang on the door. Smith stands up, and moves forward.*) I say, Dracula, you must tell me at once, this is quite a serious matter. No, lock the door again, of course, no good fooling around there. You mustn't kill me for a minute, I've something to say.

See here, Dracula, you may be trying to get money out of me, or do a pet revenge, or torture me for fun, I don't know what you're playing, anyway it's a damned dull melodrama. This is what matters. I'm a scientist. If I was in England, safe, and I heard you were lord of the wolves, and I believed it, I should be bowled over, broken. I am now. (*Dracula steps back, takes the lantern and holds it to his face between them.*) Dracula, does the world work the way I like, or not? It isn't a thing it's fair to cheat about. If you could possibly be a werewolf, I shall kill myself, Dracula, if you spare me. I shall despise the cosmos, and turn from the investigation of the world.

DRACULA: (*hanging the lantern on its hook, over the door*) Really, Mr Smith, your attitude seems very puzzling. (*He bolts the door.*) I should have thought the only thing that could depress a scientist would be to find *no* uniformity in the natural world. I should have thought the additional uniformity in virtue of which, by the recitation of certain spells or what not, I am or am not able to collect the wolves of the neighbourhood, can only give additional pleasure, offer a new field of research, into animal psychology perhaps, or whatever subject-heading it may be most convenient to employ. If you don't despise the cosmos for obeying one equation, why despise it for obeying another? I am at a loss to understand this emotional phraseology.

SMITH: The scientist, Dracula, can only live in a very odd universe indeed. And to start with, it must be in some way impersonal, it must obey a law and not a master. You don't know what you are saying; it matters, Dracula, you must tell me at once.

DRACULA: I must tell you, must I, whether the universe is the sort of universe you would like it to be?

SMITH: Or a tuppenny nightmare, a sick man's fancy we couldn't trust while we were sleeping. Must I be afraid of the dark again, and when you're dead will the bogeys get you? Oh, is the world sound, Dracula, can we sleep tonight?

DRACULA: My friend, I have my plans, and I think you are beaten. But there's no doubt, *I* shall sleep all right.

SMITH: Saved again. I say, thanks awfully, Dracula, you've quite set me up again; if you'd gone on putting across the wicked fairy business I'd have knuckled under altogether. All right, that's how we stand. I can't leave the castle, and you can kill me as soon as you like. Go on being a wicked man; you'd better start being polite again, I should think.

DRACULA: I should be more than charmed, sir, to treat you with any courtesy you may think proper. And now, since you appear to be detained, will you accept a little supper?

SMITH: (*gay and comfortable*) You alarm me, Dracula, more than I can say.

James's study again. Gerald sits in James's chair still, looking at the sword, about six weeks later; and Margery.

MARGERY: (*hurried urgent whisper*) Gerald, what have you bought *that* for? You know what I mean, I know you've got it in the house. Gerald, what is it? Oh Gerald, what are you going to do with it? Gerald, I can't *begin* to understand you. You fool, can't you see it isn't any use? (*with rational gusto*) Let it slide. Unconstipate yourself, boy. Put your nightmare down the water closet. Here we are and the sun's shining, and James has finished that deplorably bad novel, and there's nothing in the world to worry about any more. (*whispering again*) Don't you see, Gerald, nobody will say a word about [the] silly forgery business now? Only keep quiet and we're safe.

GERALD: I remember when I was first taken shooting, and as the keeper said at the time, it's a thing that may always come in useful. (*He is amused, she shrinks.*) I was always glad when I winged a bird and got it in the leg and couldn't find it and left it to die of thirst before hunger, to be gnawed on in passing and to pray for owls. I was always glad, since I was doing a cruel thing, to force into my mind, to keep clearly in front of me, just what a bloody cruel thing it was; I was always careful, at the time, to be neither a fool for my disapproval nor a worm for my blindness. These things are well and widely rooted, they call for many admirable qualities; I admire but dare not, Margery, for my soul's sake, palliate them.

MARGERY: (*the whisper*) Give it me, Gerald. Give it me, and I'll lock it up at once in a drawer and you'll never see it again.

GERALD: And when she took it out again there were half a dozen more. No, Margery, I never have believed in dishcovers. Day by day and in every way I shoot James less and less. That's what you'd like, isn't it?

MARGERY: (*after a pause*) P'raps I'm being rather hysterical. You know you couldn't say it if you meant it, nobody could. Where were we? You mean James's cheque.

GERALD: (*pleased, slowly*) There are, also, other applications.

MARGERY: (*screaming*) Say what you mean. Fool.

GERALD: (*arguing*) Anything the modern mind has a bad conscience about. That's a wide enough field for anybody.

MARGERY: Really, Gerald, you know I can believe a lot, there are limits. I mean, it's rather odd it should be simple stern disapproval of industrialism that made you play little games with James's cheque.

GERALD: Margery, it's perfectly simple, it's an exactly parallel case.

MARGERY: I call it perfectly childish. Really, Gerald, it was too bad of you to go on like that. I know I said something you might have thought meant something like that, but I obviously didn't mean anything perfectly ridiculous, (*turning away*) and anyway you might have gone through with it afterwards.

GERALD: See here, Margery. First, property's mean.

MARGERY: Theft *is* property, Gerald. It's the youngest act of property to come and steal the spoons.

GERALD: Property's mean. I made up my mind I wanted to do an act of property. So I picked out the meanest act of property I could find anywhere and did that. Then I decided, having property fairly in front of me, I didn't want to commit an act of property. So I didn't. It took six weeks.

MARGERY: And we could have got away with it even then. Gerald, really.

GERALD: As for you, Harlot, you positively enjoy property; you go wallowing about in it.

MARGERY: You may say what you like, *I* don't go forging my best friend's . . . *I* don't refuse, with an air of personal injury, to cash them afterwards. *I* don't – Give it me, Gerald. Give it me give it me oh you must give it me at once. (*turning from the sword he looks up at her*) I want your revolver.

GERALD: I may put up with this civilisation, you see, Margery, but I shan't palliate it. It may twist me into some funny poses, it can't shut my eyes.

MARGERY: Oh, *can't* it? It'll put *pennies* in your eyes if you aren't careful, or don't they do that nowadays? (Romantic literature is so misleading.) (*She sits down.*) Poor Gerald, you'd much rather have half-crowns, wouldn't you?

GERALD: I assure you, I'd just as soon have pennies. (*stretching his legs out*) Wonderful how the pleasures and amenities of civilisation seem to lose all importance, Margery, (*slowly, almost to himself*) once you've really made up your mind.

Enter James abruptly.

JAMES: Gerald my boy, there's something I've decided I ought to say to you; I've come to say it at once. I've been thinking about it for several days. After all, when all's said and done, one has one's duty to the public; I mean, I quite see it isn't a very pleasant thing to have said to you by anyone, but now that you'll be leaving us soon I do think it's my duty as a responsible householder to try and come to some sort of understanding about your intentions. You see –

MARGERY: James, what do you mean?

GERALD: How d'you know I'm leaving you soon?

JAMES: Well, you said you'd stay and see me through *Careful Susan*, so naturally I thought you would be going soon after it was published. I didn't like to ask you what arrangements you'd made about your work and so on, because I knew I only irritated you by what I'm sure was always meant very kindly. And afterwards when you won through about the horrible cheque business and behaved in your own way, so finely, so so –

GERALD: Go away, James. (*He is glowering – hunched up, chin on fists – at the sword.*)

MARGERY: Be quiet, Gerald.

JAMES: I could only offer you sympathy and really a great deal of admiration, because I do understand what you've been struggling against. Your whole outlook on life and even what seems to us quite elementary morality was only forced on you, when it came to the point, quite in the teeth of all your childish rebellion and anarchism and so on. But I didn't gather, and I never have been able to gather yet, and I do think before I let you go into the difficulties, the rather hazardous renunciation of your new life, I ought to make sure –

MARGERY: James, why is he going into anything?

GERALD: Shut up, Margery. He thinks I'm going to South Borneo, don't you remember? The Mission Field.

JAMES: Yes, of course, dear boy, I quite understand. All I am saying is I want to feel quite sure, Gerald, you don't approve of burgling and forging and murdering any longer. I mean I'm sorry to doubt you after the splendid way you came and told me all about it, but really you spoke about it very strangely afterwards, and I can't be quite sure in my own mind it wasn't simply that the claims of friendship proved too strong, that you found you couldn't quite act up to your principles even though you still think modern civilisation so wicked and intolerable that all scruple in taking whatever you may care for would – would be absurd. You *have* found out for yourself that wickedness is dreadful, Gerald, haven't you; you don't still fancy yourself as a danger to the public, you aren't fighting still against the whole system of life, the whole organisation of the world? Are you, Gerald?

GERALD: The nightmare is always in front of me, Margery, of being like James. Of liking myself for touching pitch, fancying myself as good a pitch-toucher as any man, and calling it the glorious constitution.

JAMES: Gerald, I don't understand. You have given up that silly way of thinking, haven't you?

GERALD: Make yourself easy, James, I have given up all ways of thinking; I have one little protest, I shall make that and go. (*He takes it out of his pocket.*)

JAMES: (*full of concern*) Whatever's the matter, Gerald, you can't be thinking of shooting yourself, are you? Don't be such a fool, child; (*Gerald, crossly shuddering, puts it back*) give me a chance and tell me all about it; at one time we were such good friends, weren't we? I'm sure I could help if you'd only let me.

GERALD: Oh yes, you can be of some use, James; you might look up the number of the police station.

JAMES: My poor Gerald, I know you better than you know yourself. You'd never really bring yourself to do wrong, (*this shatters Margery, sitting waiting*) and anyway the police haven't got a number, you just say 'police'.

(*It comes out again.*)

MARGERY: (*getting up*) Stop, Gerald. Oh you can't. Fool. Gerald, if you do I – I – I'll never speak to you again.

GERALD: You wouldn't anyway, silly, they'd hang me.

MARGERY: Give it me, Gerald, give it me, give it me. (*retiring*) Oh my fool.

GERALD: Why don't you come and take it from me, Margery? I should think you probably could if you were quick. I wouldn't shoot you if I could help it, you know. (*He offers it to her, amused, snatching it back again; she shrinks as far away as possible; he plays catch with it for a minute.*)

MARGERY: Oh, I am weak. I am weak. I am weak. (*Face to the wall, up by the still hanging chains. Once she turns to loose her whole resentment on him.*) It's no use.

JAMES: Gerald, you complicated untidy child, how have you managed to make a revolver grow out of the situation?

GERALD: (*He pockets it, absentmindedly.*) It's true I don't hate you awfully now; that's because I'm so pleased. (*Margery thinks of something to say, and turns back, to shiver.*) I mean, I know what I want to do, I'm going to do it: you can put up with a lot then.

JAMES: Gerald, it hurts me to see you suffering like this. (*Gerald, amused, crows.*) Put down that silly toy and tell me why. Your old friend, Gerald, I've a right to know.

GERALD: The just man made perfect, Margery, James standing up for his rights.

JAMES: But how have I forfeited my rights? Margery, do explain, I'm sure he's told you.

MARGERY: I don't think – (*contemptuously*)

GERALD: (*louder*) If you want to know what makes my flesh creep worst, it's the pious chaste virtuous young woman who beds only with her grandfather.

MARGERY: It's a lie. Peeping Tom, that's all that is. Prurient little fool, i – i – if I didn't love James I should divorce him; anything more uncalled-for than you and your ridiculous revolver I – I –

GERALD: Very respectable, I'm sure, and as I shall leave you a bouncing widow anyway, quite harmless under the circumstances. (*turning from her*) You're right, of course, I don't care a rap about you.

JAMES: Well, then, *that* isn't why you're waving the thing about. Analyse yourself, Gerald, tell us why you want to kill me. Anyway make up some sort of excuse. I mean, anybody can *do* it.

GERALD: (*chatty*) I know the story you mean, James, the keeper told the lunatic he'd better come down and throw him up the tower, because after all anybody could throw him down. So he did, so he didn't do anything. That's what they call a triumph of psycho-analysis, that is.

JAMES: Listen to me, Gerald. Stop hugging your daydreams and think what really happened. Six weeks ago you did a fairly good forgery of one of my cheques. You spent about three weeks working very hard at *Susan*, getting crosser and crosser, and finally you made a huge scene full of righteous indignation and threw it back at me. Now I ask you, Gerald, is that material for a tragedy? (*leaning forward*) Look at it, child, prepare to write memoirs, think how everybody else will see you. Think of it in the ha'penny papers, how flat, how unexplained you'll be.

GERALD: Have you ever read the ha'penny papers, what they call the tragedies, people shooting each other? Ever noticed how flat and unexplained they are, all of them? People don't explain themselves nowadays, it'd take too long.

MARGERY: (*bursting round*) Gerald, you're loathsome. James has treated you impossibly generously; you behave like a monster and you don't pretend to see any sense in it! (*back again*)

GERALD: (*just after her*) Good God, James, can't you see how you've won? How I can't move against you? You sit there smug and placid and gratified, you tell me with laborious triumph how I'm perfectly reformed and good and pious. Can't you see I crawled back and betrayed myself, I'm so steeped in your humbug your own weapons rot in my hands? I can't touch your money, I've tried, it's too loathsome to bear with. You've won, smile at me, I am bound like Samson, (*placidly to the sword*) I shall die like Samson, (*over his shoulder*) Papa.

JAMES: A few people have always revolted, Gerald, against marriage and property and the secure presumptions of the world. In [an] orderly generation they are kept in monasteries. They are only ridiculous when they try to make everybody agree with them. It is true you'd be an ornament to the cloister, but there's nothing to shoot me about in that. As for South Borneo, it would be ideal; I can't think why you haven't gone there.

GERALD: And the sensible men, safe in their pigsty, quiet and happy. Everybody can go Jericho except you and your little sensible friends, all stinking in a pile together. Ahhr, can't you see how *loath*some you are, James? (*He starts feeling about for the revolver.*) Groan, scream, go on.

JAMES: (*stalking forward*) Put it down, child. Buy a catapult.

GERALD: (*amused*) Unfortunately, James, bad luck, it nearly worked. I happen to belong to that class (*waving the revolver*) no member of which can with any profit be treated as a child.

JAMES: And what class is that, Gerald? I am your foil to the last.

MARGERY: Oh you are stupid. *Children*! Guess quicker, James! Snatch at it. Stop him, stop him.

GERALD: (*He shoots him, and takes out the cartridge slowly; Margery to her chains.*) I was right, wasn't I, Margery? Say I was right. Margery, I've dared everything, I've broken it all. Say I was right. (*She has her back to him, and the old man falls off the chair. Gerald steps over him to the telephone.*) I want the police station, please – yes – Oh hello! You might send a man along to number four Cheshire Avenue. No, Cheshire, yes Cheshire Avenue. Oh, there's been a murder done. What? Handcuffs? Oh yes, bring them along if you like, it doesn't matter. (*goes left*) Margery, I can do without you; I'd *rather* you said I was right. Oh very well, it doesn't matter. (*He bends over the sword. Grasping it tightly, crouched down, he turns to look up at her. The old man's study lights go out, and the noble wild apronstage backcloth covers him decently from view. Gerald speaks the first two words in a low tone of suppressed excitement, before rising to loud pleasurable self-satisfaction and a romantic pose.*)

> Sword sword Princess I with my sword have slain
> Your ogre ghastly that forged sure the chain.
> Make no long tarrying my dove's heart pass through
> The uplifted drawbridge and the slaughtered crew.
> Pass unmolested, yours all earth to roam,
> Or gain the enraptured palace as your home.

MARGERY: Now you have slain the dragon, and I know
> No other ever can now please me so;
> Pace, sir, I beg you surely by my side,
> And clasp me lastly a well eager bride.
> The king my father will, of course, consent.
> The palace is behind you. Time we went.

GERALD: The adventurous heart, the capable right hand
> Poise me the youth that shall true victor stand.
> Nought else I bring you, lady, nor can find
> Portion or gift but the preparèd mind.
> Love you I must, make happy if I can,
> And I remain your managing young man.

(*leaning on the sword, legs crossed, with negligent self-satisfaction*)

Unpublished Poems
and Fragments

I

Empson's first recorded poem, written by 29 June 1920, aetat 13; text taken from the autograph book of a school contemporary, J. A. Simson.

Mother, saying Anne good night,
Feared the dark would cause her fright.
'Four angels guard you,' low she said,
'One at the foot and one at the head – '

'Mother – quick – the pillow!! – There!!!
Missed that angel, skimmed his hair.
Never mind, we'll get the next.
Ooh! but angels make me vexed!!'

Mother, shocked, gasped feebly 'Anne!!!'
(A pillow disabled the water-can.)
Said Anne, 'I won't have things in white
Chant prayers about my bed all night.'

11

Song of the amateur psychologist

[1926]

Directly after writing out an untitled fair copy of this poem in his contemporary notebook, Empson added the comment: 'It is good rousing stuff, I still think.'

It is a deep-rooted
far stirring in strong shadow kingdoms
and ripens among
the slow rustle
of that midnight orchard
whose woven branches are*
soft, plump or stretching, are too small
to dream of, myriad,
intercellular;
in timid contact
of whose slow rhythmic fingers
are woven the proud worlds.

Cathedral caverns
in not glinting limestone
water there changing always
the fretted hollow curves;
high vaulted arches
of the uncharted cellars,
and, it is a discovery,
too large for a short stride
too steep, there pass
downwards beneath them
these narrow and stone stairs.

---

*Braincell Pseudopodia. [Empson]

But now rest yourself a moment, and lean
on the great pillars, feel
how in darkness they hum softly
holding the lit palace
and hearing riot in the halls.

Men come here often
with lanterns carefully,
looking over their shoulders
and feeling it something of an expedition
to choose just the one vintage
that is called for.
Also on great occasions
they unbrick old archways
and there lie guarded
the rich tawny
secret potions;
they that were buried
in an autumn
long past; are ruby,
are precious, aged
now, potent, secure.

Strike a light before we go on;
we need, rather, the sane assurance
and yellow courage of your candle.
Guard him well however do not let him
peer from your fist too rashly at the groining
there is a strong and cold wind up the stairs.

Let us descend now
but carefully, they are high steps
and steep, for walking.
After a dozen of them
there is an even darkness
that has waited so long
it is not a light thing to disturb,
and they go on down

beyond that, it is not easy
to imagine what we might see
if we were holding a light house in our hands.
Might there not be – might there not –
the unchained
the insane perspective
the no end
and your cry recoiling –

ah, I can quite imagine you saying it, with an
        air of apocalyptic
and desperate capability, sincerity, security
        almost –

'The low roof goes
down, the stairs
arriving proudly
at no final pinpoint
go straight down
only, down always.'

III
Two centos
[1926; annotations by Empson]

i

At Algezir,[1] and will in overplus,[2]
Their herdsmen,[3] well content to think thee page,[4] divided.[3]
Tell Isabel the queen, I looked not[5] thus
Leander, Mr Ekenhead, and I did.[6]

ii

of them that are overcome with. Woe[1]
stay me with flagons,[2] civilly delight.[3]
So lovers contracts, images of those,[4]
so be I equalled with,[5] as dark as night.[6]

Do thy worst, blind Cupid,[7] dark amid the blaze of.[8] Woe
to the crown of pride,[1] and Phineus prophets old,[5]
did cry To-whoo To-whoo, and the sun did shine so[9]
(the lords and owners of,[10] poor Toms-a)[11] cold.

1. Chaucer Prologue l.57.
2. Shakespeare Sonnet no. cxxxv.
3. Genesis, chapter 13.
4. Donne Elegy xvi.
5. Marlowe Ed II.
6. Don Juan, canto 2, stanza 105.

1. Isaiah. xxviii.1.
2. Song of Solomon. ii.5.
3. Pope. Arbuthnot. 313.
4. Donne. Songs and Sonets. Womans constancy.
5. Paradise Lost. iii.34.
6. Shakespeare Sonet cxlvii.
7. Lear. Act iv scene 6.
8. Sams. Ag. 80.
9. Wordsworth. Idiot Boy.
10. Shakespeare Sonnet xciv.
11. Lear. Act iv scene 1.

IV

Address to a tennis-player

This prose poem presumably dates from the period of Empson's first printed poem, 'Poem about a Ball in the Nineteenth Century' (published in June 1927): like that poem – 'There is a good case for hating this sort of poetry and calling it meaningless,' Empson wrote in the Notes to Collected Poems *– 'Address to a tennis-player' is influenced by the work of Gertrude Stein.*

Gracious are you still unaltered, halted, untired no larger, Peter, still lively competent 'So long' and so long after, laughter and after all no, thou art Peter, upon this rock I build.

(Oh petering out no, unhaltered but very rocky, very trying, flying the Blue Peter, beaten why, on the rocks, crying, an old crock, cracking up breaking up, even trying making up, oh never mind, a mind made up.)

Peter Pan, Scarborough Rock. I crack up Peter.

Unbeaten, beaten gold, a gold repeater, unhand me, minute hand, cold clock that rocks the cradle, lifeline crack rocket racquet, planned stand caught first-court grand stand, unbeaten, racks the world. Knock, it stays unaltered, all rock, sweeter to pay Paul meeter to run amok, to shock St Paul's dean and chapeetre, sheet attraction, ossi-assuefaction, petri- or putri, Peter a better faction, knock knock it shall remain unlocked, third not the clock stopped, rocked, dropped, cock cocked amidden promptly crew to grew to dears, beautied but grouted ears, pouted about his peers, boudoired abounded, powdered or peerless, reappears.

Biers, a rock of peat as, bares bears purr peering to his burrs. Bar star, starring poor staring Peter; thus far no, burthen rock-girt, further; three-crowned, weeping, a triple crowing; bitter to butter, goes out, to fair well, Simple to Simon Peter; a rock for bread, a roc's egg for a pie. I Am That is it I Lord, give them Peter, they dare, he bears, scarlet, Herod's purple, not Christ's, Pall's. Speech mitre Peter, key and lock bewray thee, he carrying, Iscariot, can they deny Peter, mock wearing Christopher renamed. Pie rock bun spy Lord, Peter face-owner hungry, tossed Pan-cake arse-end, Peter across ascending, upside scream cream down, once rot, hot cross buns.

V

Two fragments

i

Moaning inadequately
and without sufficient despair
several town councillors
were there.

Desperate ladders, mid bison, weeps
green green, unstable, a flame,
round, sweet, the tulip-face too certain
oh centred viewed enclosed.

The shift, the fine fault in flint,
fine packed and central grit, troglodyte
in the great parting centred.

Two teeth not meeting

The just irregular crystal,
needles not quite, the glanced sliding lances,
dual piercing, a reach-me-down, on edge.

ii

One cut as seizin from the turf the cross
Whose arch of branches are the best for fire
And made a fire enter their flue of cloud
Who swallow into vaults a double cross
And all the flounces of the trees made arches
Whose offered branches were the first despair

Whose rounded thought could hold a court of fire
With which the raptured Adam could not cope
And like a cow over the moon to fiddles
We leapt in turn across the cope of fire.

VI

Two songs from a libretto

[? October 1927]

i

You advise me coldly then to accept whatever
Drifts from the casual turning of the day;
Not to order an assured heart; never
To look down the coherent vestige of my way;

Secure in my bars, only, to let all pass;
Hear now my marriage, now my funeral bell;
Sure of a safe continuance of darkness,
Of remaining, in my heart, inviolable.

ii

Simply we do not know what are the turnings
Expound our poising of obscure desires,
What Minotaur in irritable matched burnings
Yearns and shall gore her intricate my fires.

Simply that no despair known of knowing
Inn continent compact continuable
Would mine the minor* rapture of her going
Would leave me liefless but not despicable.

---

*'Undermining, mining for metal, lesser, in minor key, under age.' [Empson]

Simply I shall not answer for what answer
She may on her return return, or helms
Or masters the same tortured dancer.
Simply the mechanism overwhelms.

These two songs are the only passages that Empson typed out from his notebook jottings; it is not otherwise possible to construct the story of his proposed libretto from the few remaining holograph fragments.

In one passage two aunts try to persuade a girl (presumably their niece) to take heed of a promising parti:

Aunt (1) You'll hardly if ever
     (2)   You'll never discover
     (1) So handsome rich clever
     (2)   A more worthy lover

to which the girl shortly replies:

          Search for him out some worthy lass
          Ere my affection cow him.
     (1) So must the Spring name dawns in vain,
          And pullulent, uncurling,
          Leave you sequestered, cold inane
          Pale tendrils curling?
     (2) Girl, have you never turned to see,
          Nor caught your breath in turning?
          Have you no sighing after tea
          For sharp romance's burning?
          . . .
     (1) Ah you may waive the more convulsive passions,
          So to be sober, elegant, endears
          One who can see your heart and feel your fashions
          And know the intimate sympathy of years.

Another passage begins with the girl asking about the passage from F. H. Bradley's Appearance and Reality *quoted by T. S. Eliot in his note to line 411 of* The Waste Land:

What did Professor Bradley say whom
T. S. Eliot quotes?
(1) Surely but only in the notes
(2) Why, should I have read *all* the notes?
Girl. His notes are *part* of what he quotes
(2) These modern writers get my goats
(1) The girl is overstrung and dotes
(2) Come, let's be daring, burn our boats,
Have you the notes here?
Read out the notes dear.
                              (*The note is intoned.*)
(2) Well, if that isn't bonny.

Aunt (1) presently opines,

Since so far May this remarkable Law
And the world at large seem to have got together
Let them get on together a bit *more*.

*to which the first song above is the girl's response; her song is
followed by these lines*:

(2) May do try and make a good impression
Johnny is coming and will take possession.
(1) Be plain and unsilly like us
He says he don't mind if he does.

VII
Rebuke for a dropped brick
[? 1929*]

Vulture, to eat his heart, staked down,
Known suicide's, Prometheus', Jove-hated
And still at cross-roads; to have shown renown
Twisted, and leave him fumigated

Whose heart draped for a sleeve, beaten purple,
Gold leaf, a laurel and a covering,
Fretted buttressed ball made, ant-like, of church bell,
Contains pulp Nessus of not knowing.

---

*'Myth', the poem which follows, appears in a holograph version on the typescript of this poem.

VIII
Myth
[1929]

Young Theseus makes a mission of his doom
And strides from narrow to more narrow room.
His hand, a flame on the sand powder-train,
Hisses, well certain that the clue will find,
And crumbles it behind,
The Minotaur to gain.

No victim yet could the sand rope renew.
At least he holds a secondary clue.
He, least surprised, has this escape devised:
Wind he the spinster's wool, his sail unfolds
Where Ariadne holds
Her cobweb, ill-advised.

*The autograph fair copy from which this text is taken is followed by
this abstract (see* Seven Types of Ambiguity)*:*

The seven classes of ambiguity.

1. Mere richness; (a metaphor valid from many points of view).
2. Two different meanings conveying the same point.
3. Two unconnected meanings, both wanted but not illuminating
   one another.
4. Irony: two apparently opposite meanings combined into a
   judgement.
5. Transition of meaning; (a metaphor applying halfway between
   two comparisons).

6. Tautology or contradiction, allowing of a variety of guesses as to its meaning.
7. Two meanings that are the two opposites created by the context.

IX

Warning to undergraduates

My friends who have not yet gone down
From that strange cackling little town,
Attend, before you burn your boats,
To these few simple College Notes.

Lock up whatever it appears
Might give a celibate Ideas.
You'd best import your own stout box;
They keep the keys of College locks
(Not that they wish, especially, to;
It is their duty, and they do).

Remember what a porter's for;
He hears *ad portam*, at the door;
He carries (*portat*) as he ought
(Dons love a Latin pun, with port)
All tales and all exciting letters
Straight to the councils of his betters[1]
(Not that he wishes so to thrill;
But it's his duty, and he will).

Remember that a bedder's dreams
Are very active on such themes.
Don't let her fancies loose one minute
(Take most care when there's nothing in it).
'Don't clear the table, please, today,
Till we have started for the play.'
– She'll know what *that* means, right away.

Remember, though it's wise to chat,
She's getting 'evidence' from that.

Which, kept the necessary years,
At last will tickle the right ears.

Remember nobody will *say*
When talk is getting under way.
A perfect freedom they allow,
Eagerly hoping for a row.

Which, when it comes, I hope you'll try
To counter with a working lie.
Without deceiving, this endears.
They have been practising for years.

But oh, whatever game you play
(Here is the moral of my lay)
Never believe the words they say
To make you give yourself away.

For oh, to such too careless men
What awful things will happen then.
See where the chaste good dons in rows
(A squinting, lily-like repose)
Have heard more tattle than one knows.
See where the Majesty of Cambridge towers;
Gives orders far beyond its powers;
Wields the unwieldy keys of Hell,
And shoos you from the town as well.
See, peeping, anxious, and discreet,
And listening for each other's feet,
Your various *kinderhearted* judges;
They hope you will not bear them grudges.
Their friendship is now much enhanced.
You must not think they're not advanced.[2]
Their minds are desperately broad;
They sat in terror on the festive Board
And damned you hardly of their own accord.
It is not *them* you must abuse.
And have you any further news?

Oh do be warned by what will happen there,
And go to Bedford or to Leicester Square.

Or would you please those who control your ends
Follow where their high patronage commends,
And stick to what you learned at school, my friends.

NOTES   1. Do not suppose these facts are wrong;
                I learn in suffering what I teach in song.

          2. The noblest art's the art to blot,
             Just there I've blotted a whole lot.

X

Letter vi. A marriage.

[1935]

Rejoice where possible all hares of March
And any daffodils not forced at this date.
I too attempt an epithalamion
Never to be thrust on your unwilling notice
Still less before the public, annotated.
    Life's not more strange than this traditional theme.

Terrified by the purity of your dry beauty
Dry tough and fresh as the grass on chalk downs –
The metaphor now seems stale to me only because
It drove me younger to as empty a love –
I have not dared mention to you even the ideal
Version of love sent neatly in typescript
Not altered before publication
And drowned on meeting in my interminable yattering
       conversation.
    My life's more weak than this traditional theme.

Envisioning however the same beauty in taxiboys
And failing to recognise in one case
What with drink and the infantilism of the Japanese type
The fact that it had not yet attained puberty
I was most rightly (because of another case
Where the jealousy of the driver seemed the chief factor)
– Not indeed technically, named only in vernacular
       newspapers,
And who knows who knows –
Deported from that virtuous and aesthetic country;
    Life being as strange as this traditional theme.

I remember only once bathing in the sight of your eyes
Paying some attention to this bloodless series
– One would think to the first – the grey eyes open
Large milky lit fastened steadily on me
Not knowing what to think of what might come next
Supposing I was ever to stop haranguing the tea party;
   There is a social weight on the traditional theme.

It seemed to me impossible to admit that such a signal
(Of which I was certain, which you would now certainly deny)
So dissolving and so noble, had been even recognised,
Still less, having sent them to their owner out of a clownish
       honesty,
To make sensual capital out of writings
Of a sort so much lectured on
As to be practised with decency only for clinical purposes.
   Life is allied to this traditional theme.

Nor am I sure I did not imagine a comparison
– I was at least hushed and ashamed by those perhaps
       misinterpreted eyes –
To the eyes I was to see not long after on my mother,
Thank God not since as yet, cool, liquid, larger than possible,
Expecting ill-treatment, inquiring, a young girl's,
When after inducing a goodnatured virgin to seduce me
In a morass of mutual misunderstandings, I was kicked out
From a settled job, and hoped I had escaped from you.
   But life was as strange as this traditional theme.

One of these poems at least occurred, long after being written.
In the next bed to you in a pub in Vienna
I watched the moon shadow of the window upright
Walk clear across neck and face, in perhaps half an hour,
Continually illuminating new beauties,
Placing in you one minute after another everything
I know of admirable in the history of man.
   There is not much more in this traditional theme.

I as in one instant felt during that time
By a trick with time I have known otherwise
Only in the absurd race of an ill-designed chemistry examination
Where the quarters struck consecutively; but that I won;
Perhaps inversely too in the still photograph
Of shooting a snipe, already behind me, before I knew I had tried
– I am trying to remember triumphs –
　　What else but this is the traditional theme?

Maintained one exhausting ecstasy
Interrupted only at moments by a nuisance
A foam of self-consciousness and delight, through which I now
　　　　know that this occurred.
As the shadow passed to your hair, leaving only truth, I spoke.
You woke and understood this at once. A porcine
Expression of complacent pleasure
Rounded with a fine clang my series
Before you turned over and hid the face under the bedclothes.
　　One could fit this into the traditional theme.

XI

The ages change, and they impose their rules.
It would not do much good to miss the bus.
We must endure, and stand between two fools.

Two colonies of Europe now form schools
Holding absolute power, both of them fatuous.
The ages change, and they impose their rules.

One claims the State is naked between ghouls
The other makes it total Octopus.
We must endure, and stand between two fools.

A says No Bath not Superheated Steam. B cools
This off by Only Solid Ice. For us
The ages change, and they impose their rules.

Both base their pride upon ill-gotten tools
And boast their history an Exodus.
We must endure, and stand between two fools.

There is world and time; the Fates have got large spools;
There need not only Europe make a fuss.
The ages change, and they impose their rules.
We must endure, and stand between two fools.

XII

Not but they die, the terrors and the dreams,
Not but they die. In the long run the sane man
Comes out best. He is dead too. The themes

Of despair and triumph so far always outran
Rumination in writing. The short view
Could be so long it saw where it began.

But what reflections are much gain to you.
Not to imagine is a thing to claim.
Remember what you once wanted to do

And will want to have done when the time came,
Then you need seldom feel and short sight
Is the magnifying glass able for the flame.

Uncollected Poems

Une Brioche pour Cerbère

Tom nods. No senior angels see or grapple.
Tom enters Eden, nodding, the back way.
Borrows from Adam, and then eats, the Apple.
'Thank you so much for a delightful stay.'

If it works, it works. Nod to the man at the door.
Nor heed what gulfs, how much of earth between.
If radio light, from the last sphere before
Outer dark, reflects you, you are seen.

So can the poles look in each other's eyes.
Within that charmed last vacuate of air
Who is my neighbour, and who safe from spies?
Earth sees me nod. No, nothing to declare.

Porter, report not my heart contraband.
Of you, you primitive culture, stored flame,
I scoptophile, friend by short cut, had planned
To view the rites, no high priest first to tame.

My dear, my earth, how offer me your halls?
Grant me your Eden, I see Eden Station,
Whence stationed gauge you whose full scale appalls
And all whose porters would ask explanation?

Cambridge Review, 4 May 1928.

The fourth stanza printed does not figure on an autograph MS (fair copy), which begins with this unpublished but notable stanza:

> To show the career in the womb of wit
> Partly I use the method I expound,
> Partly give birth to the heads of it,
> Last count the feet, and try to soothe the sound.

New World Bistres

The darkest is near dawn, we are almost butter.
The churning is fixed now; we have 'gone to sleep'
In body, and become a living pat;
It is then that the arm churning it aches most
And dares least pause against the ceaseless turning.
I am sure he will soon stumble upon the gift,
Maypole his membranes, Ciro be his eyes,
A secret order, assumptive distillation;
Fitting together it will be won and seem nothing,
Mild artifact, false pearl, corpse margarine.
　　Oh socketed too deep, oh more than tears,
Than any faint unhurrying resurrection,
That even rain, manna (the manner born,
The man born of the manor, and that bourne
No traveller returns. Turn Athanasius,
Turn Cardinal Bourne. The Palace, Washing Day.
Lux and her cherub, here is a myth handy).
Those glacial, dried soap film, shaken packets,
That rain of hushing elixir-centred sequins,
Falling through space, gracious, a feather swaying.
　　Rising, triumphant, hooter, whine, mosquito,
The separator, pausing by violent movement
Stands at the even not skimming of stood cream.
Moss can be grown on tops. Gyroscopes
Holed with grim jewels set in resounding brass
Rector and tractor of earth's vertiges,
Claw, widely patented, pierce, sinking,
Armoured resentience their lead fathom line.

Cambridge Review, 6 June 1928.

Insomnia

Satan when ultimate chaos he would fly
battered at random by hot dry wet cold
(Probably nor Probability
his view the total cauldron of a sky
Milton nor Brownian hesitance foretold)
One purposed whirlwind helpless whole hours could hold.

   From Bottomless Pit's bottom originally
   who durst his sail-broad vans unfold
   thence till (God's help the rival gust came by)
   Hell seemed as Heaven undistinguished high
   through pudding still unstirred of Anarch old
   had sunk yet, down for ever, by one blast controlled.

So to the naked chaos that am I,
potion whose cooling boat grates crystal shoaled
gears on a mixed bank allotropically
untempered patchwork to the naked eye,
one hour the snow's one pattern, and I bold,
gale knew its point all night, though nine through compass
     rolled.

   Though large charged carpet units insulately
   alone processed, each from the former's mould,
   each further angle could new shades supply,
   roads every earlier opposite to tie
   in single type Hell's very warders scrolled,
   Nine intersterile species nightmare's full Nine were foaled.

Cambridge Review, 19 April 1929; *a draft notebook version carries
the title 'Indecision and Insomnia'.*

Essay*

Let Rome in Tiber melt, and the wide arch
Of the ranged empire fall.

The wide arch of free stones that did not fall
(High through gravity, unmoved, unmortared)
Budded to Bows of Promise in small skies
Of many Norman recessed painted porches;
Jerked into Gothic as it cracked; melted
Only to flow towards heaven into spires.
    The cream-bowl of that arch (reflected sky)
One must observe by ski-ing its crisp flakes
And needs dynamics to approve its calm.
The roar of wind freezing your ears, the hiss
Of ploughed snow, only, insisting speed,
You watch the unchanged tarpaulin of white surface
(Sail in the wind, or sheet when stairs are burning)
And the huge valley and more distant dado
Move not the calm perspective of their Bonzo,
Maintain the nursery of their cart-horse curves.
Or you may skim (ten times that scale) in buses
The vast and hollow English skulls of cloud-banks,
(I have not done so) or compute the sun's
Intolerable curve (he rides straight as yet)
And let him not aim merely at Hercules.
    These casual remarks would only claim
Such legacies arrive at least inverted;
The larger the estates, the more diffuse;
The more admired, the more extraordinary,
The more as the third son, on milk-white palfrey,

*This printing of the poem incorporates two alterations – Empson's own emendations on a cutting taken from *Magdalene College Magazine*.

Taking your bailiff as your Sancho Panza,
(To find your fortune somewhere in the next village)
You set off with no hope of riding round.

Magdalene College Magazine, no. 61, June 1929.

UFA Nightmare*

Gramophony. Telephony. Photophony.
The mighty handles and persensate dials
That rule my liner multi-implicate
Ring round, Stonehenge, a wide cold concrete room.
(I run the row from A to O, and so
– To and fro; periscope, radio –
We know which way we go.)
    'If we can reach the point
Before the tide, there is another style.
I shall checkmate, given the whole board;
Juggling the very tittles in the air
Shall counterblast the dreadnought machiner.'
    (Scamper, scamper, scamper.
Huge elbows tumble toward chaos.
Lurch, sag, and hesitation on the dials.)
    A tiny figure, seated in the engine,
    Weevil clicking in a hollow oak,
    Pedals, parched with the fear of solitude.

Experiment, no. 4, November 1929.

*'UFA' stands for 'Universum Film Aktiengesellschaft', the German film production company. Empson reviewed the movie *Metropolis* (1927, directed by Fritz Lang) in *Granta*, 4 November 1927, p. 84:

Of course everybody will see this; it is a feast I cannot review in detail. The UFA people's mastery of technical tricks [etc.] . . . are more than can be reconnoitred here.
    The story has been much maligned, partly from its simple solution of all possible economic problems . . . For Metropolis is the Greek city state . . . obviously, after that, we had to kill the inventor, and purge our suspicion of contrivances.

    See also his review of *Berlin* in *Granta*, 27 April 1928, p. 375; and a letter from Desmond Flower, with Empson's reply to it, in *Granta*, 11 May 1928, pp. 412–13.

The Royal Beasts

[1937]

I

An ambitious man would have fretted, but George Bickersteth was very contented, rather more so than his wife. The trouble with the African Crown Colonies as a profession is that you get so much more nuisance as you rise higher. The first step upward is being moved about and having to learn new dialects, and after that you become an office wallah in a town, with ice and fans to be sure, but always under somebody's eye and asking somebody else's opinion. So long as you sit on a soapbox in one place in the backwoods and administer justice you can live like a gentleman, but it takes a bit of wangling even to avoid being moved. Indeed on this point, if this only, the French method is better; they don't keep shoving a man into a new district. George Bickersteth was capable of wangling, and had stayed up in a place near some mountains where the climate was pretty tolerable; he did not claim credit for happening on it in the first place. He had been married about four years. Six years ago there had been one of the rises of pay, going by length of service, and shortly after that his native mistress had been recalled by her family, owing to some complex disaster or money trouble into which he did not deeply enquire; it seemed a convenient thing, and he was pleased to find the girl not much distressed. He would not have taken a native mistress if it had been thought eccentric, but this was one of the British colonies where it isn't. The road was now clear to marry on the rise of salary, and he planned his next leave with this intention clearly in view. It struck him when he got to England that the blacks and the French for that matter arrange the thing much more sensibly. A cultivated man, with plenty of delicacy of feeling in its proper place, he had not much time, and he was a clear and determined speaker. There were some rather pathetic embarrassments, and it was in a disgruntled mood that he married a girl of twenty-six who had not previously contrived to leave her rectory home. As he paced the deck alone on the return journey (by the boat he had selected before leaving Africa) he felt himself almost a ruined man, sustained only by the glum pride of having done what he meant. It is fair to say that his wife in her bunk below was never made to realise the intensity of this sentiment. Never, because the tradition of diplomacy held good over the crisis; within six months she had turned out very well.

It is difficult to describe George Bickersteth without making him seem rather disagreeable, but perhaps this is only because we most of us envy him. A man who can arrange his life with such blank independence is an impressive figure as well as a national asset. But he really is rather disagreeable if you come across him in the course of travel – that is, if you travel past the place where he lives; he is very much an overseas Englishman. He does not see why he should speak to you at all, much less hear about your troubles. This is not only because he is selfish but also because the enormous mass of human suffering, now at this moment being endured, is more real to him than you would think. Your interest in your own troubles rather shocks him. His appearance of depression, however, is not so much due to this solemn cause as to his real dislike of being spoken to by strangers. So far he is a stock enough type; the extra difficulty with a man like George is that it is particularly hard to stop being a stranger. A stupider version of George Bickersteth, supposing for instance he is the British consul who has just told you the hotels are probably all full, will look at you with a dull gleam of interest and goodwill if you run after him as he retreats and say you knew when you were at Eton the brother of a man who was at Charterhouse with him. 'Baines,' he will say. 'J. D. Baines? Yes, there *was* a J. D. Baines.' After testing your reference his depression will come back, and he will walk off saying, 'I don't suppose he's done too well.' He will still be no help, but you are no longer a stranger. Under these conditions the intelligence of George Bickersteth will make him noticeably nastier; he too will be no help, and he will show that he disapproves of this gambit. Besides, you can't guess which public school he was at. He is well-informed, wise and cultivated, though in the furtive manner of British culture outside Bloomsbury. It is a great pity he is so hard to speak to.

Mrs Bickersteth was fair and plump, with the quality which I believe the word 'blowsy' is used for, though it can be very delicious. She would have been clever enough to get to a university on scholarships, probably, and she wanted to leave home, but she was too lazy. Instead of that, while at school, she had developed a kind of permanent imitation of the traditional barmaid of the nineties: 'Ow my goodness me', 'If you dare' and so on; very popular and amusing among her school friends, beautifully fitted to her physical type, and appalling to her parents. It struck George Bickersteth, in the first place, that she would be all right in bed. After some years with a negress, as he understood very well, many attractive Englishwomen aren't. He gave her his further attention, and paid none whatever to her tricks. This soon forced her to admit to a good deal of information and taste about music and books. That, he felt, he had to insist on in his wife; not merely so that he could talk to her, but so that she needn't talk to him; she had to be able to live in the wilds and find something to do. In the third place, it was pretty clear she would be willing to come. What else was there? Four, health and so on; strong as a horse. Five, a lady: well, she couldn't get away from it; thing you could prove; she could pretend she wasn't if it amused her. And there had been a great deal too much nonsense and nuisance already. He proposed the second time they met, and she said, 'Ow, Mr Bicker-steth, but this is so sudden.' It was really the first thing that came into her mind, that here at least was a good time to use this enchanting absurd phrase. He remained quite blank; rather as if he had been struck in the face, but he would have stayed blank then too. An impulse of good nature stopped her from going on with the gambit about 'a simple girl like me', and she said in her normal tone, 'Why on earth do you want to do that?' In the pause which followed it began to occur to her that she wanted it whether he did or not. Her set of jokes had been developed as one of those mechanisms which can keep us with frightful strength from recognising an unconscious and probably unreasonable despair. The clothes of the period did not fit her, it seemed to her odd to be a young lady in a rectory, she disliked most men she saw there; only as the absurd barmaid could she have been happy. She now felt obscurely grateful to George because he had not attended to all this confusion. 'Well, well,' she said, just as he began to voice a dignified retreat, 'we girls will have our fun with the gentlemen, won't we? But I'd like to marry you really. It's . . . very good of you to ask me, I think. I will,' she ended, with her lips trembling, and trying to use the marriage service as a comic cliché. It had an appalling ring of finality to George. It was final, both as regards the marriage and the perpetual use of comic clichés. From this point the thing began to grow in his mind as he had never thought possible, irritating beyond all bearing, ugly and stupid to an almost mystical degree. In a way she knew what was wrong, during the engagement, but she could hardly find any other way to speak. The only cheerful reflection George could find was that he might be able to stop her once they got to bed together, so long as she didn't make him impotent. Till then he did not trust himself to say how much he hated it without overdoing the thing into positive savagery; and then again, you couldn't ask the girl to give up all that, and apparently it was nearly her whole life, without putting something in its place, he thought. Meanwhile he talked about selecting books and gramophone records for her. And indeed the specific he had in view worked pretty well, but it took much longer than he expected. He was reduced before they got off the boat to inventing imitations of the more typical noises of her trick of speech and making them at her again and again and again, though only in bed, in the hope that in time she would get as sick of them as he was. There seemed no other possible way out; it was such a trivial thing really, and he was equally ashamed of being either brutal or pathetic about it. This was a good plan, though for a reason he could not have foreseen; she would have cheerfully gone on making these noises back at him for ever, but he began to enjoy the hideous parody himself. They settled down to letting her use the mannerisms he did not mind particularly badly. She would have altered her whole manner to please him if she could, but she couldn't, and she knew she had to keep her end up about it. Both of them always felt it was good of him to have married her, though in every other way she was just what he wanted. She enjoyed the house and the riding in Africa, learned easily to speak the language badly, and started a clinic in which she often did good without being either equipped or informed. At the time I am speaking of she had produced two children, a number held to be sufficient. She was grateful to him again for being willing to have any, and surprised to find that he thought Africa a healthy enough country to rear them. But the place, as I say, was high, and near some mountains.

Into this household an excited messenger arrived one afternoon saying that one of the terrible hairy men from over the mountain wished for an interview; he had been kept out of the village but would come to the house if allowed.

'How hairy is he?' said George.

'Quite, quite hairy, all over.'

'Where does he come from?'

'The terrible hairy men live up in the mountains, in the wild country; we never go near.'

'What does he want?'

'He won't say. He says the king sent him. He is carrying a great bag.'

'Well, we might as well have him here and see *how* hairy he is. What language is he talking?'

'He has three interpreters who make a chain of interpreters. They are all very frightened.'

'Why are they frightened? What is wrong with the hairy men anyway?'

'They do not know why they are frightened. Everybody is frightened of the terrible hairy men.'

'Well, keep an eye on them and see they don't run away. You can bring the whole deputation up to the verandah here.'

The person who advanced about half an hour later, with his interpreters huddled in the background, was in fact entirely covered with smooth black fur. He was a tall creature though a bit short in the legs for our proportions, long in the arm, his ears hung down like a dog's, and good Lord, he had a long black tail. It was a firm swinging walk, a suggestion of formal respect about it already visible, the end of the tail, slightly curved, about six inches off the ground. The bag was slung over his back; apart from fur he was naked. Then as he came up the eyes turned much too big, near twice human size, and the broad nose with large nostrils of the negro was exaggerated into a kind of soft snout rather like a horse's. The shape of lip was human, not horse, but the mouth was absurdly wide, coming round the side of the face; however, perhaps he was smiling (he was not). He halted under the verandah and gave George Bickersteth a short curt bow, then looked round for his interpreters with an effect of irritation, frisking his tail. He seemed very sleek after the journey, George thought; probably they had all sat in the river while the deputation was being arranged. This sort of thing did George good; he was not bored, and he was willing to be fairly civil.

A short speech, when the interpreters were herded up, seemed to get through them quite smoothly, about how the hairy man had come to do honour to the representative of the white king and wished to ask for his advice. George said he was in fact representative of a king and expressed willingness to hear; this was echoed patiently across the three languages. The next remark was more surprising; the hairy man wants to be alone with you to show you what he has in his bag. The interpreters were strongly against this move, having already cheered up in the course of talk, and it took a bit of pressing to get it through. They explained at their various removes of dialect that they had all felt the bag, and it had nothing in it but stones. George wondered if there was any serious loss of dignity in letting an apeman into the office. But evidently the natives wouldn't think so, and he was curious; he showed the creature in. There was a knot in the gut to be managed – the apeman had very long fingers, the usual number, black skin instead of fur under the tips and in the palm. Then a pile of yellow lumps and dust was emptied onto the table, and the apeman said an English word: Gold. This was a certain amount of evidence, George reflected, getting his pipe out, that the stuff really was gold; it looked as if a prospector speaking English had got involved somehow, and that might easily mean nuisance of some kind for himself as District Officer. The apeman then pushed the stuff back into the bag, tied it up, and offered it to George with a slight bow, the second so far. This was alarming; the stuff might be worth a couple of thousand pounds. George shook his head violently, and after a certain amount of bafflement they left it on the table and went back to the verandah.

There was now a period of repose for George Bickersteth while various points were pushed through the interpreters. The hairy men would give the king of the white men as many bags like that as he wanted. They would make these gifts only and directly to the king. They would not however allow white men or men of any kind to enter their country. Men who did that were always given a sound beating before being conducted to the frontier; this was an old custom (corroboration from interpreters). The hairy men were not men; they were Wurroos; they did not allow men in their country. The name of this particular Wurroo was Wuzzoo. What Wuzzoo wanted at the moment was to learn the language of the white men as soon as possible, and after that he wanted to speak to the king. The white men could do that in exchange for the bag (indignant clamour from interpreters). At this point George spoke up. So no man was allowed to enter Wur-rooland? (Prolonged translation and continual assent.) Did the Wur-roos think they had treated well the white man who had already done so? This was a difficult bit of grammar, but seemed to be translated conscientiously and with awe. Wuzzoo gave an approving smile, or at any rate kept calm and made his eyes and his mouth still bigger. 'He gave me the word' came back first. So he had seen through that. Then 'He is angry but he is treated well.' 'If you keep a white man prisoner you will be punished' – probably the conditional wouldn't survive the round, but it didn't matter. 'He will be set free,' came the answer, 'as soon as I have agreed with your king.'

George Bickersteth was inclined to ride the high horse about that; the thing was becoming a question of prestige. But a sudden squeak announced the arrival of his wife, who had been riding and now advanced from the stable. 'What a *delicious* man,' she said. 'And a *tail* too. I never *heard* of such a thing. Whyever didn't you *tell* me about them, George. Well, the gentlemen do *keep* things from a girl, *don't* they? There seems to be a difficulty,' she added with that sudden dropping of her manner which is so enormously endearing in women with a manner. As usual it made George feel quite grateful to her. 'It's all new to me,' he said. 'There's gold up where they come from, and they've kidnapped a prospector.' 'But why, George, he looks very sweet. What does he want?' 'He wants to talk to the King of England. The usual nonsense. What *I* want is to get hold of that prospector. And then we'll probably have to have the mines vetted and maybe hold up a gold rush, closing all frontiers and God knows what. The whole thing is going to be a damned nuisance.' 'Oh nonsense, darling,' said Mrs Bickersteth, moving into the house, 'why, if you haven't heard of these people before, they belong to Barney-Barnatoland.'

This was very clever of Mrs Bickersteth, though there was no need to make a triumph of it by moving away. George knew that the three interpreters all came from within the colony, but the last certainly came from near the border. It simply had not occurred to him that anybody would come over a difficult range of mountains to talk to the wrong authority. Also it would be the wrong authority in a marked degree; Western Barnatoland was very suspicious of what it called British imperialism, had taken to flying its own flag and so forth. Not that it had left the Empire or anything like that, but there wasn't much crossing of the frontier even where nature made it easy. Lucky to have got on to this at once; if the Crown Colony had started messing about with a Barnatoland goldfield there might have been hell to pay. George plunged back into the dialect of the first interpreter. But an orgy of comparative linguistics gave only one result. Nobody knew where the boundary was. The Wurroos did not live exactly on the far side of the mountains, because there was a pass and there were other mountains (where?); Wuzzoo had heard the name of a tribe that lived in Barnatoland, but he said it lived a long way away. He also said it was not encouraged to come nearer, and this sounded like intimate contact. George Bickersteth brought out a map, which delighted Wuzzoo; it held up the discussion for a long time because he wanted the interpreters to do three successive translations of the scale of distances, each time into new units. An abacus was demanded and refused (showing the penetrating power of the Mohammedans). But he could say about where the Wurroos lived, in the end, and this was about where the frontier reduced itself to the fatal admission of indeterminacy. It became a thin dotted straight line. George straightened himself up. There was nothing for it but to send a boat down river to the telegraph, give full information, and ask for all details about the determination of the boundary. Of course this gold might be a mere pocket, but that prospector would certainly want to make a row with somebody.

Mrs Bickersteth had now finished her bath, and came out to watch the performance. George told her in an exhausted voice that the frontier was certainly important in this, and he hoped to God she was right and the creatures came from the far side. 'Ow, for shame, George,' she said, 'and let them all go, and the gold too? I don't know what you're dreaming of. They aren't going to do any good with gold in Barnatoland, are they, George? They're a nasty unpatriotic lot there, that's what they are. And they treat their natives dreadfully, you saw it as well as I did, with your own eyes. D'you want that nice

Wuzzoo man there to get caught by those beastly slavedrivers, with his clean fur, and his tail too? Of course you want to keep him, don't be a fool, George.' She was giving in very few words, seeing how diffuse she sounded, the whole line of public sentiment in the subsequent case. George felt enough truth in it to find it very annoying. 'My good Mary, you know as well as I do I can't manage the frontier. What kind of lie do you expect me to tell?' 'I don't expect there is any frontier, darling; if there was they wouldn't just put spots on the map, would they? I know you only suggest things in your report, but they pay a great deal of attention to what you say, because they'd have promoted you if you'd let them, wouldn't they, darling?' George wondered why she was being deliberately annoying. 'Do for God's sake not wheedle,' he said. 'The thing's trying enough as it is. I've lost the whole afternoon.'

This idea that the colonists of Western Barnatoland are particularly cruel needs to be cleared up at once. They are no more cruel than the rest of us, and it is no wonder that they resented the suggestion so deeply, later on. But it is also true that the Wurroos would be much better off under the Crown Colony. The reason is a matter of geography and economics; it is about maps not about chaps. Barnatoland is a white man's country, high, cool, open and so forth, and there are mines. The colonists want to live on the land, so they want to take it from the negroes, and whether they are mining or farming they want labour, so they want the negroes to do it and obey orders. You may say that this is very wicked of them, but you are only saying that their ancestors ought not to have come to the place at all. You can also truly say, to be sure, that they do it more unpleasantly than they need do, and ought to do it better, but if you live in the adjacent Crown Colony this is no reason for thinking yourself a better man. The land there is hot, low, damp, and immensely fertile under its present cultivators. All you want to do is to buy the stuff cheap, and your only temptation is to 'stimulate' the crop by piling on the taxes. This is the more easily resisted, at least to a decent extent, because the main European population are Government servants who wouldn't immediately gain by it. So that the laws the Wurroos would come under on this side of the boundary would not involve forced labour at a distance or any threat to their ownership of land; the taxes would be higher, but they could pay them. The contrast is not a matter of personal wickedness nor yet of the superiority of Crown Colonies, and they would have been exposed to it, if they had got the contrast of geography, anywhere in British Africa.

At this point Wuzzoo began talking again at the end of the line of interpreters, who as his remarks reached them appeared much shocked. As the respected man would be busy with the work of his king, he was saying, he proposed to be taught English by the respected woman. Mary gave a squeak of pleasure as soon as this reached the dialect she knew, and said that she would be very willing but didn't know how to start. So that was what she had been butting in for. Fur; and the tail of course went a long way. Well, he had let the fellow into the house himself. And just as well to keep hold of him from the start, come to think of it. 'The only thing I insist on,' he said loudly, 'is Berlitz. I will not have three interpreters about the place. You must do it by pointing and making farmyard noises or whatever they use.' '*George*, you must *teach* me *all* your farmyard noises,' she said entranced. Harshly, but with pay, he dismissed the interpreters. Wuzzoo walked onto the verandah. George raised his eyebrows but did not turn him off. 'Yes, all right, he'd better *sleep* on the verandah,' he said after a moment, fighting a strong rearguard action. 'Get him a rug out here. Look here, Mary, don't make him any more uppish than he is already. The general footing is the family dog. Have you got that?' 'How delicious, George,' she said, without reassuring him.

Over the busy life of the next few weeks any novelist must draw a veil. The facts about talk, so the literary have felt in all ages, cannot be admitted by the written word. When Wuzzoo talks I shall report him as talking tolerably well. But it was natural enough that he learnt quickly. He was interested, he had nothing else to do, he was so much annoyed by the confusion of his own language that he thought in English as soon as he could, and he had as remarkable a memory for trivial detail as most negroes. It gave the Bickersteths a rather misleading impression of his intellectual powers; they were startled.[1] To be sure it was an over-thorough use of the Berlitz system, which only works well if you cheat a good deal and translate odd words under your breath. But Wuzzoo had various things he wanted to say, and immediately began drawing pictures to say them, and once you have begun to exchange real information there is something for the Direct Method to work on. A twist of delicacy in the first week led him to a more ambitious effort on these lines, which startled Mary so much that she appealed to George. 'Listen, George,' she said at lunch, 'I think he's really a very *nice* man, I mean he's not at all *suggestive*, but I can't Make it Out' (flattening the voice into pathos), 'He keeps drawing obscene pictures.' 'I should fancy,' said George glumly, 'that sooner or later I shall have to see *all* his obscene pictures.' 'Well, my gracious, you *do* have a lot of hardship, don't you? *To* be sure.' And indeed the sheets of typing paper looked more like the Lamaist Wheel of Life than any more deliberately pornographic work. The revolving year was roughly illustrated by stages of vegetables, and Wurroos were shown variously employed at different dates; gathering reeds or something in the autumn, brewing something in pots during the winter, driving up cattle to pasture in early spring. The pictures that Mary found surprising only appeared in a brief interval between spring and summer, apparently about a month long. The segment was too small to hold more than one copulating couple, but there was an extension for dances of an interesting character (as far as you could make out) and apparently fights between males before crowds. Wuzzoo's style of drawing was the kind of quick outline that seems very vivid and lifelike so long as you know the thing meant, but becomes baffling if you don't. For this month and the ones before and after there were also closeups of the male Wurroo genital, the middle one with enlarged testicles. The present stage of the year, which was about midsummer, had been picked out by a heavy line. 'Good Lord,' said George. Then: 'But did you really not see what he meant? It's extraordinary how you can make yourself stupid as soon as you feel inclined. I suppose you thought it would be more amusing not to understand him.' 'But d'you think he really means . . .' 'He's telling you he's outside the breeding season, of course. I must say they're a very outoftheway lot. The next thing is going to be a herd of anthropologists camping on the verandah,' said George, not looking at all displeased.

The reply from headquarters took about a month; it was nearly ten days down river to the telegraph, but still there must have been ten days' wait at the other end. George had gone so far as to point out that the new tribe wished to belong to the Crown Colony, with their gold, and that he himself thought this would be a suitable arrangement if the boundary conditions made it possible. He was surprised that the long reply, when it came, paid so much attention to what at the time had seemed a rather absurd piece of pious hoping. 'As regards the boundary question,' the thing said, 'no satisfactory answer is available, as the matter has not been the subject of recent arbitration. It falls under a clause in the charter of Western Barnatoland to the effect that previous agreements as to the boundaries of the Crown Colony shall be respected. In this region the only known previous agreement is a treaty with King Murawayo in 1862. His sovereignty was then admitted over all the tribes south of the Ghandesi range, and within certain other boundaries not here relevant. In 1887 King Murawayo was defeated by what was then the colony of Barney-Barnatoland. They took over the whole territory he then ruled, leaving him the territory of his own tribe as personal property. This is clearly stated in the treaty of 1889. So far as concerns the present question, these boundary arrangements were not altered by the formation of Western Barnatoland as an autonomous state within the Empire. Now there is no doubt, if your informants can be trusted, that the Wurroo tribe lives south of the watershed of the Ghandesi. On these grounds the territory which the tribe inhabits, being *ipso facto* an inhabited territory, will belong to Western Barnatoland together with any minerals it may contain; as also the land south of this territory, with its minerals.

'This conclusion, however, is open to dispute on several grounds. It is not yet certain whether the deposits of gold are actually within the territory normally occupied by the tribe; they may abut on the northern side of that territory. Also the expression "south of the Ghandesi range" may be taken to mean, not south of the watershed of the mountains, but south of the mountains as a whole including their foothills. This is what it would often mean in common parlance; furthermore, all the other tribes concerned live on the plateau at a considerable distance south of the foothills, so that the expression would naturally be used of them in this sense. Thirdly, whatever the precise meaning of the terms used in the treaty with King Murawayo, the treaty cannot have been intended to cover the case of this tribe, since nobody at that time had heard of it. The purpose of this clause of the treaty was to assert the sovereignty of King Murawayo over those tribes which then acknowledged his allegiance, while reserving the British right to claim territory beyond them. The treaty therefore cannot reasonably be invoked to obtain jurisdiction over a tribe of which King Murawayo never heard, or at least to whose territory he never laid claim.'

'Golly,' said George, 'he's going to fight the case. He must be bursting with it if he sends all this hot air to me.'

'You are to make all possible further enquiries about the state of the case in view of these considerations, and keep me fully informed. Two surveyors with a posse of police have already set off to examine the goldfield in question, and will obtain information from you as to its site. The matter must be treated with strict secrecy, and any unauthorised person in the neighbourhood must be carefully examined. It is expected that the territory will be closed to prospectors within a short time. Western Barnatoland has been informed that a tribe, of uncertain locality but claiming to be under our jurisdiction, is now holding by force a Barnatoland prospector, though so far as we know not ill-treating him; and that we are taking immediate steps for his release.'

'Golly,' said George, 'and we don't even know if it *is* a Barnatoland prospector. He seems to be heading for a row pretty firmly.'

He walked out of the office to look for Mary in the sitting room, feeling the need of an audience, and found Wuzzoo grinning at him from the depths of an armchair. It is well known that a family dog cannot at all easily be kept out of the armchairs, if he is allowed into the house at all; and Mary had truly pointed out that she would only collect a crowd if she gave English lessons on the verandah. 'What does he say?' said Wuzzoo. 'I can see he says plenty.' The arrival of the messenger of course had created a stir, from which Wuzzoo had held aloof. It struck George that the creature was disagreeably good at this kind of manoeuvre. 'He doesn't know where you belong,' he said shortly. 'He thinks you belong over the mountains.' 'Why?' said Wuzzoo placidly but firmly. After all, the thing would have to be done some time; and George abandoned himself to explaining the conditions of the boundary in words of two syllables. It so happened that he had an historical type of mind, and this type of mind thinks that the only way to get a present-day arrangement understood is to explain several quite different arrangements which existed beforehand. As he wanted to speak very clearly and simply about the boundary he started from King Murawayo. This may have affected Wuzzoo's whole reaction to the situation; at any rate it made him sit up indignantly as soon as he understood. 'We,' he said, 'the Wurroos, they were servants of Murawayo? Murawayo dare not come near. Murawayo dare not come near any hill country because of Wurroos. One time he thought maybe he dare come near, then we send him word, then he stopped.' George felt curious to know what word was sent, because if the Wurroos were a straightforward military power surely they would have been heard of before? There must be some kind of superstition about them; in fact there obviously was from the interpreters. And was he talking about the right man? It was seventy years ago, say, and Wuzzoo had only managed one past tense, or two. But he was too old a hand at this kind of thing to get off the point. 'It does not matter, it is not important, we are not asking,' he said slowly, 'if the Wurroos were servants of Murawayo. We said to Murawayo that the land of all tribes south of the mountains was not our land, because he wanted it, and now all that land belongs to the other white men.' 'We are not a tribe,' said Wuzzoo at once. 'A tribe is a lot of black men, like here. We are not black men. We are Wurroos.' 'No, a tribe is any lot of men, a small lot, but any kind of men.' 'We are not men,' said Wuzzoo indignantly. 'Of course we are not men. I said that when I came. Do I look like a man? Ask any of the black men if I am a man. We think very badly of men,' he went on chattily, finding that George did nothing but stare at him. 'Of course that was black men; we don't know what we think of white men, so we take care. But we always said we were not men. We know that well.'

George sat down heavily in the other armchair, and took a pipe out. The governor would have to be told about this, seeing how he was heading for a fight over that gold. He looked like making a fool of himself, George thought, but that wasn't the business of the District Officer. This might be more like a legal argument than any trumped up so far. Of course it didn't matter what the tribe said; for that matter, there was a tribe in Central America who stuck to it that they weren't men because they were parrots. Totemism. Probably they still do. But hang it all, fur and a tail and a breeding season. It looked as if you could get a lot of expert evidence to say they weren't human. Or would they still be a tribe? A tribe of monkeys. Special pleading. After all, what this chap said in a law court would carry a certain weight. Or would he not be allowed to give evidence, if he wasn't human? And would he stick to it?

'Why,' said George, and paused to let that sink in, anyway, 'why do you Wurroos want to belong to us and not to the other white men?' 'Two things,' said Wuzzoo, sitting up. 'First, I start this way, over the mountains, because we know the other white men very bad, so we think maybe you not so bad. We don't know. But now, second thing, I do what my father said. My father very clever man, I think. He just see white men doing bad things, and he see the gun. He say, no good keeping quiet now they come here, we must make treaty, because of the gun. He say maybe all right where they make the gun, big people, much thinking, not interested in us. He say, we get bad white men here, because bad men can't stay home. So he say, first, go to government men not trading men; second, go far away, go right up to top government man, go to king or very near king. Then he say, third, maybe one place you can get to top man, another place you can't get to top man. That very important, he say, maybe you have to change across, make sure you find place where you can get to top man. So he think of all this, just from the gun.'

This struck George as touching but rather nigger. The boasting about his father contradicted itself, because obviously they knew something about the Barnatoland people, not only about the gun. Heaven knows, he thought, what Mary has been stuffing him up with. Still, in an abstract ill-informed way, it was a sensible argument. It didn't look as if this not-being-human business would be held to fanatically, regardless of cost and so on.

'I talk English very badly,' said Wuzzoo suddenly. 'I say my father very clever *man*. Of course he is not a man. I want to say he is very clever.'

The hell you do, thought George. 'Listen,' he said, 'if you say the Wurroos are not men, there is much danger. You can say you are men easily. Maybe you are not men, maybe what you say is true, but if you say you are men nobody will say you are not men. But if you are not men, then there is no law for you. You cannot make any contract, any promise, any agreement in our law; all agreements in our law are agreements between men. You cannot keep your gold, you cannot keep anything you have, you cannot keep your land; all property in our law belongs to men, if you are not men nothing belongs to you, nothing is yours. If you are men a man cannot kill you for pleasure; but if you are not men, and you do not belong to some man, if you are not some man's animal, then any man can come and shoot you with a gun and kill you. And they will want your fur, because it is very nice fur and we make fur into clothes to keep us warm, so they will all come with guns and kill you and take your fur. And if you are not men nobody can stop them.'

Wuzzoo was silent. 'What do you think?' said George after a full minute, pressing the thing home. 'Will you say you are men or not?'

'I think the government men are not so weak as you say,' said Wuzzoo. George opened his mouth and shut it again. 'These are three important things, promises in law, and keep what belongs to us, and no guns after fur. All these three things, we must make treaty about them. If you want make treaty, that will be easy. I think we just say we belong your king. You all belong your king, but we belong like his horses and dogs. Your horses there, you take much more care your horses than your servants. If we are men we are just like black men. You say very bad things come if we are not men. Very bad things come if we are black men, just the same. Nobody can shoot the king's horses for fur, I know that. The other two things: we must make treaty with the king before we say we are his horses and dogs, and everybody must know what the king said. Then I think he keep his promise, because he would be shamed, and he is very far away, I know that, he not want us, he just want gold. We give him gold, why he want break his promise? Of course, maybe he break his promise, maybe very bad things come, maybe very bad things come anyway. I just have to make plans. My father said, it's a long way to go, he said, but get as near the king as you can. Now I see the nearest thing. The nearest thing is belong to the king like his horses and his dogs. And then another thing. It is true. We are not men, we always said we are not men. Now we make treaty with men the first time; I have to make plans, I have to think a long time ahead. No good say we are men, when we are not men. That make trouble some time. Of course, if you all too bad, then we must play tricks. But I think you two here very kind to me, and I know your guns very strong. A long time we keep quiet, never come out. Now we come out, I think best come out a long way. We are not men. I think best say we are not men.'

'You always said you were not men,' said George, after the pause that is necessary between the speeches in this kind of conversation – and by the way it is a quite possible and satisfying kind of conversation, though it has never been in fashion in England since the Civil War – 'only because you wanted to say you are not negroes, not black men. The world is very big, and there are all kinds of men. It is no good you saying you are not men. You do not know what you are saying. There are all kinds of men. There are yellow men and red men as well as white men and black men. How do you know there are not furry men, how do you know Wurroos are not men? You say you are sure, but you are only saying you are sure about a word in the English language. You cannot be sure about a word in the English language. How do you know how many kinds of animal we call men in English?'

Wuzzoo heaved a deep sigh. It may have only been George's conscience, but it seemed to George that Wuzzoo was impressed and interested by the linguistic line of argument, saw that he could not answer it in any dignified manner, and at the same time recognised its unfairness and futility. And obviously, thought George in the pause that followed, if there were any other men as unlike men as Wurroos I should have brought them out, so if he's [as] clever as all that he won't believe me.

'I think you are very good to me,' said Wuzzoo at last. 'I believe what you say; I make plans by it. Now I want two questions. One is not important; it is just part of making plans. That is all right what you say about men in English. First question: if we say we are not men, will the white men believe us? The second question is important. I know you are my friend, I know you are thinking about your king and your work. You talk about the dangers for us; that is good; I want to know that. Second question: do you want me to say the Wurroos are men, do you want me to say the Wurroos are not men?'

George got out of his chair and ignored both questions. 'I am writing to the governor of the Crown Colony,' he said, 'that is, I send word to my head man. I tell him, I make him know, what you say. And I mean to see, I watch out, I make sure, that the Wurroos are not treated too badly, do not get bad time.' Wuzzoo got up too, and he was a quick enough guesser to put his right hand into the right hand offered to him. George was really moved by this conversation, partly to be sure by his own eloquence to start with, and even though he had done that as a businesslike test. And the effect of making George moved about the Wurroos was that he felt their only chance was to be kept in George's own Crown Colony, on any terms, whether they were classed as men or rats.

II

'I must beg you, Sir Reginald, really I must, to think the matter over. The claim is too ridiculous, I doubt if the British government would take it up even on your direct advice, and if they do they will have all the religious people against them and all the democrats. It is an attempt to turn back the clock of history. You cannot do it; it will break your career.'

'Well, as to the career, old man, I've pretty well had it, and a little yapping won't disturb me when I retire. You must consider that the old country really needs the gold very badly, and letting Eastern Rhodesia have it practically means giving it to an unfriendly independent state. So long as you've a sporting chance, I can't see any sense in not having a try for it. Then there's another thing, though I don't say it weighs very heavily, this Wuzzoo seems to be a decent chap, and I like the line he's taking over it, and it's quite true they'll have a hell of a thin time slaving in their own mines under Eastern Rhodesia. And as to fluttering the democratic and religious dovecotes, good God, you can't expect me to worry about that. Nothing I should enjoy better; nothing in the whole world; damn it, it gives me a hobby to retire on. What I've always said about a tribe of this sort is that they want firm kindly paternal rules; we want to treat them as a valuable kind of inferior animal, and take entirely for granted that we know what's good for them. Entirely for granted. The only surprising thing is that one of them has had the sense to see it. It's always seemed to me one of the great ironies of history, Weston, that the American cottongrowers should have cut the ground from under their own feet. And what's more nobody ever seems to see it. They sat there owning thousands of slaves apiece and voted that all men had an inalienable right to liberty, and what they can have had in their heads people don't so much as think of asking. I know they hedged about mentioning slaves in the same document, but that was just a blind piece of caution. The whole thing shows how as soon as a man sits down to argue theoretically, above all when he borrows smart ideas from abroad to back up some small immediate demand, then he forgets right out of hand the plainest truths that have been under his own nose all his life. And in the end the bluff was called and they had to smash a perfectly good working arrangement about negroes, a thing that may never happen again, in fact hardly can happen again. And it was only Calhoun[2] right at the end who had the guts to preach what they were all practising, and doing very effectively.'

'The remarkable thing about Calhoun was this,' broke in the secretary, who drew the line at defence of flat slavery. '(Apart from the fact that he was a grave embarrassment to his own side, which is enough I should have thought to show you are misunderstanding the whole position,) Calhoun was always saying that great civilisations with great arts had always been built on slavery, and therefore slavery was a good thing for the civilisation of the South. Now the remarkable thing about the South, you might almost call it a unique thing, is that it produced no art of any kind; even the portrait painters were imported. Anyway no new *idea* in art. And all the time the slaves, who were supposed to be just supporting this refined culture, were working up an artform which good or bad swept the whole civilised world within two generations.'

'I've got it,' said Sir Reginald. 'I saw the crux of the thing while you were talking. Obviously they didn't believe the negroes were human at all, any more than these Muggoos are, only they didn't dare say so because of the churches. That whole democratic set of tricks was in with free thought and had to watch its feet. And in the long run the fatal thing was not to speak their minds. I'm very glad to have understood that, it's a bit of history that's always puzzled me. Mind you, I think they were wrong, but they were wrong simply on this scientific test, the interbreeding question. You can't have a hybrid who's half man and half not, because neither law nor religion nor the state know where to get hold of him. But that was just bad luck; it was all the more urgent, really, to get a working formula because you were going to get the interbreeding once the thing broke up.'

'Most of the interbreeding happened in the slave latifundia,'[3] said the secretary from a considerable height, 'because the owners took all the women they could manage.'

'No they did not,' said Sir Reginald. 'What the hell are we talking about the blacks for anyway? I was telling you I mean to back this Tuggoo plan up to the hilt. It's the first sane solution of the native question I've heard in Africa, or anywhere else for that matter. And for that matter the first decent natives,' he shouted after the retreating secretary.

III

'You have heard the evidence of the scientists, my lords, and I submit that it could hardly support my case more strongly. A considerable similarity of morphology between the two types undoubtedly exists, and nobody will be surprised at it; nobody here is concerned to deny that the Wurroos and the human race belong to closely allied species. As closely allied, let us say, as the cat and the tiger. But you do not treat a tiger like a cat, nor a cat like a tiger. Mere common sense, my lords, is enough to tell us that species may be closely allied from the aspect of morphology and yet profoundly distinct for the purposes of mankind. You have to make a great decision here, my lords; you have to make a precedent here, if I may so express myself, of an unprecedented kind. I hope I may be allowed, my lords, to beg of you, with the utmost respect, not to be swayed in this matter by previous decisions in law which may appear relevant but are in fact wholly irrelevant, and are in themselves often of a somewhat absurd character. Law in its last analysis, my lords, is merely the codifying of common sense within a certain field, and the same is true of the labours of the scientists. In this important and as it were fundamental case, my lords, science and the law are equally concerned, and equally concerned to codify common sense; and it seems to me that if they give different pronouncements then one of them must be wrong. Now the scientists, my lords, whether they be right or wrong, are almost unanimous; I might I think say wholly unanimous, because the reverend and learned gentleman who appeared for the other side did in fact, by common consent of the informed opinion, abandon the whole basis of modern taxonomy. On all definite tests that are commonly applied to determine the distinction or identity of species the Wurroos are definitely distinct from man.

'In the first place it has so far proved impossible, and enough experiments have now been performed to give the matter virtual certainty, it has proved impossible, I say, my lords, to interbreed even in the first generation between the two species. The two species, I say, almost as a result of definition, for that was in history the fundamental distinction between species. On this count a Wurroo and a human being, whether white, black, or yellow, are more surely distinct than a horse and an ass, who can in fact produce offspring; though this offspring, and I refer, my lords, to the well-known mule, is in itself, being always a product of the second generation, sterile, thus proving the distinction of the two species. Now it may be objected that merely mechanical difficulties may produce intersterility, as for example between a Pomeranian and a St Bernard, though both these animals fall within the species of dogs. Indeed I understand that in the present case the mechanical difficulties were found severe by the early experimenters. But I have to remind you, my lords, of the modern scientific methods of insemination, which allow the act of generation to take place even through the agency of the public post; methods that are now in common use to obtain progeny from distinguished racehorses, prize rabbits, accomplished pointers or truffle-hunters, and I believe even exceptionally gymnastic seals. These methods are capable of overcoming every mechanical difficulty so far known to science in this matter, my lords. These methods, my lords, as you have heard, have been unsparingly employed. The results of this test, so far as the test can give evidence on the point at issue, are already complete, and I would like here to associate myself wholeheartedly with the point raised or warning delivered by Lord Brancombe; that if the decision of this court is such as it must I think in reason be, if the case passes, as I think it must, in favour of our distant cousins the Wurroos, then no further evidence of this kind can ever be considered by British law. So far the intentions of the experimental gentlemen, and naturally in discussing a complete test, my lords, I must add the experimental women, their intentions, I say, so far, cannot be called in question. But from now onwards, my lords, if this case be decided as I believe it must, and I confess that I am thankful to think of this consequence of the law, their activities will cease. The crime of bestiality, my lords, with whatever honourable motive, will have been committed by any future experimenter; and I need not remind you that no evidence may be based upon an act of conscious crime. No blackmailer, my lords, may come before the law of England and state the success of his machinations as evidence for a criminal charge; no bookmaker, equipped with evidence of whatever collaboration, may demand from these courts the reward of evil. On this head, therefore, my lords, and I think I may say this unsavoury head, the question, if you are willing to close it, is for ever closed. To boast before a British court of an act of horror, my lords, if I may speak frankly, would have appeared to me enough for the most fantastic appetite. These people have boasted of an act of horror committed, so far as I can understand them, solely in order to obtain servitude for a happy and an improving tribe. I cannot believe, my lords, that you have any wish to allow the continuance of a practice which I have had to describe in almost detailed terms.

'Passing to more agreeable topics, but by no means to more trivial ones, I may add that three Wurroos, selected by vote, one self-devoted English lady, one hired negro, and one Chinese malefactor of advanced age, have all succumbed to the effects of blood-transfusion between the Wurroo and the human stock, though carried out, I understand, to a reasonably merciful degree. You have already heard that this is considered by modern science to be a test not only less unsavoury but more convincing than the former, and I must remind you, my lords, that the sacrifice of these six lives has been carried out by persons already expecting the result, and concerned only to satisfy the claims of the law. I need not stress, my lords, the other features of the scientific evidence, neither the covering of fur, which is perhaps more striking than convincing, and in any case faintly reminiscent of the Hairy Ainu,[4] nor the far more solid evidence of the tail and the breeding season, unknown even among the great apes, let alone among mankind. Suffice it to say, my lords, that while you deliberate the decision of science has already been made.

'I know very well that your lordships are not in any danger of being swayed by some trivial or party issue, but I should wish, if I may without impertinence, to express a fear that your lordships think it necessary to rest your decision upon some obscure letter of some obsolete law. There is no such necessity before you, my lords; the matter now before [you] lies in a clear field of jurisdiction. We have heard what has been fancied by ignorance or imputed by malignity on this topic in the Middle Ages, and I make bold to say that such precedents have no claim whatever, in such a case as the present, to fetter the majesty of British law. The question has not previously, in any serious sense, been raised, for the good reason that no such creatures as the Wurroos have ever previously been known to mankind. The gulf between the human race and the various animal species has always up to now, if I may use a curious phrase, my lords, been conveniently enormous; there has been no need to codify what was already certain. This convenience has now been withdrawn by the shock of a new experience, and it falls to you, for the first time, my lords, to explain what all previous lawyers have been able to take for granted, what they meant when they spoke of man. Whether these worthy creations of God are human or no must be decided by modern evidence, and I have no need to remind you of the mass of happiness or misery that may hang upon your decision. Six lives, my lords, and surely they are enough, have already been sacrificed to convince you that this question is decided already, in the only way, I make bold to assert, in which it can finally be decided, by fact.

'And when I speak of facts, my lords, you know as well as I do that irrelevant facts must not be allowed to pervert the action of the mind. Now apart from what I may call the absurd arguments, the medieval trials upon the persons of disastrous bulls and magic cats, we have the admitted but certainly irrelevant fact that the Wurroos are intelligent enough to argue their case and honourable enough (as I feel sure we may assume) to respect such agreements as they may by special arrangement have undertaken. This fact only seems relevant, my lords, by confusion with another fact, which is also readily admitted by the defendants, that the Wurroos are of a species closely allied to the human stock. Now I feel sure that it will prevent any confused alliance of these two facts, my lords, if you will keep clearly in your minds another case that might conceivably have arisen. Let us suppose the imaginary and perhaps impossible case of a rational ant, of the normal insect size; such a creature might easily become a serious danger to mankind, and it is at least certain that the existence of Wurroos does not put us in any danger. Now would any of you, my lords, be tempted to rule that an intelligent ant, however rational and talkative and conscientious, was thereby inherently a member of the race of man? Arguments have appeared in the public press, my lords, based on religious grounds, to the effect that the Wurroos must necessarily be human because they are capable of morality, and therefore within reach of religious considerations. I venture to say that no sect of Christianity, my lords, would have raised this argument for the humanity of a talking ant. And if they would not, their argument falls to the ground; for it is evident that they are considering not only the moral powers of the creature but also its likeness to humanity. Now if each of two characters would alone yield an insufficient argument, and this is certainly true in the present case, we cannot obtain a sufficient argument by their mere combination. However, I say this, in any case, only in refutation of a better argument which these authors might have devised; their argument as it stands is evidently fallacious. And it is not my intention to suggest, my lords, nor I think would the best scientific evidence agree, that this fantasy of the talking ant has any inherent absurdity. You are only here, my lords, to make a precedent on the case of the Wurroos; and I think there is a very alarming prospect before us, in the long and mysterious processes of evolution, if you here undertake to admit any rational animal into the comradeship of the British empire. This is no question, my lords, of the temporary and trivial ownership of an exhaustible goldmine; it is a question of the future of the race of man. Indeed it seems to me almost providential that the question should have been raised at so convenient a time by so friendly and so public-spirited a tribe of creatures. You must remember, my lords, that evolution is going on all the time, and at any moment the supremacy of the human race may be challenged by who knows what mystery or horror. If the talking ant is too improbable, let us suggest the talking rat; I think I need say no more, my lords. And let us remember that this precedent that makes safe our liberties will also give to the friendly race of Wurroos a release that they ardently desire and demand, a position in the world which they both enjoy and understand. The occasion seems to me so splendid, my lords, as to exceed in its implications the normal jurisdiction of this Court. You are here to plan for the happiness both of the Wurroos and the race of man. So far your course is plain. You are here also to plan for the defence of the human race against any further product of insurgent evolution, and there, if I may presume to tell you so, my lords, there your duty is clear.'

'My lords, I must first try to sweep away this chatter about talking ants.

It is well known on biological grounds that we are in no such danger whatever from talking ants; the insects work by instinct; they have no possible bodily structure from which to discover reason. What my learned colleague treats as an accident is the crux of the whole matter. We are all agreed that the Wurroos are rational, and that they are almost men. I submit that on scientific evidence which I have produced, they *could* not be rational if they were *not* very nearly men; so nearly so that they might as well be called men. I agree, as the scientists agree, that it is very curious to find rational mammals with a breeding season. Very curious, but nothing to disturb – man.

'The arguments from precedence are by no means as he supposes; our magistrates may still condemn a dog to death for proved savagery, and this very reasonable step was all that our legal ancestors were concerned to obtain; therefore one, as I may say I think after a more thorough study of the precedents than my learned colleague, that cannot be argued from precedence. But such precedence as may be adduced from the more curious trials of beasts and from the suspicion of half-beastly parentage in the Middle Ages, have I think been dealt with by my learned colleague, who might surely have assumed that I would base no argument upon them. It seems to me, my lords, upon this unusual occasion, that I have a more confident part to play. What I would suggest to you, my lords, is the profound absurdity of the professional expert in science, when concerned in a simple matter of humanity, simple I say because simple for the plain man to judge, but complex enough in its substance and complex indeed in its consequences.

'Can Europe already have forgotten, my lords, that great decision of the Catholic Church in the seventeenth century in Tierra del Fuego offering that even the Indians were men? Is not this a fundamental instrument of progress from which the English could decently and securely build an empire? Are we at this late date, and even less progressive than the advanced spirits of what was then Christianity, to deny mere humanity to a suffering and intelligent people? Are we to cut them off blind and helpless from all communion with their only teachers and their own kind?'

'I do not see, Mr Thompson, that you can argue, on mere grounds of humanity, that these creatures or people ought to be denied a thing they in fact ask for very urgently. I should like you to explain why they are so much to be [ ]? Do you mean they are to be cheated if they get what they want?'

'When you say humanity, my lord, you settle the question. Certainly they are not to be cheated by the parties with whom they agree. Indeed the Crown, whose property they wish to be, cannot possibly by constitution cheat. I appreciate it. I only ask you to remember the enormous citizenship, greater even than that of the British Empire, which they are already trying to give away. I ask you to remember that in the distant future all races of mankind may make a homogeneous body and yet this single tribe will necessarily be still alien, still unique, still open to oppression, still perhaps feeling itself a monster neither man nor beast, if you my lords do not decide now with a mercy beyond their understanding.'

'And still, if I understand you, Mr Thompson, ready somehow to be kept in order by the race of man; unless you want them superior to it?'

'Silence' (after consultation). 'The court is agreed that the judges do not feel bound by precedent. As you have rightly said, there are no precedents here clear enough to bind us; and you no less rightly call this an important decision. I think I can speak for my colleagues, and say we are ready to take a permanent decision, intending by that a decision to hold for thousands of years after the collapse of this court. We think such an assurance unreasonable, unwarranted, not to be anticipated, and only within our normal powers as individuals, but naturally we are content, here as elsewhere, to accept the permanent moral responsibility which is inherent in our judicial responsibility. In so special a case, we are prepared to let you raise the question, but we deny that it need be raised.'

'There are so many other questions, my lord. There is the religious question. Are these Wurroos for ever, by one act of this court, to be shut out from heaven?'

'I do not understand you, Mr Thompson. The Wurroo candidate made a clear and I thought [ ] statement that he and all his tribe were physically non-[ ] for heaven. Do I understand you are eager to condemn this entire race to hell – or, at least, except only such members of it as are exceptionally fortunate?'

'That, my lord, is the normal condition of humanity.'

'This might be a very proper claim before an ecclesiastical court,

Mr Thompson, but before a civil court it cannot well be [ ] under humanitarian grounds towards an entire species.'

'I warn you, my lords, that no religious body will accept the decision towards which you seem to be tending.'

'This seems a normal case of self-determination in the British empire. In case of any question a plebiscite under instructed officers on the question of humanity can easily be arranged . . .[']

IV

Meanwhile other legal bodies were necessarily concerned to arrive at their own ruling. A Eucharistic Congress decided that since the creatures were rational and possessed some vestiges of a moral sense (granting that this was at present exiguous and condoned great evil) therefore they were necessarily human. As to the question whether they were derived from the human stock, the Congress was reminded of the text that God 'even out of these stones could raise up children unto Abraham' [*Luke*, 3:8]. Probably, it was maintained, as a matter of human reason, they were in fact part of the human stock, and as to scientific evidence, the method of science was admittedly incapable of reaching certainty on any question. If however they were not part of the human stock, they were a race of men independently created by God, and the Catholic Church could not renounce its duties towards them. A strong movement of the English Catholics demanded the immediate right to introduce missionaries in the tribe (Rome gave its approval but declined to make the matter a political question). To the argument that the tribe had its own rights of internal government, and did in fact conduct any human intruder to the frontier after a sound beating, it was retorted that if the tribe was not human it had neither the right of government nor the power. A compromise was suggested, to the effect that Catholic missionaries might be admitted to determine by experience whether the tribe was human; it was then found that the compromise was more unsatisfactory to both parties than any suggestion so far put forward by either.

Sir Reginald Tompkinson very wisely tried to remove Catholic missionaries from the entire Crown Colony, on the ground that their presence was liable to disturb public order; the question was taken up by the Labour Party and threatened to split the Government. It was found that Protestant feeling was no less firm, though on entirely different grounds which took longer to determine. The Church Congress showed an unusual degree of responsibility towards British law. The Established Church of England could not so long as it accepted the establishment, it was rightly though surprisingly argued, take up a position towards the legal authorities which amounted to open war. An attempted comparison to the position of the divorce laws was firmly quashed. On the other hand it was evident from the first that the delegates would not be able to reconcile with their consciences any mere abandonment of the tribe to heathendom.

The way out of this impasse was first found in a brilliant speech by the Archbishop of Canterbury. There was no reason, he maintained with ample learning and with his noble gift of rhetoric, why the benefits of the Church of England should be confined and cloistered to the race of man. The baptism of dogs he would for ever continue firmly to discountenance, but any visit to the remoter habitations of the universe, such as might any day be expected from English men of science, and he had in mind the planet Mars, would find him prepared and even determined to include in the party an ordained clergyman of the Church of England with full missionary rights. As to the text of Holy Writ which he was pleased to hear had been given due prominence by a Roman Catholic body, its meaning to an enlightened common sense was clearly and exactly opposite to the meaning which their ingenuity had extracted. Nobody supposed that men made from stones by an act of God would in fact also be children of Abraham, since this would be a direct contradiction in terms. The undoubted meaning of the text was that they ought to be treated *as if* they were children of Abraham, supposing they had already shown themselves to deserve it. In the same way the Wurroos ought to be treated spiritually as men, because spiritually they were held to deserve it; even though they were not in fact children of Adam, or whatever other name for our first progenitor the palaeontologists might now employ.

Taking a broader or deeper view, he continued, the question what living creatures were to be called men was in itself a merely verbal question, and one which the law had already been called upon to decide. He could not imagine why the Established Church of England need differ from the Law of England upon what was after all a mere legal technicality. And on the other hand the spiritual responsibilities of the Church were entirely unaffected by such a technicality; they must be decided in the last resort by the living consciences of Christian men and women, and he conceived that in the present case, with its remarkable unanimity of Christian feeling, the verdict of those consciences was no longer in doubt. The immediate need therefore was undoubtedly to press forward in the field of missionary endeavour, and he was prepared to establish a committee to authorise and decide upon any slight changes in the wording of the liturgy when translated into Wurroo, changes dealing only with such references as were made to 'men' or 'persons', which the special circumstances of their case might now seem to require.

At this point Wuzzoo himself gave in; indeed he suddenly apologised for having made so much fuss about the matter. There could be no danger, he pointed out, in sending any number of missionaries as long as they kept within certain reasonable restrictions; among these he suggested the avoidance of actual sedition and a decent withdrawal during the breeding season. He would be grateful if the tribe was given free medical attendance, though doctors had already been sent in 'on a gold basis' without individual Wurroos having to pay. There would be no restrictions on the educational work of missionaries, except that they might not offer rewards of any kind for successful learning. In the hope, he said, of avoiding waste of their time, money and labour, he wished to add that he would advise the tribe strongly against conversion, on all the grounds that had occurred to him, and fully expected that no converts would be made. His position in this matter was not actuated by any animus against Christianity, which indeed he thought a quite suitable religion for mankind.

Opinion in America was vocal and to a surprising degree fundamentalist; the incident put the fundamentalist cause in a dangerously strong position. There was a widespread distaste both for British imperialism in general and for the fantastic shifts to which it now seemed to be reduced, and this tendency, as so often in America, accepted the leadership of the strongest political body in its ranks. What one might vaguely call the Methodist vote had no strong line of its own; it followed the Church of England (as against Rome) in England and the fundamentalists in America. Any acceptance of evolutionary doctrine (meaning by this term the mere family tree of the various species, not as in Roman Catholic objections the causes by which it is to be explained) had now been shown by facts, so it was widely claimed in America, to involve a revoltingly inhuman and *a fortiori* unChristian attitude towards the subordinate races of mankind. The indignant pity felt towards a confiding dupe and his impending oppressor was invariably connected with the name of Wurroo, and poor Wuzzoo was trapped into a grave mistake by American reporters when (in an attempt to show that his position was not merely abject) he confessed that he admired the negroes as little as they. This put the whole negro press against him and convinced the whites that he had been made to swallow contradictory propaganda. It is almost true to say that no person in the USA believed he was responsible for the sudden change of front about missionaries, though his official advisers in England (who had worn themselves out in trying to convince him) were all astonished when he came round. In America it was the final proof that he was used as a puppet; and the story that he was kept permanently under drugs, though no drug could be suggested that would fit the facts, was widely printed and believed.

Probably three reasons must be given for his change of front. The effect of his first anti-Christian advisers was working off, and he was gradually coming to recognise that religion does not produce as much chastity and fear of hell as it had been natural for him to infer on *a priori* grounds. Secondly the genuine outburst of public indignation against the wild though casual action of the governor of the colony affected him not merely as showing the current of public feeling but as a piece of trouble out of which he could help a friend. Actually Sir Reginald had done this not to help Wuzzoo but out of a steadily growing sense of irresponsibility; the size of the thing had gone to his head, and the more fuss was made the more he wanted. But in any case it was probably the third reason that set off the other two. Wuzzoo had been approached by a delegation of neo-Buddhists, which except for a couple of Anglo-Saxon ornaments was entirely Japanese in personnel. They pointed out to him that the religion of the Blessed One lay wide open to the entire animal kingdom, and furthermore that by accepting it he and his race would join the great and growing fellowship of the oppressed peoples of the world. The topic of Buddhism had rather naturally been left out of his English education. He listened to the delegation with great interest, agreed with nearly everything they said, and as soon as they had gone cancelled his engagements for the evening on grounds of ill-health. It was on the following day (so I am afraid he can hardly have taken enough advice) that he changed his front and admitted any kind of missionary to Wurrooland.

One item in the rather melancholy list of consequences from this intellectual disturbance may be called a healthy sign. The question of the spiritual status of the inhabitants of Mars, or of whatever planet (perhaps enormously more remote) may contain rational inhabitants, had been raised for the devout of England in a speech by the Archbishop of Canterbury. It therefore received their attention, for the first time in the four centuries or thereabouts since it had first been plausibly broached. The utmost efforts of apologetic neo-physicists had not yet reduced the probable number of habitable worlds in the universe to less than a few hundred, and a section of younger Anglican clergy adopted as usable in the pulpit the doctrine that Christ had visited all of these planets, in turn or (by miracle) simultaneously, and on all of them passed through a similar ritual of extinction. Otherwise, they maintained, the arrangements of the divine mercy must almost certainly be pronounced unjust. On the final consequences of this movement (denounced after a time as heresy by name in the Papal encyclical *Necnon Humanum*) it is premature to pronounce, but it has already led to a position ambiguous between pantheism and Arianism, in which the historical importance of the events related in the gospels is reduced to a reassuring unimportance. One aspect of it may be illustrated by the words of Pfumpf, who at least will not be accused of an anti-Christian leaning from his wholehearted support of this school: 'Christ cannot be escaped, therefore no question of history need be considered. If men wrongly deny the existence of the historical Christ they will rightly be punished, but if they all deny it the Christ will again appear and again be crucified. If we are wrong in supposing that Christ was crucified in Galilee, our position is none the less secure. He will eventually appear on this planet as he has certainly appeared on others. He will eventually appear, and will eventually be crucified.'

V

'You mean it disturbs the cosiness of the universe if there are other intelligent creatures; man isn't unique; we can't feel it's all arranged for us? Like the trouble about Copernicus, in fact?'

'Yes, like Copernicus, all right, but there was a real theological difficulty about Copernicus; it wasn't just a vague feeling. And the curious thing is that everybody seems to have forgotten what it was. People knew at the time well enough; it was brought up against Bruno and Galileo when they were tried. That is, in the first trial of Bruno; of course the second isn't known about. But the only version you get in histories is what you were saying just now; they wanted the earth in the middle of things so that men could look important. That wasn't the point at all. They wanted the earth to be the only habitable planet so that Christ could be unique. The inquisitors actually asked Galileo whether Christ died for the inhabitants of other planets, and the first point against Bruno was that he stood for the plurality of worlds. Of course he brought in pantheism and so forth as well, but he thought you could deduce the new philosophy from the new fact.'[5]

'But you can't, so it doesn't matter. Nobody did deduce it when they accepted the new fact.'

'Yes, I know, that's just a curious thing; nobody did. But you can. There was a lot of very careful intellectual politics going on. I don't say it comes very directly, but the plurality of worlds was the last straw. The justice of God was under a great strain anyway, because the vast majority of men hadn't been given a chance. There were all the great classical pagans before Christ appeared at all, and even then the Chinese didn't hear of him for a thousand years. I daresay it seems easier now that the missionaries have got about a good deal, but Dante felt it all right; how God can be just at all had to be made a supreme mystery with a whole crowd of interlocking allegories. Of course, I ought to have said before, it was an essential claim for Christianity as a powerful centralised religion that you couldn't possibly get to heaven without it. But another of its chief claims was that it relieved the injustice of life on earth by perfect justice after death; the two dogmas made a bad conflict. Still, maybe somebody ought to have got to China and the Chinese ought to have listened; as long as it was all on one earth you could find somebody to blame. But once there were any number of worlds that Christ hadn't died on and where people couldn't possibly hear the gospel the injustice of the thing would become intolerable. The only way out is to say that Christ does it on all the different worlds, probably does it all the time in several places at once, and that gives you quite a different idea of the historical Jesus; for one thing, Christ may just as well have other incarnations as a man.[6] Then of course you got the discovery of America and the split in the Christian church; it all works from a feeling that you can't centralise things round a single person. But people were determined to forget about the central difficulty, and so you get this idea that the astronomers were only persecuted out of stupidity and vanity. It wasn't stupid at all; it was remarkably far-seeing.'

'That sounds very tidy, you know, but I can't help feeling, if it was all as clear-cut as that, it wouldn't have been possible to hush it up. People may have felt these implications, but they can't have thought them out.'

'Exactly; some daren't tell, and most wouldn't think. So it comes to be an obscure force working powerfully in the background.'

'Well, well; we can agree it was an obscure one. And the Wurroos come in because Christ ought to have appeared as a Wurroo?'

'No, not that; they can hear the gospel as they are. They come in as an argument that it didn't take a sudden supernatural change to make men out of apes.'

'Nonsense; God might as well do it twice as once.'

'Yes, indeed; but if twice then probably often, probably on any suitable occasion. You can't say there was any urgent need for God to break the ordinary laws of nature to make Wurroos, when the planet had Christians on it already. Unless you say they are designed to supersede the intolerably wicked race of man, and nobody is going to say that. Well then, if it's only a thing that God does in the ordinary course of nature, it's likely to be gradual, like the rest of evolution, and that's the whole crux. I don't say it's a proof, but it alters the whole balance of probabilities.'

'But, good gracious, man, why is being gradual the whole crux? What does it matter how fast he does it?'

'Now isn't it a curious thing that people feel like that? When

Darwin first came out they all saw the point; well; what the popular imagination seized on was the Missing Link, the creature that ought to have been missed out of the scheme of the world. But nobody mentions it now; they lose interest in theology, except in a fairly mushy form, that's the only way it affects them. I looked up that controversy between Wells and Belloc about Wells's *History*, for instance, and they seemed to have a gentleman's agreement to keep it out. At least I suppose Belloc knew it was a dangerous part, because he blustered about nominalism when it came onto the horizon, but Wells didn't even see it mattered.'

'They may have left out some pet dogma of yours, but they were talking about Missing Links and such all the time.'[7]

'There's no reason why Christianity should worry in the smallest degree about ingenious monkeys or about a low tribe of men descended from them. Nor need it worry about the particular machinery of evolution; however the thing was done it could be done by the will of God. The only thing Christian theology must have is a clear-cut distinction between the two. The first man had the choice between heaven and hell; he couldn't half go and half not. His father was an animal; he had no soul, he had no afterlife, he had no prospect of either heaven or hell. The eerie thing about the Missing Link was that it had half a soul though the soul is indivisible. Of course any actual Missing Link would be easy enough to deal with; you could just say it was either an ape or a man and stick to your choice. But in principle the thing has got to be clear-cut; otherwise all the dogmas are only half true, and hell only half real, and so on.'

'I don't see why you shouldn't have more or less soul, in fact I should have thought people obviously do, if the word has any meaning. Why shouldn't you partake of hell in the degree to which you have soul enough to appreciate it? Or heaven, I mean.'[8]

'Ah, that's the liberal note; they've all been playing around that, naturally. But it won't do. The whole line of Christianity has been to make every individual soul completely real, as real as God so to speak; equal in the eye of God, made in the likeness of God, able to know God in heaven; God became a man to show that men have full-size souls. Once you give up that you give up individualism, and you're right outside Europe; you may as well be a Hindu at once. They can't do it; you'll see.'[9]

VI

'Come back, Mary. You mustn't wince away from me like that. It's bad for my psychology. You had better hold my hand for one minute.'

What Rudyard Kipling described as unclean dismay descended on the room, as if the lights had gone off. After all, there was fair ground for disapproving, the girl was badly embarrassed. It took the form of being determined to get things clear.

'It's a misunderstanding, really it is, Mr Wuzzoo. I don't feel like that a bit. I got a kind of shock but it was quite different . . . I'll kiss you if you like.'

'But, my dear girl, you must never kiss an animal on the mouth,' said Wuzzoo, with so effective a smile that the social lights turned on again. 'It may have all *kinds* of germs there. What you want to do is to nudge it under the ears, when you go by.'

'I know, I really feel that from behind you,' she said eagerly, holding him by the shoulders. 'It is like having an agreeable kind of large dog in the room. Only when you see the eyes suddenly, you jump because they are not less than human, they are much more. It is an angel in the room and . . . that was what made me jump.'

'An angel. Oh Lord. Yes, I know you are being very nice but this is real bad news. I thought it was turning out all right about that sort of thing.'

'Why is it bad to be an angel,' she said, giggling a little. 'I think it is splendid.'

'I haven't anything to do with angels,' he said pettishly. 'You are going to heaven and being an angel and all that, and I haven't got a soul at all. Surely that's easy to get hold of.'

'But nonsense, I don't mean the dogmas about angels. I daresay none of us are going to heaven really. I just mean you are that kind of person.'

'Well, of course,' he said, but still not cheerfully, 'if you just call me an angel like you might call a spaniel an angel, I am very pleased to have people pat me on the head. Because that might be important. But you mustn't mean I have got spiritual heights. It really isn't just a matter of dogma. You have got all the spiritual heights in the human race and all the spiritual depths too; that is why you are so cruel. I have to explain it because it is so important, I am very sorry it sounds insulting. I have been going into this, and I'm not sure I ought to talk about it.'

'Nonsense,' she said, shaking him by the shoulders which she still held. 'I mean, go on and talk about it, though it *is* nonsense too.'

'It's all because we have kept to a tidy breeding season and you haven't. That is why you feel it's all right, for one thing, to treat me like this in the middle of a teaparty.' (She let go of his shoulders.) 'And it's why we haven't got a soul and aren't men. Because you have worked all your mental life off repression of sex; I mean you did millions of years ago when it all started' (he realised that the thing needed softening somehow); 'and I don't mean that wasn't a good thing, it gave you all your heights and depths and made you angels. But we haven't started that at all. We are very flat kind of people beside you, that is one reason we just want to be left alone. And it is very frightening if you start to call us angels, that is just what we want to avoid. You understand that now, don't you?' he ended with a kindly but schoolmastering tone.

'But don't you see it's ridiculous for you to stand there and spout Freud at me,' she said with considerably more detachment. 'You are a living refutation of the whole Freudian theory. According to Freud you couldn't be a rational creature at all, and here you are more than human, as I said. So it can't be as important as all that.'

'Now listen, it's just a mistake what you think about my face,' he said earnestly. 'You aren't used to big eyes like a horse's with about as much intelligence in them as a man's. You don't know how to interpret them, so you try to think of men with eyes like that. And then you go off into angels and call me more than human. You mustn't do it, it's very dangerous. Look, it's like that even inside the human race, only not so much. You are used to Englishmen with small noses being short of willpower, so you think the Japanese must be short of willpower because they are a race with small noses, and it isn't true. A racial difference doesn't work the same way as an individual difference, it is quite a separate thing.'

'But I don't believe it is,' she said, beginning to argue cheerfully. 'I think the Japanese really are short of willpower; that's why they have to train themselves so frightfully and always stick together, to get enough. I think we know about animal faces too; I mean, lions really are noble and camels really are supercilious. I believe you are just like your face too, only you don't want it pointed out.'

'Your eyes are frightening me at this minute quite as much as mine can have frightened you,' he said steadily. 'You feel I am unnatural, and you are a generous-minded girl so you turn it into calling me an angel. But the others are not going to do that. I am only giving way to fancy, like you. But I fancy I see a war of extermination behind the awe in your eyes . . . Not of course for some time,' he went on before the impressive pause could be interrupted. 'Not till it would mean a lot of trouble.'

'Mr Wuzzoo, you were going to play the piano for us,' screamed out Lady Hurston too suddenly. 'You said you had adapted some Wurroo music for the piano, and we *must* hear it. You must come along at once, because we want to hear a great deal.'

'And what are we to do to stop this war?' Mary went on firmly.

'Yes, I'll come to the piano at once, Lady Hurston, though I don't think people will want it to go on very long . . . If you are willing to be very helpful, can you dress for Ascot and come to the Zoo with me next Saturday afternoon? I warn you I mean to get talked about, and if I get a chance I'll make a speech.'

VII

'Of course what you can do on the piano is only a sort of parody,' said Wuzzoo, ambling to the instrument, 'you must imagine it on Pan's pipes and tom-toms. It's a very narrow form really, but it has a certain dramatic power. It excites me all right. You'll find I'm very clumsy with the keyboard, but I can do the timing properly, and that's the difficult part.' Then, fidgeting with the keys, 'This is a very fine piano.'

'Oh, how wonderful, Mr Wuzzoo,' said Lady Hurston at the first pause, 'why, it's real music, isn't it? And so firm and clear-minded, and brave. And yet all the time that deep savage note underneath, the hopelessness of the forests, you feel in it, don't you? I think it's extraordinary you should understand all that about your lives, somehow, out there.'

Wuzzoo spun round on the music stool grinning from ear to ear. 'How awful,' he said, 'you'll never forgive me. I didn't do it on purpose. I was just getting my hand in. That was Bach. But what you say about him is quite true,' he went on, firmly drowning the laughter, 'and people don't see it enough. That's what I was trying to explain about the jungles; of course he's a very Christian composer. There has to be some talk before I play our own music,' he went on, standing up and addressing the room, 'or it will seem just nonsense. You know how the negroes use complicated rhythms; well, we do it more. There are three tunes played together, and the notes only come together at the beginning and the end. Then the singing man starts and goes on for as long. The music is meant to go with ballads. Of course the dance-music during the breeding season is quite different, but you aren't allowed to play that at other times.'

'Oh nonsense, Wuzzoo, you can play it here. We aren't at all squeamish about indecent music in this country, whatever the other arts have to put up with. Anything but.'

'Yes, but I don't know it, because I'm not allowed to practise. That is, not outside the breeding season, and inside it I have other things to do. The musicians of the breeding season are considered a very low lot; of course they [ ], but they have to do it very secretly and far away from the others. No ordinary person wants to be a musician, because it cuts you out of the best things in the breeding season. They come from special families, and at one time they were castrated before they were allowed to perform. I don't think they were ever forced into it, because there was always a supply of willing ones. They got privileges and a kind of notoriety. Anyway it is straightforward orgy music, just what you would expect. The ballad music outside the breeding season, which everybody learns to play, is much more surprising for you, I should think, and I am going to play some. But it needs a bit of explaining, which I couldn't do properly, and I have now to introduce Mr Jenkins, to those who don't know him, who as I am sure you all know is a very learned musician, and he has been working on this music from my playing and knows a great deal about it.' Wuzzoo sat down abruptly.

Mr Jenkins advanced with notes and a large foolscap sheet with figures on it. Like most musicians, he had an air of habitual constipation; or perhaps a more poetical figure is more just: he looked as if he lived in an unusual world under water. But at the moment he had a healthy glow, because he was enjoying the experience, very unusual to a music critic, of having something to say which could be said in the English language. A modest and rather unsuccessful man, he was not annoyed at having Wuzzoo treat him as a rabbit to be brought out of the hat at a dramatic moment; or perhaps he hardly realised it had happened. He began lecturing at once.

'I am very much honoured,' he said rapidly, 'at being selected by Prince Wuzzoo to speak to this assembly about the extraordinary development of music among his people. Many attempts have been made to extend the range of music by tampering with the diatonic scale. I cannot find evidence that the Wurroos use anything else, though what I may call their keys are sometimes an odd selection from it. One could not of course make a definite assertion here without examining the actual instruments, as I hope in time to do; but Prince Wuzzoo expresses himself as satisfied with the piano keyboard. His own performances as a singer, involving as they do a continual slide from one note to the next, give I am afraid little evidence to decide the question, remarkable as they are. However in any case it is no departure from the scale that gives this music its interesting character, and I do not see why a more informed use of the full scale should not yield still more valuable results. The other possible means of extending the range of music, as I need hardly inform you, is by complexity of rhythm, and here Prince Wuzzoo himself has already made the essential points. But I venture to think he gave a wrong impression about the effect of the ballad music of his country when he spoke of the power of rhythmical intuition in the negroes, true though his actual statements were. Dramatic and indeed exciting as the effect of the Wurroo ballad can be, it is at the opposite pole from the dance music of the American negro. The painful aridity, the merely intellectual excitement, that we find in the panchromatic scales of Bartók and of Schöenberg, these are at first sight the basis of Wurroo music; and yet we find it fused into the plain drama of a popular ballad. It is essentially, if I may venture for a moment into what is perhaps sociology rather than music, it is essentially the music of a sexless people . . . These general remarks are I think sufficient as an introduction, and I shall now try to explain the principle of the technique. I do not want to hold you from the actual music longer than necessary, but, as Prince Wuzzoo pointed out, the music itself is hardly intelligible unless you know what to listen for.

'It is based on what I suppose must be called a single isolated bar, comprising three wholly disparate rhythms. There are three melodies, one with three intervals, one with five, one with seven. They need not be used all at once, but they are always, so to speak, within reach, and at all crucial points they are used together. I am not sure that any European performer could play a single bar of this music, even with three metronomes before him; certainly I have not yet learned to do so myself. Prince Wuzzoo will often tap out the combined rhythms with his fingers when he is in doubt how to answer a question. We can only, I think, learn it quickly by using space instead of time, and I have prepared a chart, which I want to hang up in the room, showing the relations of the notes as clearly as possible.'

The chart when pushed up over the mantelpiece looked like this:

Times from the start to successive notes in whole numbers:

0	15	30	45	60	75	90	105
0	21	42	63	84		105	
0		35		70		105	

Time-intervals between notes in whole numbers:

15   6   9   5   7   3   15   3   7   5   9   6   15

'The arrangement of intervals, as you see, is symmetrical. Three intervals of the seven-time beat are not crossed by others; namely, those at the two ends and in the middle. Probably all you hear at first will be these three intervals with two jangles between them, each twice as long as the intervals. But there is also a principle of harmony at work. At the first instant and the last, where the three instruments sound together, we have either unison or what the Wurroo people consider a satisfying chord. Furthermore, any two notes closer together than half the seven-time beat are expected to harmonise; the player of the first note of the two holds it long enough to make them overlap. Naturally, as the divisions go by odd numbers, no note can be half-way between its two neighbours, and therefore each note is required to harmonise with some other. Thus after the initial chord the first seven-time note and the first five-time note will harmonise, though they are at an evident distance; then the third seven-time note and the second five-time note also harmonise, coming almost on top of one another. A more dramatic duty is assigned to the notes of the three-time beat. The first of these is nicely within reach of the second seven-time beat and also just within reach of the second five-time beat, which is already harmonised to the third seven-time beat. After the triumph of reconciling these conflicting claims we have a kind of caesura, and then the same succession of dragged intervals has to be worked out backwards with new harmonies. I think I may leave you to imagine the extraordinary musicianship required to compose a bar in this medium at all. In composing a second bar after a first, however, there is an added difficulty imposed by the relation of the music to the singing.

'The singing is not directly accompanied, and while it may hold particular notes it will commonly follow the glides and abrupt intervals of actual impassioned speech. Each cry of the performer, however, must glide from some one note to some other of the previous bar, giving them their exact time-intervals. So far we have merely an ingenious device for reducing a realistic reproduction of speech to a complex but as a whole rhythmical time-order. But the succeeding bar has to reproduce or echo, at the same intervals, each of the notes from which the glides of the previous singing started and stopped. At the same time, of course, it carries the notes that will be used by the singer to follow; if the hero is to answer the villain, both their sentences are as it were dissolved in the intervening bar. It is not necessary on every occasion to use all three rhythms; indeed a single melody may be played alone, and then caught up later in a complex unit. But neither singer nor orchestra is allowed to repeat a melody immediately after it has been used, and therefore the frequent use of single melodies, which might appear a simplification, is in fact even in this music considered a tour-de-force.'[10]

VIII

'How unfinished they look!' Wuzzoo said, as the creature craning from its stretched arms achieved a Michael Angelo pose of generosity

and exaltation, and the disagreement with the habitual cramped [ ]
of the thighs made it a deformed archangel. 'It was impossible that
they were meant like that. I always feel the same about you. It is a
great aspiring stock; I feel very humble beside it,' said Wuzzoo,
looking however with distaste at the chimpanzee.

'You must not get into a habit of tittering, Wuzzoo,' said Mary.
'You are always ringing the changes on one joke. I shan't try to argue
with you because I don't believe you mean what you say.'

'Well, but I really feel uneasy,' said Wuzzoo, undisturbed by this
attack. 'I was reading Swift about the intelligent horses whose name
you can't pronounce. It is so clear that there's no point in them going
on, they are quite all right and no good, they might as well die out.
They have no presence of madness behind them, so they have no
religion and they will never do anything new. He meant it as the ideal
creature, but it turned into a complete satire on his ideals, and it feels
to me like a satire on the Wurroos.[11] You all seem so much more
interesting than I am, usually nastier but far richer in the creative
follies. That is why Buddhism won't do for us really; we want
something much madder. Why should we believe that all desire is
suffering?[12] Our desires are not. I feel that Christianity is the thing for
us. I must come here on Fridays and study the apes at night to learn
how to chatter at the moon,' and he began singing the *Dies Irae* very
loudly.

'*Ne me perdas illa die.*'

'Are you discovering your soul, Wuzzoo, or wailing at the moon
because you haven't got one?'

'Neither. I am in a mystical condition. I am beyond belief and
disbelief. I am curious of the [ ] of both, and only this binds me to my
terrestrial condition.

'*Oro supplex.*

' – though that is all wrong, by the way, it is not my end I want
looking after. What I don't like is the effect of finality. I need divine
discontent.

[*1 page of manuscript missing*]

'I must say I am excessively contented,' he said, grinning at her after a
glance at the crowd. 'Now I shall make a speech if we can get outside.'

'You are drunk, Wuzzoo, and you will make a fool of yourself. If you aren't careful you will pull all the strings of popular sentiment the wrong way.'

IX

The following tantalising passages are Empson's notes and ideas for further scenes; square brackets indicate indecipherable words.

i

So long as the Wurroos weren't heard of it was still very arguable that no other creature but man could possibly be rational. You can say there are suggestive analogies from the animal kingdom, but they don't go at all far. The truth is simply that we don't know how men became rational, how unlikely a thing to happen it was, what machinery was required. It may be a unique event.

ii

People sometimes talk as if the Noble Savage was a ridiculous piece of sentiment, because savages aren't noble. This is very narrow and stupid. The point about the noble savage was that he was supposed to be the pure mind, not duped by king and priests and so forth, sitting at the door of his hut and brooding [. . .]. Wuzzoo has considerable claims as a noble savage, because with his lot the obvious line of development hasn't occurred.

iii

We are much less fitted for travel than you . . . no I can't sublimate the desire for fun: we don't sublimate things.

iv

I don't want to play at tragedy and don't want to make the thing too milky. The appalling world situation ought to come in. [Evelyn Waugh's] *Black Mischief* was a powerful book because he kept telling you 'blacks are like this' – I can't do anything but say 'suppose Wuzzoo was nice'.

v

Idea that tragedy is peculiar to Europe and the sacrificed god.[13] Pleasure in sad stories of course much more widespread.

Feeling that everybody gains by seeing the death of such a valuable one? A proof of human dignity, godlikeness etc. (Final test idea independent of this)

One must suppose the Wurroos to have an elaborate hierarchy and to unite about situations of dominance, with death as test of value. Do they have enough *anti-herd* feelings for *one* hero to become crucial? I suspect their hero will be one with nature – they are working out much too like the Chinese. Have they enough individualist feeling to work out the state – individual paradoxes, pastoral and so on? How demonstrate it? They are working out much too like Chinese.

vi

'Of course, I make a much better contrast here than I would in China, say, because you work such an enormous amount of your culture off sex. You might think that we would be adolescents in the breeding season, having Weltschmertz and discovering beauty in nature and all that. But you do that because you are running it through your whole system, and we don't. It brings out a pugnacious side, and the music is quite different then (the musicians have to hide when they practise – even so it is thought a rather disgraceful profession). "The palpable and obvious love of man for man" is a great deal more palpable in the case of Wurroos, because they aren't competing for women all the time and afraid of seeming buggers.'

vii

Meeting of Wuzzoo with distinguished Freudian. Proves he can't exist.

viii

'Why do all your babies scream like that?' Wuzzoo asked during a lull. 'Our babies don't. I don't think I know any animals' babies that do. Oh I remember, of course,' he went on, 'Freud. They all have unappeasable desires which inherently can't be satisfied. But it seems very extraordinary.' The infant produced another furious masterpiece of hysterical and fundamental despair.[14] 'Do your women *like* having to look after these things?' Wuzzoo wanted to know. 'Of course they are only raving lunatics for a year or so, but then they only get on to nagging and whining. Is that why women have to be kept under, because otherwise they wouldn't let you breed the things at all?'

ix

'I had three children,' said Wuzzoo simply. 'I suppose you could call it favouritism rather, but I had three one year after another. And they were all by the same female. People thought it rather pretty, you know, evidently we liked each other a lot and so on. Rather eccentric though.'

x

'I understand you all send yourselves to sleep with erotic daydreams,' remarked Wuzzoo into a blank silence. 'It's a difficult trick to learn at my time of life, and I can't think a very sensible one. Very like teaching your digestion to work in a wasp waist. I had never slept alone in my life when I left my country: I should be thought queerly of if I did. But there again, apparently, your people carry the human perversions to a fantastic extreme; there are plenty of human tribes where nobody goes to sleep alone.'

xi

'I am getting to feel that you ought to envy me very much,' said Wuzzoo. 'Whenever I hear of a fundamental problem I find I am safely and entirely outside it. Theories about money – we haven't any; communism – we haven't any classes; psychology – we haven't any repressed sex. The only danger is you may find out how dull we are compared to you, and lose interest, because we want all the public interest we can get for protection.'

xii

Meeting of Wuzzoo with Eliot

xiii

'It must seem wonderful to you, Prince Wuzzoo, to come here straight out of the jungle and find all this luxury.'

'Extraordinary,' said Wuzzoo, with a friendly smile, munching his Ryvita, and showing about as much wonder as a stalled ox.

'I mean, after the jungle, it must seem so different.'

'Tell me about the jungle: what do you think about it?'

'Well of course to me it seems full of such extraordinary things, I mean the animals and so on, anything may crop up, and the Africans doing magic, and so on. And yet though it's wonderful it's frightfully cruel, and the queer things are so wonderfully queer, you may be tripped up anywhere. And then again all these things don't happen most of the time; most of the time it's just fearfully boring; it's very stark; all the light and shade of life seems to have gone. That's how I imagine the jungle.'

'That is very cleverly [ ], and well put. I am glad you have said it for me. I know what you say is quite true, I mean you really would feel that about the jungle. Because it is all just what I feel about England. But still, I try not to let it worry me too much.'

X

Empson's draft outline of the novel:

Station of district officer. Arrival of creature, language issue, wishes to explain and desires isolation, will hand over gold if wanted. First told wrong country, wants to deal direct with King. Boundary issue turns up. Animals better treated than coolies. Says agreement refers to negroes, he is not. Hence non-human claim. Sent on to governor. World situation particularly trying re gold. Breezy governor delighted to make gentleman's agreement with gentlemanly animals. Then the representation coming in. Suggests [ ], impossible; [ ]. Decides to fight case. Fur incident on boat? Clothes problem earlier; induced to wear loincloth. Attempt to keep him on English side; social success. Music. Visit to zoo. Newspapers. Frank talk about how [ ] of bloods. The Case. Royal Beasts? Sudden return by aeroplane for breeding season. (Told to run fur issue: mistaken for claim to be human; stopping this to run gold issue discreetly, without attacking Southern Rhodesia.) Negro movement claim not to be human disowned by Paul Robeson. Deputation from Liberia. Catholics claim they are human still, British law no right to decide. Protestant discovery that

Martians e.g. should be claimed for Christ – no reason they should be human. Basis of contrast – are all persons human? Joint Stock Company a person but not human. Hence they can come under most laws as companies. Would e.g. decency laws however apply to a company?

– Area closed from both sides and official prospectors sent in at once.

– want a *subsequent* case for contrast point.

– claim to recent mutation brought out as part of independence claim? Offers to show himself on 200 certain days as personal loan animal.

Notes on 'The Royal Beasts':

1. Empson's draft notes expand the observations made in the first part of this paragraph: 'The original language and personal situation is interesting enough to be put down in some detail, but from that point on I shall pretend that Wuzzoo could talk fairly well. The business of explaining things with limited language is very tedious to write down, and not intelligible even when written down completely. You go on till you see a gleam in the other man's eye which does not appear in print, and though of course you can make mistakes about the gleam a reader can't know whether it was a stupid mistake merely by looking at the transcript. Also W. was in fact a very quick learner; he was much cheered up after his experience of his own language by finding a goat could always be called a goat; he was very indifferent to grammatical mistakes and the fear of absurdity to which they can lead; and he had things he wanted to say as soon as he could get hold of enough language. Any fresh mind will make rapid progress at the start with these conditions. One result of this was that the [Bickersteth] household swung round from thinking him an alarming kind of monkey to thinking him a creature with superhuman intellectual power. People have been teased a lot about the superman, and this suspicion was one of the underground currents that ran for sufficiently long in Wuzzoo's favour. Actually if the [Bickersteths] had tried to teach English to a negro under these conditions they would have thought him fantastically receptive too, but they had not done it.'

2. John Caldwell Calhoun (1782–1850), American statesman and congressman; vice-president from 1825 to 1832, serving part of his term in the administration of his then friend and admirer, John Quincy Adams. Partly provoked by the tariff acts of 1828 and 1832, Calhoun later led the Southern states in their supposed right to nullify a Congressional act; above all, to maintain the property rights of slave-owners. Claiming to protect the minority against the 'tyranny of the majority', his fight to secure the slave-holding interests of the South (which he regarded as a 'positive good') bitterly estranged many of his erstwhile political allies. 'Calhoun is the high-priest of Moloch – the embodied spirit of slavery,' wrote John Quincy Adams in 1843 (Allen Nevins (ed.), *The Diary of John Quincy Adams 1794–1845*, New York: Scribner's, 1951, p. 544).

Empson seems to have looked at both Adams's memoirs and Calhoun's own writings, from which he noted: 'Slave and freeman can work in a field together: but freeman must eat at master's table, and mustn't do the work of "menial or body servants": "They are unsuited to the spirit of a freeman."

'With us the two great divisions of society are not rich and poor, but white and black; and all the former, the poor as well as the rich belong to the upper class, and are respected and treated as equals, if honest and industrious; and hence have a position and pride of character of which neither poverty nor misfortune can deprive them.'

3. *Latifundium*: a large ancient Roman estate on which slaves were legally deemed to be movable property, like cattle.

4. The Ainu people, who are believed to be of Caucasian rather than Mongoloid extraction, have more copious body hair than any other known human group. Cf. Empson's review of *The Secret History of the Mongols*: 'The courtesy of [Arthur] Waley is finely seen when he reports that the Ainu, in the northern island of Japan, are famous for their long beards. The Japanese say that they are covered with fur, and merrily showed them to a visiting prince (within living memory, in the interests of Asiatic solidarity) as typical Aryans; they are Caucasians like ourselves, but so was the prince, so this was a sad gaffe' ('Waley's Courtesy', *New Statesman & Nation*, 13 March 1964, p. 410).

5. Cf. Empson's untitled review of *A Study of 'Love's Labour's Lost'*, by F. A. Yates: 'The final eight questions on which Bruno [1548–1600] died rather than retract are not known, but in the recorded trial at Venice he is clearly connecting his belief in the infinity of worlds with his doubt of the divinity of Christ, and in the trial of Galileo we have the straight question – "did Christ die for the inhabitants of other worlds?" If there are many worlds, either Christianity is intolerably unjust or Christ went to all of them; if there are many Christs there may be a bit of Christ in everybody, and you can write as Donne did about Elizabeth Drury. People seem to have agreed that it was a foolish error of the Inquisition to make a fuss about Copernicus. It might, I think, as plausibly be maintained that the Copernican view really does involve pantheism, and that the questions he unwittingly put to the church have never been answered' (*Life and Letters*, vol. 15, 1936, p. 204).

6. Empson's thinking and its background anticipate Aldous Huxley's (1946): 'The doctrine that God can be incarnated in human form is found in most of the principal historic expositions of the Perennial Philosophy ... Krishna is an incarnation of Brahman, Gautama Buddha of what the Mahayanists called the Dharmakaya, Suchness, Mind, the spiritual Ground of all being. The Christian doctrine of the incarnation of the Godhead in human form differs from that of India and the Far East inasmuch as it affirms that there has been and can be only one Avatar ... Because Christians believed that there had been only one Avatar, Christian history has been disgraced by more and bloodier crusades, interdenominational wars, persecutions and proselytizing imperialism than has the history of Hinduism and Buddhism ... Here it may be remarked that the vast numbers of Buddhas and Bodhisattvas, of whom the Mahayanist theologians speak, are commensurate with the vastness of their cosmology. Time, for them, is beginningless, and the innumerable universes, every one of them supporting sentient beings of every possible variety, are born, evolve, decay and die, only to repeat the same cycle – again and again, until the final inconceivably remote

consummation, when every sentient being in all the worlds shall have won to deliverance out of time into eternal Suchness or Buddhahood. This cosmological background to Buddhism has affinities with the world picture of modern astronomy . . . If, as we have no choice but to believe, spiritual laws governing consciousness are uniform throughout the whole planet-bearing and presumably life-supporting universe, then certainly there is plenty of room, and at the same time, no doubt, the most agonising and desperate need, for those innumerably redemptive incarnations of Suchness, upon whose shining multitudes the Mahayanists love to dwell' (*The Perennial Philosophy*, London: Triad Grafton, 1985, pp. 74–5, 78).

7. In response to Hilaire Belloc's criticisms of his *Outline of History*, H. G. Wells alleged that Belloc was 'running away from . . . a grisly beast, neither ape nor true man, called the Neanderthaler, *Homo Neanderthalensis* . . . For three quarters of the "palaeolithic" age he was the only sort of man . . . The poor Neanderthaler has to go to the dogs, I fear, by implication, for Mr Belloc puts it with all the convincing force of italics, that "*Man is a fixed type.*" . . . Apart from Mr Belloc's assertion, there is no evidence that man is any exception to the rest of living creatures . . . his absurd reasonings about Natural Selection and his deliberate and tedious bemuddlement of the early Palaeolithic sub-men with the late Reindeer man and the Capsian men are all conditioned by the necessity he is under to declare and believe that "man" is, as he puts it, a "Fixed Type", the same in the past and now and always. He is under this necessity because he believes that otherwise the Christian faith cannot be made to stand up as a rational system . . . I believe a far better case could be made for Catholicism by an insistence that . . . the truth of the history it tells of space and time is entirely in relation to the development of these spiritual aspects, and has no necessary connection whatever with scientific truth' (*Mr Belloc objects to 'The Outline of History'*, London: Watts & Co., 1926, pp. 40–41, 46).

Belloc responded to Wells's blithely progressive optimism by pointing out that in the course of describing later Palaeolithic Man in the *Outline of History* Wells 'tells us that later Paleolithic Man disappeared and that a new culture took his place, possessing (what Paleolithic Man had not) domesticated animals, a knowledge of husbandry, bows and arrows, and the rest of it.

'This, of course, is the orthodox doctrine of the famous Gap between Paleolithic Man and Neolithic Man on which our generation were all brought up. It is true that there are now guesses at the discovery of a link between them; still the gap is very marked' (*Mr Belloc still objects to Mr Wells's 'Outline of History'*, London: Sheed & Ward, 1926, p. 32).

For a general survey of the controversy, see A. N. Wilson, *Hilaire Belloc*, London: Hamish Hamilton, 1984, pp. 298–302; in view of Empson's later admiration for Aldous Huxley's *The Perennial Philosophy* (1946), he would not have appreciated Wilson's glibly dismissive summing-up: 'Wells's vague notion that all religions were ultimately one, and that there would come a dawn when the more agreeable aspects of Buddhist and Christian morality would be embraced by a secular society which had discarded the troublesome doctrines of the supernatural, was such nonsense that Belloc had no trouble in demolishing it' (p. 302).

8. Empson pencilled among his notes: 'why can't Christian theology admit

degrees of soul anyway? individual stuff, but degrees in hell apparently. Removes the last reality after time if you only partly go to heaven.'

9. Cf. Empson on T. S. Eliot's pronouncements against the importance of 'personality': 'Mr Eliot himself says in "Tradition and the Individual Talent" that "the point of view I am striving to attack is perhaps related to the metaphysical view of the substantial unity of the soul" – I believe I am right in calling this the central issue between Christianity and Buddhism . . . The fact is simply that . . . no human system can work without the free judgement of the individual. The dogma of the eternal unity of the soul is at bottom only a device for insisting on this fact; whether or not, in practice, there is no other means for making men recognise it adequately. Certainly in theory there is nothing against it in Buddhism' ('Introduction' to T. S. Eliot, *Selected Essays*; Tokyo: Kinseido, 1933).

10. Cf. Empson's review of *In the Realm of Mind* by C. S. Myers: 'The later sections centre round Dr Myers' belief in the principle of Directive Purpose, a fundamental thing opposed to Mechanism, Determinism, or Blind Chance, and found in all living matter, also in the plan of the universe as a whole. Psychology is forced to recognise this principle, and the other sciences would do well to follow its example. Dr Myers frequently says that this view is different from Vitalism, but it can hardly be any different in any important respect without becoming null. As a matter of philosophy or religion I myself find it attractive, but it seems very little use to the practising scientist . . . You can see it influence his judgements in a roundabout way; for instance, when he says that the most primitive music is enjoyed because of complex harmonies, though it seems only to work by small equal intervals of tone, and though simple harmonies were invented later – he wants this just as he wants the amoeba to be intelligent, the complex development to be inherent in the simple origin. But surely, if this point is important, the first thing is to get evidence; whether these savages *can* hear harmonies, and so on. Dr Myers is not thinking on these lines. He is taking a broad, philosophical view . . .' ('Two Psychologists', *The Spectator*, vol. 159, 20 August 1937, p. 325). Empson is referring to the following remarks by Myers, which clearly have a bearing on his own development of the Wurroo music:

'An important step making possible the evolution of music in man appears to have been the appreciation of equal tone distances: some of the most primitive examples of human music consist in a phrase of two, three or more descending tones separated by small, more or less definite and equal distances one from the other. Then came an important development based on absolute pitch, which also arose early in animal life . . . In savage music it is sometimes the first, sometimes the last note, which plays this role, influencing the number of descending steps and ensuring that the melody as it recurs in the song shall always recommence or terminate on the same note.

'There can be no little doubt that the memory for absolute pitch is also responsible for the development of tone *intervals* as contrasted with tone *distances*. Tone intervals are based on the experience of "harmony" between two successive tones, the remembered pitch of the first tone appearing in a certain degree "harmonious" with the heard pitch of the following tone. Whereas the tone distances first employed in primitive music were narrow, the tone intervals, on the contrary, were relatively wide. But these relatively wide intervals arose through an awareness of harmony, not from the summation of small tone distances . . . The first use of tone intervals seems therefore to depend on the pleasure derived from the relation of two *consecutive* tones, not from the consonant effects of fusion obtained by hearing the two tones *simultaneously*' (*In the Realm of Mind*, Cambridge: CUP, 1937, pp. 54–6).

Even while devising his Wurroo–Schöenbergian musical excursion – a mathematician's gambit, fantastically extreme but not unfeasible as music (as a trained mathematician, he made a lifelong habit of doodling algebraic prob-lems: 'It's as good as masturbation,' he once remarked) – Empson pondered the question of whether the Wurroos would be able to experience a sense of tragedy; at the foot of his MS page he noted with gay self-irony: 'They obviously *have* got tragedy if they use this form.'

11. Cf. Empson in 'Literary Criticism and the Christian Revival': 'T. S. Eliot wrote in an early number of the *Criterion*, but I think did not reprint, that the last chapter of *Gulliver's Travels* is one of the greatest productions of the human mind. The degree of contempt for the world expressed by Eliot here would in Swift's time be called Manichaean or Calvinist, and he was uneasy when he tried to explain the chapter himself . . . The chapter is very good as a description of persecution mania, and Swift no doubt arrived at it by an immense release of personal spite, mixed with some public spirit. In America, on the other hand, about ten literary dons have produced arguments that Swift meant to satirise the horses too, because they were eighteenth-century rationalists. This is the real Buddhist contempt for all existence, even in the highest heaven, as found in the Fire Sermon; but I believe the theory has now been quietly dropped' (*Rationalist Annual*, 1966, pp. 28–9).

12. Cf. Empson letter to I. A. Richards, written on his first visit to Peking, 2 April 1933: 'The Buddhist position as I understand it is that impulses within causation are essentially avoidances of pain, and that (apparent) satisfactions are harmful because they are creators of desire which eventually produce more pain. One might say that some satisfactions are obviously positive because the aged bewail the failure of their desires, but the Buddhist answer does for this. The Mahayana business then claims that there are positive satisfactions but they are essentially apart from causation and therefore "impersonal": you get in Money-Kyrle's *Development of Sexual Impulses* [London: Kegan Paul, 1932] e.g. an early-Buddhist pessimism which obviously excites this sort of escape . . . I certainly do not see what other means would introduce positive satisfaction: on the whole, you understand, since the pleasure is defined as the removal of an equal pain. A conceivable loophole is in his definitions of "desire" – a sensation of a need together with the idea of the means of quieting it; "appetite" – a sensation of a need together with the sensation of the means of quieting it. It is the intellectuality of the creature, the fact of its consciousness, which alone makes a state of want able to be a state of pleasure. This at least gives consciousness a legitimate importance: in [Money-Kyrle's] book there is no suggestion as to why it should occur or whether anything would be the same if it didn't. Counting the impulses satisfied in a creature with an appetite relieved without consciousness the total value is nil; counting in the consciousness the value is positive . . . It seems clear that consciousness is somehow involved in value, because if there was no consciousness we would at any rate feel there was no value . . . It really seems clear that there are positive satisfactions, and that a majority of the people in this bar, like myself, are receiving them as I write. But

I do not see how they can be accounted for if all action is attempt to escape immediate pain: and if there are no such satisfactions there is no complete thing, no whole individual, which you would call valuable' (Empson Papers).

13. Cf. 'Greek tragedy is the reverberation after the fall of human sacrifice; no wonder its theology is adventurous and rather confused' (*Milton's God*, Cambridge: CUP, 1981, p. 238).

14. Cf. Empson's unpublished essay on Buddhism and Death (1933): 'the special Buddhist version of a deathwish . . . is that no sort of temporal life whatever can satisfy the human spirit, and therefore we must work for an existence outside time on whatever terms.' This concept is not a psychological perversion, Empson goes on to insist, but 'at the back, I believe, of all the grand examples in the aesthetic of the deathwishes. Shakespeare makes Lear hint at an odd and interesting reflection on this topic when faced with the despair of Gloucester: "Thou must be patient. We came crying hither. Thou knowest, the first time that we smell the air, we waul and cry." Alone among the young of the mammals the human infant is subject to blind fits of fury at finding itself thrust into the world; it is nasty, he feels, to the point of mysticism, and I suppose Freud could hardly disagree . . . the desires for absence of stimulus and return to the womb are the obviously Buddhist deathwishes, and are clearly a large element anyway in all but the most primitive religions' (Empson Papers).

The Elephant and the Birds
A plan for a ballet
[1942]

The dance tells the story of two legends; the Greek story of Philomel and Procne, and the Indian story of what the Buddha did in his incarnation as an elephant. There are seven scenes, and the dance could occupy a whole evening or be reduced to about an hour. Both stories of course should be told in the programme, but the Buddhist one is obvious on the stage and the Greek one already well known, so they need not be told elaborately.

The Greeks had several versions of the Philomel–Procne legend, even doubting which of them was which, so it is fair to choose a convenient one, as follows. Procne (swallow) after being married to King Tereus (we need not worry about his subsequent status as a Hoopoe) insisted on having her sister Philomel (the nightingale) to stay with her at the court. The result was that Tereus raped Philomel); he then cut off her tongue and hands to stop her from telling. She told Procne by writing in the sand with her toe. They plotted to kill Procne's son by Tereus and serve it to him for dinner; this revenge was what somehow turned them into birds.

The usual story is that Philomel only had her tongue cut out; she did not know how to write, but made a tapestry telling the fatal truth with her hands. We do not now easily assume that a princess cannot write, and a ballet cannot be bothered with weaving a tapestry. The Shakespearean parallel in *Titus Andronicus* cuts off both tongue and hands and uses the wounded mouth to poke a stick around in the sand with the letters of the name accused. This mouth business seems too appalling to dance as well as unnecessary in practice, and the possibility of writing with a toe is one that the tyrant might plausibly overlook. I think the movements would make good ballet, granting that they are meant to express tragic strain.

The Buddha in his incarnation as an elephant offered his body to a hunter, I am not sure whether to save the other elephants or to comfort a hunter who clearly needed an elephant, but anyhow it was through this act of wilful self-sacrifice that he contrived to be reborn as a man, the man who has now become famous as the Buddha. (The hunter would be chiefly hunting ivory tusks.) Both stories take for granted the idea of reincarnation between human being and animal, but the Buddha goes the opposite way round from the tormented and revengeful women who are reborn as birds. Such being the basic material, the two stories have next to be worked into a unity.

However the question 'What is the point of the thing?' ought perhaps to be faced at once. What has seemed to me finest in ballet is its power of bringing out the feeling of mystery in an already known legend, as in the *Swan Lake* and the *Fire Bird*, so that the audience is eager to see the 'interpretation' in the dancing. It is in this kind of way that I think the two stories would make a good ballet, and so far there need not be an obvious point, indeed should not be. At the same time of course a ballet ought not to feel pointless either, not in its first impact, not after reflection when you know it well. I should claim that this ballet does feel in some general way 'like life', and will try to describe in the text the suggestions that a production ought to aim at bringing out.

SETS

There are only two sets, a forest and a court, but these are combined in the last scene when the court is a ruin. Both are painted drop-curtains with side-objects along the wings; one has tree-trunks, the other pillars. It should be possible to change over in a quick black-out. The court backcloth is behind the forest backcloth, and be-tween them in the centre is a pedestal about one foot high. For the final scene the pedestal is pushed forward in front of the forest curtain (at least this plan seems the least trouble); all that survive of the court are stumps of pillar and a live dancer pretending to be a statue.

The best mechanical arrangement, I think, would be to make the side tree-trunks permanent and have pillars pushed in to hide them for court scenes. These pillars are divisible along jagged lines near the base, and the tops can be moved out separately. But of course it might be more convenient to have a separate lot of stumps. The effect to be aimed at, I think, is a rather contradictory one; the coiling tree-trunks seem to have grown all round the pillars, and yet it is just the same forest scene that we had before. What the aesthetics of the thing require is an obviously simple but surprising transformation.

The backdrop for the court would be elaborate and preferably a mixture of Greek and Indian architecture. There is a white-stone life-size Buddha statue on it sitting cross-legged in the centre, just higher than the real pedestal. This statue is a habitual ornament of the court in scenes 2 and 4 but is replaced by a live dancer in scenes 6 and 7. The best way to get the effect in ballet is I think the crudest one; paint the statue on the backcloth and fix a black cloth, completely rectangular, across it when it isn't wanted. There would be no harm in having the statue stand if the dancer can't sit crosslegged, except that there would be a different and I think rather unwanted dramatic effect in scene 6. If the statue squats it is forgotten till the centre of the stage clears and it begins to move. If it stands it is always in view and may appear to be biding its time in a threatening manner; perhaps there is no harm in this, but the Buddha ought not to seem in control of the situation.

The forest ought not to be made very hot and thick. I have actually pushed through dense tropical jungle around Angkor till I was bumped by the huge Buddha statue I was looking for, and even then what you see overhead is quite like ordinary temperate woodland. The designer must not confuse this kind of affair, which is frightening enough in itself, with the deep 'rain forest' of Central Africa or South America, where there is a solid belt of life fifty feet above you. No such incident has occurred in such country. In any case, the ballet is not intended to make us feel that the characters are all deep jungle objects though of course the trees go right up. But he is asked to have some fun over huge coiling white tree-trunks near the ground; these serpent-like objects have in fact torn apart the stones of Angkor, and the ground jungle there, up to about six feet high, can become impenetrable again within about fifteen years of being cleared. I am all for having the scenery dramatic so long as it doesn't put in the wrong drama. The remarks about Angkor of course apply to India too.

The general assumption of the story is that a colonial Greek princess has married a north-eastern Indian king some time after the conquests of Alexander the Great, when the two countries are in regular contact and can influence one another's architecture; this implies that we aren't seeing either the original Buddha or the original Philomel and Procne, but there is no reason why we should because their claim is to be fundamental types of something that recurs. The court set therefore, in rather the same way as the forest one, ought to be extravagant and eclectic without any suggestion that it is deeply primitive.

It seemed to me that the stage had to be presented before the reader was asked to imagine the scenes, which will be given next; remarks about choreography and music and so on will be given later.

SCENES

1. *Forest*. The elephants enter gradually, all from one side, at play, free from anxiety. The leading elephant, with a more regal head-dress, comes after and nudges them into their best paths. All finally follow him out on the other side of the stage; they were only passing.

2. *Court*. Tyrant and full court (male elephant and female swallow and nightingale dancers in human dress; tyrant standing back centre) receive giant tusks brought in by hunters; they express miserly admiration. Wife and her chorus (female swallow dancers) execute proud ratlike swoopings over tusks. Tyrant advances to appraise them; his dance recalls the elephant technique but crosses it with the military goose-step. Wife's sister (nightingale) hops with patient affection after wife who is preoccupied. Tyrant orders hunters to fetch more tusks and dismisses court; he withdraws to back centre. Wife and her sister dance alone, watched by tyrant; their mutual affection. On change of music, wife resumes interest in tusks; exit hugging one, leaving sister unwanted. Tyrant again advances, now to dance with wife's sister, whom he at last pursues

off stage. It is a wooing not a brutal attack, and she is coy and fluttered rather than indignant.

3. *Forest*. The chief hunter is pursuing elephants but finds only birds, the swallow and the nightingale, who tease him and ignore him. At last he becomes exhausted and lies down front centre. Though almost without incident this should be a fairly long scene marking lapse of time and establishing the bird analogue to the sisters and their ladies. The hunter's dance has no likeness to the elephant one.

4. *Court*. Wife's sister alone mutilated (mouth stained, arms tied behind back); her dance of almost passive despair. Wife enters with sharp change of music and is shocked and active. At last sister with her toe gradually scrapes message on the ground. Wife becomes increasingly zigzag and swallowlike, making pauses to plot with sister. She calls in whole female court. Growing fever. Finally baby in long swaddling clothes is rushed in held by swallow nurse from back wing to back centre. Pause. From front centre and always facing audience on tiptoe wife makes single dash backwards and stabs it.

5. *Forest*. Exhausted hunter again lying in foreground. Gradual quiet entry of elephants from one side in background. Entry of leading elephant from same side, all as scene 1. Hunter with effort starts up armed (presumably with bow). Elephant chorus flee. Leading elephant however remains and offers his body with majestic humility. Hunter displays superstitious terror, none the less kills elephant (with knife), then flees, bearing its outsize tusks. Elephant chorus return and mourn, surrounding body of leader, who removes elephant dress while hidden. Elephant chorus depart mourning. Leading elephant rises in triumph as human statue and moves in elephant dance to back centre, a slow but direct action, ending cross-legged on last bars. Both sinking to and rising from cross-legs would of course need to be done in elephant music rhythm.

6. *Court*. Long table at back with tyrant seated behind it at centre and sisters on either side of him. Buddha dancer (late chief elephant) is

behind him cross-legged as statue but hidden. Grand elephant tusks (the chief elephant's) stand as regalia on each side behind tyrant's head. Elephant music is always used somewhat coarsened for court scenes as it also represents human glory; here it comes nearest parody as it marks the entry of the court bearing the cannibal feast to the unconscious tyrant. He eats, and the music must carry the idea that *hubris* has arrived at horror; all dancing has stopped. Wife and sister rise together on a change of music and wife points hands at him (telling him what he has done). He too rises in fury and topples the whole table over (it can be constructed to make a reliable tidy fall); he must also kick aside his chair. Both sisters flee in their different manners toward front stage. Court, which was till now along wings, now crosses whole stage in alarm making confusion. Tyrant shoulders his way through them to kill both sisters. He catches the slower nightingale (wife's sister) as more easy; this is at one side of the front stage and he catches his wife later at the other. He returns slowly to front stage and stabs himself there, falling tidily dead with head directly backward. Meanwhile court separates round one or other sister in the wings; for the first time in this scene the back stage is clear with the Buddha dancer (late leading elephant) visible as statue. He now rises, seizes in elephant dance the two tusks on either side of him, and dances a slow elephant dance straight down stage towards the body of the tyrant, on whose body he reverently lays the tusks. He has a brief dance almost on the same spot expressing depth of feeling about the situation rather than any judgement about it, and ends cross-legged behind the head of the tyrant. Meanwhile the court has fallen flat without struggle as the Buddha approached it, and the result is that the nightingale and swallow dancers (like the elephant dancer in the previous scene, only the other way round) can now rise from their surrounders after a change of dress. They have shed their court regalia and are now wholly birds like those of scene 3. While the Buddha is still dancing around the corpse they rise and dodge backwards to escape him, and during his dance they dodge across and across the back stage escaping one another – their horror of one another at this stage needs to be brought out both by the music and the choreography.

7. *Court as Forest.* The scenery is to express lapse of time without the

slightest change in the trees; nothing is left of the court but some stumps of pillars and a statue of the Buddha (as is so often true). The birds return and dance before the statue in the ruin. The sisters, the leading swallow and nightingale, return and lead them. The elephants, without ending the recall of the bird themes, also return and dance before the statue. Finally the statue arises and leads the dance of the elephants. The sisters are no longer afraid of him, as in the previous scene, but they can hardly be called reconciled with him; they are more like independent forces; indeed the loving sisters are now unconscious of one another. I think there should be a final *tableau* with the sisters back to back hiding the Buddha.

CHOREOGRAPHY AND FACTS ABOUT BIRDS

Elephants are a symbol of magnanimous royalty; the notion behind the legends is that they are generous because they are so strong. The chief supporting truth is that an elephant must be careful where it puts its feet because it is so heavy; it dare not slip and fall, so gives an impression of trying not to tread on anyone. Only two points of technique are essential. One is suggested above; the elephant dancer always feels the ground with the foot before putting the weight on the foot, and normally needs two beats of music for one step. Secondly, to convey the majestic swing of the animal's movement, the dancer has to move up to a point of balance on one foot and then stay on that point of balance for a beat of the music and at last swing over; of course by the first rule he still has another beat before the weight goes on the other foot, after it has reached the ground. The first scene of the ballet ought to be a slow elephant dance, and this is gymnastically the hardest sort, but once the audience has got the feeling the effect can be given with the beats going fairly quick.

Perhaps the real difficulty is not in making the movement but in convincing the dancer that it appears regal and does not appear a form of galumphing. I have only seen it done by the dancing girls at Angkor; nobody could imagine that these exquisite little pauses were galumphing. Of course the risk of absurdity is greater in a male dancer who is actually claiming to look regal or divine (the pathos of the girl child dancer is that she is recalling qualities very unlike her own); but there is no doubt that the movement in itself is a startlingly magnificent one, and I do not see why it should not be brought off. The Cambodian dance technique I understand was imported from India, and probably there are still Indian elephant dance techniques which might be studied. But I am not recommending a wholesale borrowing of Eastern techniques for this ballet, which indeed had better be in the classical Western ballet tradition as much as possible; the only thing that needs importing is the root idea or the mechanics of the elephant dance, as described above.

The elephants are seen dancing before the Buddha or Buddha statue dances like an elephant, whereas Philomel and Procne are presented as human before the nightingales and swallows are seen dancing like them. This of course is because the reincarnations go opposite ways around. In both cases the animal dances are simply a formal stylisation of the dramatic scenes, which ought to be much freer.

The female cast is divided into swallows and nightingales, mostly swallows. The swallows present no especial difficulty except in the one dramatic *coup* of the leading swallow Procne at the end of scene 4, when she has to rush backwards on tiptoe and stab her child without looking at it. If this is thought impossible there are two saving factors. It is dramatically quite in order for her to fall after killing her child, and she is running up against the nurse, whose business it would be to catch her. Also she does this at the end of a scene and a climax of the music; it would be rather more impressive to have a 'tableau' in complete silence before the black-out, but the black-out could be used at once on a night where the trick went wrong, and the main effect would still be got.

As to swallows in general, they move very fast and tend to zigzag without sharp changes of angle (because they are catching flies); for the dancer to skim on tiptoe into the wings and out again, or straight across stage and out, would be a typical move. Mr James Fisher at the London Zoo (whose chief comment was that birds danced much better than any human beings) suggested to me that it would be fair to confuse the swallow with the swift, a bird with similar habits whose scientific name is *progne*; and that swifts hold 'corroborree mass dances' in which they 'move round and round, up and up, screaming'. This idea does suit Procne's type of madness; she makes herself too busy to remember her tragedy, chiefly by pretending to be excited and happy. In the ballet she is first seen being busy in this way in a crowd of similar ladies, and we may suppose that she married for social position – something wrong with her relations with her husband was why she was determined to have her sister to stay with her – so that she has already got this general character before the tragedy which it caused. The biological low-down about the bird movement is not irrelevant because these ladies too are always catching trivial flies.

The nightingale dance is much more difficult, and indeed this was what drove me to consult Mr Fisher. I think I may claim it as a saving grace that the human psychology is just as hard to dance as a bird; hence there is a real effect to be made. Philomel as a character is fixed in an agony of self-torture and determined not to forget what she did and suffered; she hugs it to her; therefore she would not dance at all. The nightingale of our poetical tradition 'leans its breast against a thorn' in order to produce more perfect music about an old pain which might otherwise be forgotten; this passive and rather horrible movement is not a dance. And in my version Philomel has to do her main dramatic scene with her arms tied behind her back, so that it is peculiarly hard to do any dance. Obviously the main weight of the nightingale faction has to be carried by the musician. It seems to me an important idea for the dancing that in this neurotic state she treats her pain as a form of property that she is determined not to be deprived of, just as Procne gets up an irrelevant interest in elephant tusks or flies or some other form of external property.

In the difficulty of imagining her dance it seems worth going into the facts about nightingales, though as few people ever see them they have no claim to interfere with the aesthetic requirements of the thing. They are extremely territorial birds, each occupying about an acre, and their purpose in putting out this enormously operatic singing is to warn other nightingales off their own property. Within its territory such a bird has stereotyped movements, singing only from selected posts and approaching them always along fixed paths, like a bus; so too Philomel is a case of fixation. The bird skulks under branches, and in general the nightingale chorus will keep to the wings of the stage. When other nightingales approach, a chivvying process goes on along the boundary, and special notes are used: 'rufous tail is spread and moved up and down as if on a pivot, wings fluttered and head dipped so that beak is below perch'. This item is probably no use for choreography, but the next I think might be; when at peace with no intruders the bird keeps 'cocking head to inspect ground below perch'. It is thus incessantly concerned to keep hold of a rather theoretical kind of property, and might be called introvert as opposed to the extrovert greed of the swallows. The human nightingale chorus never acts as a unit except just before the killing of Philomel in scene 6, where they gather round her; but even so they are ineffective and she is killed quite quickly. The crisis of the nightingale type in the ballet is when Philomel is persuaded to do the extremely un-ballet thing of scratching the story of her rape on the ground with her toe, 'cocking head to inspect ground'; and the whole dramatic force for ballet of the nightingale group has to be their difficulty in dancing. This is what is wrong with them, so that the medium of the dance is really not irrelevant to a study of their case. Of course the actual dancers must be given graceful thoughtful strained movements, but it seems to me that in this part of the thing the musician has to come first; given a sufficiently powerful and haunting line of nightingale music you could develop the strained movements of the nightingale dancers as an adequate interpretation of it. They are never alone on the stage. Finally we need to connect Philomel before the tragedy with Philomel after it; the point about her is that she loves her sister only, in a sort of incestuous way, refusing to go outside the family; that was why she had to go and live at her sister's court and become raped. She is therefore already this kind of intimately possessive character in the first scenes, before the tragedy which her character helped to produce; there should be dramatic variation, but she can be treated in a fairly standard way from her first appearance onwards.

It may be objected that there is a serious difficulty of interpretation or execution about all three animal types. I should claim in answer that they are all in a certain sense obvious to the audience; this makes them powerful. The whole energy, indeed the whole effect of lightness and ease, in this ballet should depend on presenting them tacitly as problems triumphantly overcome.

COSTUMES

For the avarice theme the elephants have to wear long white tusks, and they need to be impressively bigger than the birds; they had better have tall head-dresses, weighted at the back so that the tusks hang out in front, and this would help out the suggestion that they are always balancing. There is no need to hide their faces or otherwise make them look particularly like elephants. They look wild and regal, in light grey, and very broad strips of the cloth can swing out; they might have pink feet. The leading elephant differs only by an extra high and ornamented head-dress presumably with gold. He must be able to get out of his loose elephant dress while surrounded on the stage; a trap door would be convenient, but there is no need to make a fuss about hiding his abandoned clothes. As statue he is in rough (perhaps calico) white tights, looking like worn stone; he should have a thin white curled wig with the Buddha knob on the top, and might be given the long white ear-lobes.

There is room for doubt about the meaning of making him rise as a statue not as a man. He could of course rise in pink tights, loose white loincloth, and a blond curled wig, with a jewel on the brow. He would then have to change into the statue dress (which might simply be pulled over the top) either between scene 5 and scene 6 or between scene 6 and scene 7. But in any case, as the story of the ballet goes, there is no time for him to go through his life as a man, and the court is already displaying a Buddhist statue before the elephant is killed. Such being its nominal creed it had of course no business to kill elephants, and the more striking plan, I think, as well as the more convenient one, is to suppose that this elephant was simply re-born as the statue; he may have entered peace without requiring a life as a man.

The sisters also have a change of clothes while surrounded on the stage, and here there is no problem about hiding cast clothes as their choruses lie prone till the end of the scene. They have gorgeous court dresses, easy to slip out of, and of course do not wear wings as birds. The nightingale should look rather dumpy in dark grey (much darker than the elephants') and something might be made of her 'rufous' tail; her arms are no longer tied behind her back when she is resurrected, but the nightingales make little use of their arms when dancing anyway. Nor do they move fast. Procne, still in smart colours, arises stripped for incessant racing, which is all that is left to her of her career. Of course the main dramatic effect here (end of scene 6) is that the sisters have turned into the birds of scene 3. However they are somehow the archetypal swallow and nightingale or anyway the leaders of these choruses, and need to be dressed distinguishably; not I think by crowns in memory of their royalty but merely by a heightened version of the same clothes and colours.

It would be plausible to suppose that a Greek princess has married an Indian king in the first centuries after Alexander (say), and then the women's dress should be Greek but the dress of the tyrant and the hunter or hunters should be Indian. However there would be no need anyway to do more than hint at this contrast.

MUSIC

In spite of its melodrama, which of course the musician is not asked to play down, the ballet is meant to give a series of straightforward lyrical dances. There should be three plain themes allowing much repetition and not hard to recognise when transformed. The final scene, with no incidents, ought probably to be the longest; it is a recapitulation, and the feeling is that these incidents ceased to be agonising but are the way things keep going on. A musician no doubt feels that he has to interconnect the themes here, but this should not be felt to 'mean' very much – the characters are not interconnected, except so far as the girls can now be reconciled with the Buddha because they have already suffered; and till right at the end of the scene the music could be a series of repeats.

Each theme should be somewhat overlaid when its leading dancer or chorus is human and should stay fairly plain when they are animal; the human creatures are more complex, and anyway there is a story about them to be followed, but as animals they are typified and have little power of variation. This distinction however does not apply to the Buddha as elephant and statue; he is never particularly complex. Elephant music in a somewhat coarsened or broader form is always required for court scenes, because it is regal (the male chorus reappear as courtiers when not elephants). In the sixth scene the elephant music has to be parodied as false-regal for the cannibal feast and disappear for the killing, to the ordinary hearer like myself, but in fact the tyrant advances as rogue elephant and his part of the music, behind the extravagant outcry of the sisters and their choruses, should be a monstrous distortion of the elephant theme. His suicide front centre coincides with the discovery of the statue back centre which at once begins to rouse itself, so the tyrant at his death is allowed a share in the return of the elephant theme at its highest point of grandeur, which needs to be sustained to the end of the scene. For this advance of the Buddha bearing tusks to the dead tyrant it is both regal and spiritual, whereas for the reincarnation of the elephant as statue in scene 5 it was purely spiritual, or holy; the big elephant passages have thus to include more as the ballet goes on. In the final scene the elephant music is not concerned to be particularly holy or regal except as reminiscence, but should remember all that it has included.

However the Buddha must not be allowed to steal the show; the whole point of making the scenery imply a great lapse of time before the final incident is that the world is as strong as the Buddha. Even the swallows, incessantly occupying themselves with something ir-relevant, are meant to come out as impressive rivals to the Buddha. It is urgent for the musician to co-operate with the nightingales; they need to appear as forceful as the two others, and of course their strained dance must appear so, but this can only be done if the dance has meaning put into it by the music. The point about the sense of strain is that these women insist on hugging and recreating a single state of agony. I think the actual noise of the bird ought to be suggested, but then I am thinking of what is called a nightingale in England, and it is not clear that the same noise was meant by ancient Greece or is well known in modern America. It is a bubbling throbbing sustained uproar, useless of course for music as it stands; I am tempted to tell anecdotes to prove that it actually has the powers of heart-break so often ascribed to it by the poets, but this would be off the point, and in any case it is easily heard on gramophone records.

The story, choreography, dresses and scenery may well be built up as a contrast between Europe and the East, and it might seem that the composer is asked to do the same. I am rather against this. What seems to me the important difference between European and Far Eastern music is that the Far Eastern music can go slower than a heartbeat, but India does not fit this contrast neatly; and anyway the elephant music never does that, though it can very profitably for special effects be reduced like a Dead March to the pace of the heart. Anyway European music as now developed has got (for one thing) to be played on its own instruments, not on ancient Greek or Indian instruments, and I doubt whether the composer would do much good by making learned hints.

GENERAL REFLECTIONS

As I said in the first bit, the main power of ballet seems to me to lie in carrying out through a direct dance the feeling of mystery in an already known legend. So I do not feel that these themes require great subtlety of treatment; the point is rather that the audience would be intrigued and moved if they could be put over plainly.

However it is important to get the proportions right. This ballet is not a Buddhist tract. Indeed there is a certain amount of genuine mystery, as the fitting together of the two stories works out, in the relation between the Buddha and the tyrant. Both are commanding figures, and the ballet insists that they are less different than they seem; the first movement of the statue on leaving its pedestal is to honour the dead tyrant (perhaps ironically) by returning to him the tusks of the Buddha elephant, which on Buddhist principles he had no right to demand since they were got by killing an animal. It must also be supposed that the action of the Buddha statue in this scene revived the sisters as birds, so that it is a merciful one. The tyrant danced as a rogue elephant and the Buddha as a holy one, but they both performed the typical elephant process of shouldering through the complexity of the world. It is not so to speak theologically wrong for the Buddha to give tusks to the dead tyrant; he is only repeating what he did when alive as an elephant, in offering his body. This is what gives him power; and yet he seems to recognise that his kind of power is not really unlike the tyrant's, though of course very different in detail. It should be clear anyway that he does not revenge himself on the tyrant, who though undoubtedly wicked (chiefly from cowardice) has already been punished adequately by the sisters.

As a matter of making a ballet, the chief need for the elephant is that the bitterly contrasted madnesses of the birds would be too horrible without a contrast to both. It should be clear that the pacifist moral story about the Buddha elephant offering his body is grotesque because it overplays its moral; in the same way the European moral story of Patient Griselda is grotesque – it was meant to show that wives ought to be patient, and by the time all the details have been piled up it is clear to any balanced reader that wives ought to stop being patient earlier than Griselda did. The Buddha legend has the same kind of wilful moral splendour which does not depend for its effect on being taken solemnly. Nor is the jungle better than the court, or the court than the jungle; the Buddha by his elephantine nature could shoulder through both of them, and so perhaps under other circumstances might the tyrant have done, but in any case the same types of character remained.

It may be thought that the contrast between Greek and Indian legend ought to mean something important if used at all. I do not think it either does or needs to. The fact that the males are Indian and the females Greek is of course simply the effect of a royal marriage (the Greek queen would bring her ladies with her, and she chose to bring the sister with her different ladies); it does not have to be symbolical. As to the themes, self-sacrifice is not a new idea to Europe, and the Greek legend is already a Buddhist anecdote as it stands. The women whom the torture of the world leads into evil are reborn as birds, and must suffer so far for their Karma, but of course a murder in a past life would never prevent a bird from being reconciled with the Buddha. It might perhaps be said that the Western belief in the individual makes the idea of a reincarnating elephant absolutely foreign to it; but this point is a very confusing one, because the legend obviously treats the Buddha as having the same 'personality' when an elephant and when a man. In any case of course Pythagoras believed in reincarnation, and the Greeks had probably been in touch with Indian beliefs. The suggestion of confusing the Buddha with the tyrant may also seem pretty remote; especially if it is supported, in a learned manner, by the theory that the Buddha or Bodhisattva heads at Angkor (for instance) were idealised portraits of the reigning kings. But then again, the idea of the divine right of kings is a familiar and recurring one in the West. It seems rather a good thing to let the ballet recall the two historical traditions, but the only interesting reflection to be made, so far as I can see, is that there is no contrast between them.

APPENDIX
An exchange on 'The Elephant and the Birds'

In (? June) 1942 Empson asked the editor, anthologist and biblio-grapher John Hayward (1905–65) for an opinion on 'The Elephant and the Birds'. He was fully aware that Hayward sported a high reputation as an uncompromising though sympathetic editor. Even as an undergraduate, and despite a progressively paralysing muscular disease which presently confined him to a wheelchair, Hayward had edited the Nonesuch edition of Rochester – so successfully that Edmund Gosse hailed him as 'the best and, in fact, the only competent editor of Rochester'. Before the age of thirty he managed the feat of editing both the Nonesuch Donne and the Nonesuch Swift (including the first correct recension of *Gulliver's Travels* to appear since the eighteenth century). In his later years, as the erudite and stringent editor of the *Book Collector*, he became pre-eminent in the field of bibliography. His anthologies include the *Penguin Book of English Verse* and the *Oxford Book of Nineteenth-Century Verse*.

Cultivated for both his scholarship and his social presence, Hayward held a commanding position in the world of letters from the 1930s until his death. His soirées (held in the 1930s at his flat in Bina Gardens, London) with T. S. Eliot, Geoffrey Faber and Frank Morley are memorialised in *Noctes Binanianae*, a volume of verses by all four hands. He became the confidant and adviser of numerous writers including Stephen Spender, Anne Ridler and Stevie Smith; and he provided creative advice on the plays and poems (especially *Four Quartets*) of T. S. Eliot, with whom he shared a Chelsea flat from 1946 to 1957 (see Helen Gardner, *The Composition of 'Four Quartets'*, London: Faber & Faber, 1978). Like Eliot and Empson, W. H. Auden placed great faith in Hayward's critical skills, as this note from the 1940s (dated New York, 25 October) confirms: 'The opera ["The Rake's Progress"] whose libretto you so kindly vetted is going well – the second act nearly finished' (Hayward Papers, King's College, Cambridge).

Empson had known and liked Hayward for several years, and corresponded with him from the Far East. Fully reciprocating his liking, Hayward did everything he could to further Empson's interests: in October 1939, for instance, he wrote to Frank Morley: 'Ever since [Empson] sent me an extremely good poem ["Missing Dates", January 1937] by way of apology for being very drunk and uproarious and destructive in B[ina] Gardens, I've pressed his claims on Tom [Eliot]' (Hayward Papers, King's College, Cambridge). T. S. Eliot himself enormously admired Empson's poetry: he published *The Gathering Storm* (Faber & Faber) in 1940, and encouraged the American firm of Harcourt Brace to bring out *Collected Poems* in 1949.

Empson must have delivered the text of the ballet during the personal visit to which Hayward refers in his letter; the Empson letter printed below is an unsigned typescript draft (no fair copy has been located). Square brackets in the Hayward letter indicate a tear in the original note-sheet.

Letter from John Hayward

[Merton Hall, Cambridge, 12 July 1942]

My Dear William: Thank you very much indeed for allowing me to see a copy of THE ELEPHANT & THE BIRDS. It has fascinated me from first to last and I greatly hope for its production. You must know that I'm quite incompetent to criticize a work of this kind; but since you flatteringly ask me for comments and to comply is a simple way of showing you my interest, here are a few observations. –

I think there may be some considerable difficulty in finding adequate symbolism for the Elephants' weight, majesty and dignity. An oriental audience, I imagine, would understand & enjoy a stylized Elephant 'dance' much more readily than an occidental one would, though the London ballet audiences, by this time, must be pretty ready and apt to suspend their disbelief. I'm not thinking so much of the choreography as of the presentation of the Elephant dancers. It is essential to avoid any suggestion of Babar and his friends, particularly in the person of the Buddha. A solution might be found in the use of highly stylized masks to suggest, not Elephant-kind, but the abstract qualities of majesty &c.

SCENE 4. I'm inclined to think that it would be less ungainly from the choreographer's point of view and perhaps more effective from the audience's if the sister were to scrape her confession with the point of her toe rather than with wand held in her mouth. This detail in the legend would permit a variant and the audience would be none the wiser. Also, I'm inclined to cut out the Tourneuresque stabbing of the baby. Is it necessary that this incident in the legend should be demonstrated on the stage? My objection to it is that it introduces action which can only be interpreted dramatically (swaddling clothes, stabbing &c.) whereas action in ballet should be interpreted in terms of dance.

SCENE 6. If my objections to the baby-stabbing are valid, then it would be desirable, I think, to cut out the business of the feast and the toppling table, which might be technically awkward in any case. I don't think the audience would miss the incident and it might have difficulty in following its development as there is no indication given that the baby was cooked and served up! I do realize, though, that to abandon the acts of infanticide and cannibalism may lessen too much the sense of guilt of the sisters, especially Philomela's.

THE NIGHTINGALE'S DANCE. Is it necessary to try to realize choreographically the dingy, dumpy aspects of the bird[?] Most people, [ ] never having seen a nightingale (and who has?) [ ] of melody and not ornithologically [ ] uneasiness about finding an adequate dance equivalent. Let her be dressed in drab grey but could her *persona* not be interpreted as that of a singer – in other words her dance be an expression of the range and variations of her song? By the way, was there not a ballet called THE NIGHTINGALE by? Stravinsky in the early repertoire of Diaghilev's company? If there was, it might be useful to look up what choreography was devised for the bird.

PERSONAL REMARK. I imagine swallows as violins – the long sweeping bowing, the shimmering high registers, the extreme virtuosity of movement up and down the scale and so on. Nightingales I imagine as clarinets (rarely perhaps as hautbois) – not flutes or piccolos, the obvious naturalistic equivalents – thinking of, for example, the slow movement of Mozart's clarinet quintet. I wonder what your musician's choice would be.

This is all I have to say and it's not much. But I should like to hear from you again when you have time to write more about the progress of the ballet. (I'm very glad that Hurry [Leslie Hurry, the stage designer

(1909–78)] is in on it.) And, of course, in the most unlikely event of my opinions being of any use to you, do please command me.

I was so happy to see you and Henrietta [Hetta, whom Empson had married in 1941] together and hope that you will never be less so yourselves than you seemed to me to be on that all too brief visit.

Love from:

John

I shall not advertise the existence of the Ballet to anyone.

Empson's response

My dearest Hayward,

I was much shocked by your kind letter, and propose to write on the subject though I can hope only to entertain you and not to improve either you or the Western world. Your views on my little ballet show I think the appalling corruption into which the European ideas about ballet have fallen. Europe and yourself are not yet equally corrupted about the legitimate drama, so will you cast your mind back to a production of 'As You Like It' at the Festival Theatre by Terence Gray, probably in 1930, when Terence Gray thought it would be advanced and refined to give elaborate scenery and costumes but not to allow properties of any kind – the fencers had to make do without swords and so on. If you happened to see this or something like it you would agree I think that this was corruption. The thing can be done without scenery but not without properties because the person and the personal situation must be presented as real, but his background is not essential to the force of the thing; so that any producer who deliberately does it the other way round is evidently trying to kill his play. I am sure that you would not do this to a play. But you believe it to be a point of refinement to do the same thing in a ballet.

Do not suppose me to be confusing 'reality' with waking life. Perhaps all myth and probably all good ballet belong to a dream world; but these myths are nightmares, in which the presence or the lack of definite instruments is a vastly important imaginative event, the defining thing, vastly more important than any of the background material *because its supporter.*

You say that 'action in ballet must be interpreted in terms of dance'. I might view this with more respect if I had been brought up on the European ballet, in which the dancer must always skip and bounce in rapid time; but I have seen more Far Eastern ballet than any other sort, where the timing allows of and indeed demands dramatic action; and the fallacy in the operation of the platitude therefore appears to me in a positively lurid character as expressing the collapse of the entire artistic form.

The objection to my murder is not that it is not interpreted in terms of dance but that the acrobatics required in the dancing are probably more than I can get. The woman has got to run twenty or thirty feet straight backwards on tiptoe and end with her dagger in the right place as if it were a single fall. She can't have more than the last three bars of the scene for it. And unless this impression of brief release of violent force can be got into the few brief dramatic incidents all the slow lyrical reflective parts will become pointless and totally unexplained.

It is true and had not occurred to me that an armless woman could write with her toes; of course the original legend assumed that a princess couldn't write, and this doesn't make sense for a modern audience; nor do the later inventions to tighten the story up. Maybe drawing with her toes could be made to suggest enough difficulty and horror. But if you want the change because you think a ballet can't owing to its nature suggest difficulty and horror then I think you (like nearly all European balletgoers) are simply fooling with the subject. Luckily dear Hurry at least would never fall into such an error. Whether we can get a choreographer to put some nightmare into European dancing is another thing.

To sum up the point – it is clear that you tacitly define Dancing as 'skipping in time to a quick beat'. Really dramatic dancing could be a more interesting thing than that even with European music. [Incomplete]

(Both letters in Empson Papers.)